ALSO BY BEVERLY LOWRY

FICTION

Come Back, Lolly Ray

Emma Blue

Daddy's Girl

The Perfect Sonya

Breaking Gentle

The Track of Real Desires

NONFICTION

Crossed Over: A Murder, a Memoir

Her Dream of Dreams:
The Rise and Triumph of Madam C. J. Walker

Harriet Tubman: Imagining a Life

Who Killed These Girls?
The Unsolved Murders That Rocked a Texas Town

DEER CREEK DRIVE

DEER CREEK DRIVE

A Reckoning of Memory and
Murder in the Mississippi Delta

BEVERLY LOWRY

Alfred A. Knopf
New York, 2022

THIS IS A BORZOI BOOK
PUBLISHED BY ALFRED A. KNOPF

Copyright © 2022 by Beverly Lowry

www.aaknopf.com

The photographs on page 1 and page 197 appear courtesy of the Archives and
Records Services Division, Mississippi Department of Archives and History.

Knopf, Borzoi Books, and the colophon are registered trademarks of
Penguin Random House LLC.

Library of Congress Cataloging-in-Publication Data
Names: Lowry, Beverly, author.
Title: Deer Creek Drive : a reckoning of memory and murder in the
Mississippi Delta / Beverly Lowry.
Description: First edition. | New York : Alfred A. Knopf, [2022] |
Includes bibliographical references.
Identifiers: LCCN 2021053204 | ISBN 9780525657231 (hardcover) |
ISBN 9780525657248 (ebook)
Subjects: LCSH: Thompson, Idella, 1879–1948. | Dickins, Ruth Thompson,
1906–1996. | Murder—Mississippi—Leland—Case studies. | Leland (Miss.)—
Social conditions—20th century. | Leland (Miss.)—Race relations.
Classification: LCC HV6534.L45 L69 2022 |
DDC 364.152/30976242—dc23/eng/20211227
LC record available at https://lccn.loc.gov/2021053204

Jacket images: (pruning shears) *Tragedy-of-the-Month,* 1949, Triangle
Publications, Inc.; (background) Special Collections, University of
Mississippi Libraries
Jacket design by Jenny Carrow

Manufactured in the United States of America
First Edition

For Greenville friends, past and present.

In Memory: Julia Reed

Rabbit Jenkins

Leila Wynn

Charlotte Buchanan

My parents.   Their dreams.

CONTENTS

Deer Creek Drive is, fundamentally, a story about the attitudes, behavior, and language of Mississippi in the 1950s. This was the decade of *Brown v. Board of Education,* of Emmett Till, and of the beginning of the end for Jim Crow. While this material is often difficult, my aim was always to illuminate and reckon with the reality of living and growing up in that section of the state we called the Delta during this time. As such, the book uses a number of primary sources—documents, court testimony, newspaper articles—as well as a reliance on memory, much of which reflects the demeaning and problematic language that was used so freely and unsparingly at the time. It is both my story and the story of an unreconstructed South and how both of us were destined to change.

Beverly Lowry

I

THE CRIME

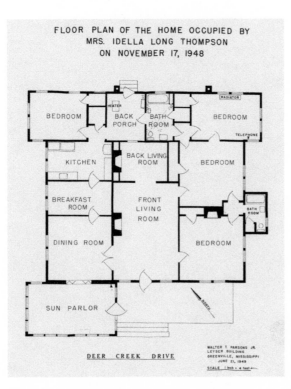

FLOOR PLAN OF THE HOME OCCUPIED BY
MRS. IDELLA LONG THOMPSON
ON NOVEMBER 17, 1948

Known as State's Exhibit No. 1, this is the architectural rendering of Idella Thompson's home in 1948, which was presented to the jury on the first day of the trial by the district attorney, Stanny Sanders. It is the only exhibit included in the digitized transcript of the trial and as such provides a kind of map to the crime and its aftermath, showing how big the rooms were and where they were located, how close the bathroom was to the back porch, how far the front door was from the crime scene, and other crucial details. It was reprinted in newspapers and in the tabloid magazine *Tragedy-of-the-Month* and is the kind of site-setting evidence lawyers like to come up with before anything else.

LOOKING BACK

Y ou'd think by now people would have forgotten or perhaps decided simply to let go of the memory of what happened in the Mississippi Delta town of Leland in the early afternoon of November 17, 1948. But nobody has. Even people too young to remember know about it. They've seen clippings pasted in old scrapbooks or heard the story (which did not, by the way, end that year or the next but went on and on, one of those stories that because people love to tell it keeps starting over). Although some local residents still refuse to engage, even briefly, in a discussion of the matter, there are those who would—if you went to Leland—gladly point out the house where it happened—still standing, freshly painted perfectly white, lawn exquisitely maintained. They might even be willing to tell you exactly where in the house the sixty-eight-year-old "society matron" was attacked, first in the enclosed back porch, and then dragged on a small rug into her own bathroom, where she, or, more than likely, her body, ended up: facedown, her daughter said, in her own blood soup, the crown of her head against the tub, beside which sat an ordinary three-legged wooden stool. And between the stool and her head, the gleaming nightmare weapon washed and wiped clean of prints and gore.

That it happened was shocking enough on its own. But there? In that neighborhood?

Until that year, both of these women, the society-matron mother and the socialite daughter, had lived pretty much their whole lives on this street, which—it is important to note—was and still is the most desirable in town, the street about which locals say, "If you want to get to heaven, you have to live on Deer Creek Drive."

Or, as some would say, simply "the Drive."

If by happenstance you did find yourself in Leland standing before the murder house, you might then want to check out the house where the dead woman's daughter lived with her cotton broker husband and two young daughters: a mere three houses away down the Drive, north toward Stoneville. You could walk there in minutes, noting as you went, thanks in great measure to the Leland Garden Club, the beauty of the surroundings: the meandering creek to your left and on its high, sloping banks the oak and sycamore trees, the occasional surviving sweet gum, the crepe myrtle and pecan, the azalea and rosebushes, the park benches, the well-fed families of proprietary ducks.

That the two women's homes were situated on what some Leland families consider the "wrong" side of the creek should also be noted. It is, of course, a measure of small-town snobbery that there exists, to some, a bad side of the best street in town, but the distinction is also significant in terms of current property values. Houses on South Deer Creek Drive, according to a longtime realtor and lifelong resident, command a higher price. Asked why this was, she answered with a sigh, as if the reason should have been obvious. Because, she said, "Black people live on the north side."

Close to? Or *on?*

These days? *Both.*

It was 2018. I'd returned to the Delta to participate in the annual Hot Tamale Festival, which took place in downtown Greenville. The realtor was driving me around Leland, pointing out places of historical interest, including a museum devoted to Kermit the Frog and his creator, the puppeteer Jim Henson, surely Leland's best-known resident, more famous even than the bluesmen James "Son" Thomas and Johnny Winter. She'd promised to get me into the murder house, which she'd personally sold five times since the killing, but when we drove there and she went inside to ask, the current residents told her no way.

Without a doubt, anybody who knows how and where, on the very day she'd been released from a weeklong stay in the hospital, Idella Stovall Long Thompson was murdered—anybody, that is, willing to remember and say so—could also let you in on the most important part of the story: the identity of the person who was eventually arrested, tried on a first-degree murder charge, convicted, and sent to Parchman, Mississippi's infamous state prison, for life. This particular detail is why a lot of Leland people want to keep the story under wraps. And while some of those who refuse to talk are relatives of the two women or members of the same social class, not all are. A furniture salesman told a friend of mine that if I was hoping to hear what people had to say about *that*, I "might as well go on back home." Because, he said, "*we're not going to talk about it,*" with no indication who he specifically meant by "we." Leland's small enough—its population barely five thousand in 1948, less than that now—to come together like that, to automatically clam up, close ranks, do the zipper thing, running pinched thumb and index finger across their lips as if to lock the information inside.

I know the story, they're saying, *but I'm not telling. Especially not to an outsider like you.*

Greenville, where I grew up, is only nine miles away, but I'd left years before and had never lived in Leland, and so there were lifelong residents who felt justified, if not obliged, to tell me to go on back to Texas and leave this thing alone. And then shut the door in my face.

. . . .

At the time of the murder, however, the news spread fast. Leland was practically a suburb of Greenville, and telephone service still depended on the "Number, please" request of the switchboard operators, the working women whose job was to put calls through and who, as a consequence, often heard important news first. And sometimes they repeated what they'd eavesdropped on, and maybe the person or persons they shared the news with then phoned somebody else, and so on. Also, once the Leland police chief followed through on his sworn duty and called the Washington County sheriff over in Greenville to let him know what had happened within his jurisdiction, the sheriff had to make calls of his own before heading east on Mississippi State Highway 82 to the crime scene.

One "Number, please" led to the next. And so we all found out one way or another, if not that afternoon then certainly by the next morning when the November 18 issue of the Greenville *Delta Democrat-Times* arrived, bearing what, in retrospect, seems an oddly worded banner headline: "Search Continues in Leland Slaying." As if the murder itself had become old news. And in some ways it had because we already knew about it, including who the victim was, who'd been at the crime scene, and who the eyewitness said had done it. Which meant the real up-to-the-minute news had moved from the event itself to its follow-up. The search.

Beneath the headline was a more straightforward subhead: "Mrs. J. W. Thompson Killed with Shears. Rites to Be Friday." The slain woman was described as the widow of the prominent Delta planter and former Mississippi Levee Board chairman J. W. Thompson, whose daughter the forty-two-year-old Ruth Dickins had reportedly surprised the killer, a man she described as a young, slightly built, dark-skinned Negro she didn't know. She was coming, she said, into her mother's home and didn't see the man right away, and before she knew it, he had slammed into her out of, it seemed, nowhere. They tussled and she wasn't sure how, but she managed to wrestle the weapon from him. After that he fled. Out the back door, she assumed.

"Ruth," a family relative told me. Nobody called her Mrs. Dickins, except maybe servants and children, many of whom addressed her in the southern manner as Miss Ruth. And she wasn't a "socialite" as the papers said. She was, her second or so cousin swore, as plain as an old shoe.

As if that mattered. As if social status in the Mississippi Delta came not from ancestry but personality and character.

. . . .

I was a big reader, but doubt I personally read the paper that next morning. But certainly my parents did. And unquestionably they would have talked about what was splashed all over the front page because it was a story not about strangers living in a whole other part of the country but about *known* people, members of a top-tier family. Being a listening, watching, imagining kind of girl, I would have paid attention, the same as, in all likelihood, every other girl my age, ten going on eleven being an age when female children are beginning to scarf up whatever information adults have been keeping from them, especially details of the most lurid, the *worst* things that have happened or still might.

But I can't honestly say I remember much from that particular day. Things had to spin out a little further. A little more time had to pass. More news reported, discussed, wondered at before imagination could take hold and sink deeply enough in to make forgetting out of the question.

Once the AP had wired the story all over the country, other newspapers covered it that same day, including the *Chicago Tribune* ("Widow of Planter Killed by Intruder"), the *Austin American-Statesman* ("Planter's Widow Hacked to Death"), *The Montgomery Advertiser* ("Prominent White Woman Slain"), the Greenwood, Mississippi, *Commonwealth* ("Leland Woman Is Killed by Negro"). And others, all emphasizing race, class, and shock value.

While splashy, unlikely murders tend to encourage long memories, this one was like no other, and in our part of Mississippi—that egg-shaped patch of ridiculously rich alluvial soil we called the Delta—nobody talked about anything else that whole fall and especially the next spring and summer when the trial provided the grisly details.

. . . .

My memory of Greenville attaches itself to houses: where we lived when certain things happened, how old I was each time we had to move from one address to another, whether it was the time I broke my arm playing Crack the Whip the first day I went roller-skating in Strange Park and didn't know enough to avoid taking the end position, or the day my brother David blasted his face open by tearing spent firecrackers apart and lighting them, not knowing one of them was live, or the time when the panel truck from Tatum Music Company came to take away my mother's beloved Baldwin Acrosonic piano for nonpayment. We mark time mostly, I think, by events. I order my and my family's Greenville life according to which house we were living in at the time. In our fourteen-year residency, there were seven, only one of which—the bungalow at the corner of Cedar and Manilla—we left by choice.

When my first novel, *Come Back, Lolly Ray*, was published in 1977, I hadn't lived in Greenville for more than twenty years. I'd gone back maybe twice during that time, brief overnight stays ending in a quick getaway before I ran into somebody who might remember the deepening financial and legal troubles that encouraged my family, the Feys, to skip town and not come back.

I never planned or even wanted to set a book in Mississippi. There was the burden of the state's literary past—Faulkner and the rest—plus I'd moved, I thought, for good. I wanted the past to stay where it was and believed that whatever I wrote would reflect the person I'd become, living in Manhattan, learning how to eat an artichoke, combing my hair across my forehead in a dramatic slant, like Delphine Seyrig in *Last Year at Marienbad*. But the past can be a nag. And sometimes a book knows what it is before the writer has a clue, including who's going to be in it and where it'll take place.

I renamed my fictional town Eunola and never said what state it was in or even which river dead-ended the main street of town. But Greenville knew. The opening line was like a secret whispered into their hometown ears: "The sun and river were to the west, back over their shoulders on the other side of the levee. The main street of town—along which they waited, impatiently—dead-ended there, at the foot of the levee."

Who among locals didn't nail it down? They knew I'd grown up there and that what I was describing was, absolutely and without a doubt, downtown Greenville, Mississippi. Within another page or so they'd have figured out other details.

Friday. Autumn. Late afternoon. The courthouse. Washington Avenue just over the railroad tracks where the street makes a sharp jag to the left toward the levee. Majorettes, marching band, drum major, special twirlers, cheerleaders. What else but the parade preceding the high point of our week: that night's high school football game?

That book wasn't about my life, and neither is this one. But both emerge from me. And here I am at this stage of my life, these seventy years later, remembering things that took hold of me then and still refuse to let go.

The story of Ruth Dickins, the murder of her mother, and what happened afterward.

The story of a girl who could not stop wanting what she couldn't have.

And the hot tamale region that birthed us both.

NOVEMBER 17, 1948

The first police officers to arrive on the scene were the Leland chief of police, Frank P. Aldridge, and Phillip P. "Pink" Gorman, one of only three regulars on the Leland police force. Aldridge wasn't feeling well, having been released from the hospital after surgery only the day before, in addition to which, barely four months earlier, he'd undergone three separate surgical procedures in one day. Although barely able to get around, he nonetheless managed to pull himself together and get to work. He was downtown on a Third Street sidewalk not far from the police telephone box when, middle of the afternoon, it rang.

Leland was one of those quiet, small towns news reporters like to call "sleepy." Because nothing much of a criminal nature happened there beyond the usual petty crimes and traffic violations, that phone didn't ring too often. With no idea how his life was about to be jiggered, Aldridge answered and, once he'd heard the message, told Gorman to go get the police car—there was only one—Mrs. Thompson had been murdered.

No need to identify the victim further. Idella Long Thompson's family had lived on the Drive since 1902. They owned acreage east of town. There was also the matter of the Thompson husband, all those years ago. Frank was chief at that time too. The family tried to keep the details of what had happened hush-hush, but people got wind of it quick. Nobody didn't know who the Thompsons were.

. . . .

The call had come from one of Leland's most respected doctors, the co-founder of the Witte Clinic and Hospital—where both Aldridge and

Mrs. Thompson had been hospitalized—Dr. Kinney Lyght Witte (pronounced "Witty"), affectionately known throughout the town as simply Doc. A noted horseman, Doc was also the murder victim's brother-in-law, having been married to her baby sister, Johnie, for forty years.

This kind of thatched connection among established Leland families was common everyday normal. Once land-rich families settled there, they married each other, kept the prestigious bloodlines going, built a big house, bought more land, joined a church, stayed put. Chief Aldridge was from a socially prominent Delta family himself and in fact was distantly related on his father's side to Idella Thompson. The Aldridges owned a large plantation in nearby Arcola, in addition to which he'd married extremely well: his wife, Katherine, called Sassy, was the granddaughter of Captain James Alexander Ventress Feltus, often called the founder of Leland. And so between his family and Sassy's, without question they knew every white person in town as well as a good many members of the majority-race Black citizenry.

· · · ·

It took the two officers less than five minutes to drive across the railroad tracks and down North Deer Creek Drive West to number 311. After parking out front, they went up the sidewalk and the front steps. The door into the house had been left open, and so when nobody came to meet them, the two men "went right on in the front door." Chief Aldridge didn't check his watch, but he figured it was about 3:30. That time of day, the neighborhood would have been utterly still; in fact one neighbor said that while, yes, he'd been home that entire afternoon, he'd heard nothing, no screams or sounds of a struggle, but then he'd been taking an after-dinner (as some southerners refer to lunch) nap at the time. Probably others living on that block of the Drive were doing the same thing.

Because Aldridge was struggling, Gorman led the way. They left the front door the way they found it, unlocked and ajar.

The day was fair, clear, and slightly cool, high in the mid-sixties, a perfect fall day, with a weather change scheduled to hit that night, thunderstorms and colder temperatures. In temperamentally humid climes like the Delta, the hours before a storm hits tend to be close, clamped down, the air thick and still with expectation. The rain would indeed start up in the late night to early morning hours and continue most of the next day as predicted, unloading almost three inches, soaking into the lush lawn of Mrs. Thompson's backyard, wreaking havoc on the murder investigation, the search for evidence.

Naturally lean, at sixty-two Aldridge was balding, with patchy gray hair, high cheekbones, and a healthy, appropriately cop-like brush mustache. He looked fairly gaunt at this time, perhaps due to weakness or pain from the surgery. Pink Gorman, on the other hand, had been a member of Leland's first football team in 1922 and a volunteer fireman for more than twenty years. At forty-three, he still maintained his vigor. The two men had worked together since 1939, the year Aldridge became police chief, an elected position at that time.

Both were outfitted in trim, fitted dark blue uniforms complete with smart Sam Browne belts across their chests. The uniforms were new, having been provided to the force only the year before. Beneath his jacket, Aldridge preferred to wear old-fashioned, thick leather Y-back suspenders, with two looped straps that attached to buttons on the waistband of his uniform trousers front and back. His large wire-framed glasses emphasized his alert, wide-eyed, slightly owlish appearance. Before the uniforms were issued, Aldridge was known for wearing an open vest that ended at his gun belt, no coat whatever the weather, his badge attached to a suspender strap.

White people called him Frank, although, when addressing him in his official capacity as police chief, some paid due respect and called him Mr. Frank, the same as Black people all over the Delta were expected to do. He was known to be a stern keeper of the law, whether monitoring speed zones or chasing potential criminals, most of them on their way either west to Greenville or north to Memphis.

The house was quiet, well cared for. "Neat as a pin," Aldridge said. Mrs. Thompson's regular cook and cleaning lady, Martha Prewitt, wasn't there and wouldn't be all week. It was late in the cotton-harvesting season but still "picking" time, when she and a whole lot of other domestic workers spent their weekdays in the fields gathering cotton bolls by hand and dropping them into large burlap sacks. During harvest months, she showed up weekends to take care of some of her regular chores but that was all. This happened every fall, and white employers found ways to accommodate the hired help they deemed worth holding on to. After all, a good picker could make three or more times the wages she earned doing domestic work, and when the harvest season ended in a few weeks, Prewitt would return to her normal schedule. Her mother had worked for Idella for more than thirty-five years, and so, as the Thompson clan told one another and even Prewitt herself, she was just like family.

Idella Thompson's other longtime employee, Jimmy Banks, spent weekdays in a room above her garage, waiting for a signal from her—the ringing of a bell wired to the house—requesting his help. Fifty-six, he worked for Idella as a yardman and general custodian. He usually went home at three. But Jimmy had grown deaf over the years. He could hear the bell but little else. Not even a noisy ruckus.

. . . .

The two men walked straight into and "right on through" the long formal front living room, past two bedrooms on the right and the dining room, a fireplace, and the kitchen on the left. As they went, their heavy shoes moving from throw rug to wooden floor, one of the policemen surely called out to announce their arrival the way people in the South do or used to, partly because back then although they made a big point of locking their back doors, a lot of people left their front doors unlocked so that as long as you were a white person, you felt welcome to enter without knocking. But pure common sense told you to deliver a kind of warning *woo-hoo* to let whoever was there know you'd come in.

Doc Witte had made no mention of Ruth's presence, and so there was no reason for them to assume she was there. Walking down the hall, they would have called out only to him, almost certainly using the nickname everybody knew. They kept going through the smaller, more casual back living room and into the door to the third bedroom, the smallest of the three, with windows overlooking the backyard. There they found Ruth half sitting on the radiator and Doc standing close by, between her and her mother's bed.

Nobody ever saw Ruth Dickins look any way but buttoned up and groomed, but that day Aldridge said she was a mess. The front of her dress was bloody, and her dark, near-black hair—usually combed off her forehead in a sleek wave she combed into a swooping curve behind her ears, ending in a blunt chop at her neck—was down in her face, and he could see scratches on her forehead and arms. Her left hand was beginning to purple and swell. As if, Frank said, she'd been in an awful scuffle.

When Aldridge asked Doc how long he'd been at the house before he called in, he said no more than five minutes and that it had been Mrs. Dickins who called him, maybe ten minutes before that. So, in terms of what happened to Idella, Doc hadn't seen anything. Everything was over and done with by the time he got there. Other than the dead woman, he and Ruth were the only people in the house.

Idella's sons, James Wynn Thompson, forty-four, and William Wood Thompson, thirty-six, still lived in their mother's house, Wood with his wife, Demetra, and James—Jimmy—alone. The back bedroom was Mrs. Thompson's. On the east wall, opposite her bed, were two doors, one leading into a closet, the other into an adjoining bathroom. From where he stood with Ruth and Doc, Aldridge could see the body of Mrs. Thompson, faceup—he said—on the white tile floor, the top of her head nearly grazing the bathtub, her body stretched diagonally across the floor toward the commode. A tiny woman, barely five feet tall and under a hundred pounds, she wore a green wool dress adorned with a small decorative pin. Her left shoe lay on the bathroom floor beside her leg. The right one hung loosely from her toes. One hand was clenched in a tight fist.

Clearly, she'd been severely assaulted, her head and hands, Aldridge said, "all cut up," her clothes and body "bloody all over." A pair of metal pruning shears lay on the bathroom floor next to her head. From the bedroom, Aldridge couldn't actually see the left side of her face and head, where the worst of her injuries were, but he made no move toward the woman to make sure she was dead. There obviously being no need.

"The whole thing," Aldridge said, "was a mass of blood." Blood covered the bathroom floor, and "there was blood all up the wall" and everywhere else. There were even splashes on the ceiling. The whole room was "as bloody as could be."

As for the condition of the pruning shears and whether they'd been wiped clean, he only glanced at them and couldn't honestly say. If at that point he'd already figured out they were the murder weapon—because otherwise why would they be there?—he didn't say so.

Some people said hedge clippers instead of pruning shears. Others said rose shears. Newspapers switched back and forth. A serious gardener like Ruth Dickins certainly knew the difference. Hedge clippers were meant for trimming bushes or lopping off a branch in a single whack. They operated like scissors and required the use of both hands. The blades were usually straight and about twelve inches long, the wooden handles approximately the same length. Opening the blades required the user to spread the handles wide, then clang the blades together in a single sharp motion. To use such an instrument in a murder would require a *plunge* from on high, arms straight up, blades closed, into the victim's body, one mighty stroke at a time. It's hard to imagine pulling off this kind of move unless the intended victim was not moving. Asleep maybe. Or bound.

Pruning shears, usually eight to ten inches in length including handles and blades, meant to fit in the palm of one hand, made for a closer, more intimate cut. Ruth called the ones on the bathroom floor "snips."

They were all metal, from the tip of the blades—curved, shaped something like a hawk's beak—to the blunt end of the handles, where there was a kind of loop device meant to lock the blades closed until you needed to use them. The murderer would have had to stand close to the victim, within inches, to hack into her body as repeatedly as Idella Thompson had been. At least 150 times, the coroner would report. Maybe more. There were too many to count. One pierced her skull, revealing her brain, dislodging that eyeball.

There was no sense to it. Dead was dead. Who would keep chopping away like that and why?

Ruth had already told Doc the snips belonged to her. She'd brought them from her house to Bit's—Idella's—to use trimming some rosebushes ahead of that night's rain. As requested by her mother.

Aldridge didn't waste time wondering about any of that. After a quick foray into the bathroom, he headed back into Idella's bedroom, noting as he went the bloody tracks he left behind and the squeaking noise the wet, sticky soles of his heavy shoes made as he traipsed across the wood floor. There were, however, no other tracks behind or beyond his that he could make out or remember.

Lifting the phone receiver on Mrs. Thompson's bedside table, he called the Washington County sheriff, Hugh W. "Hughey" (pronounced "Hew-gie") Foote, who, after hearing the news, made a few phone calls of his own—including one to Ruth Dickins's husband, John, and one to the Thompson and Dickins family lawyer and financial adviser, the man known around town as Mr. Greenville, William T. "Billy" Wynn.

Once he'd made those calls, Foote headed toward Highway 82 and turned east out of Greenville toward Leland, straight ahead on the perfectly flat ground, past fields of what we knew as "white gold," the last of that year's cotton crop, toward the scene of what seemed to all who heard of it that day an entirely unthinkable crime, a murder that could surely be understood only as an ungodly attack committed by a wild man, a man either terrified or possessed. A maniac.

Ruth told Doc and Frank Aldridge right off she didn't know the intruder, had never seen him before. And she wondered if her mother hadn't started the ruckus herself. Mrs. Thompson, after all, was known to be "right difficult" and, according to her daughter, "hot-tempered" and "fiery," especially when it came to her pecans. Oh, Ruth said, "she would go into a tantrum over those pecans." Even the ones that fell from trees planted on the creek banks, which were not her property.

This year had been bountiful and therefore especially aggravating. The creek bank, Ruth said, had been "alive with Negroes picking pecans." And if her mother discovered Black people in her yard? She would light into them, give them "unshirted hell."

Based on Ruth's account, the initial thinking was that the intruder, a Black man from somewhere else, had wandered into Mrs. Thompson's yard. To protect her pecans, Idella unleashed her fire on him. Maybe when he came close to the house, she picked up the snips to warn him off, maybe she even struck at him or in his direction. And because he was not from around here and didn't know the unspoken rules, he refused to accept her fury as his due but grabbed the snips away from her and, enraged by her language, went at her, over and over again. Weak and small as she was, released only that morning from a weeklong stay in the hospital, what could she do?

. . . .

Sheriff Foote's path to police work was a little like Aldridge's, nothing he'd planned or thought about while growing up the son of a plantation owner in nearby Rolling Fork, Mississippi. But his father loved gambling more than managing crops, and as a result he'd had to sell off the land to cover his debts. By the time Hughey graduated from the University of the South in Sewanee, Tennessee, his father had moved north to Greenville, and so Hughey went there too, settling in the nearby Lake Washington area, where, like everybody else who lived there, he planned to engage in cotton planting. When that didn't work out, he moved in to town, where he worked for a couple of years for his father, then decided to go for something different.

To gain employment with the Greenville Police Department, you had to be a white man between twenty-five and forty-five years old. Hughey signed on. Within a year or so he'd been appointed deputy, and thus gained a leg up on the job he'd set his sights on. Like a lot of other men he longed to be county sheriff. He'd come close when the governor appointed him to serve out the term of a man who died in office, but his tenure was cut short when the late sheriff's widow was elected. Undaunted, he ran again but lost to the Greenville funeral director John Askew Stovall. When Stovall appointed him chief deputy, Hughey appeared to be climbing the right ladder, but when the two men managed to get crosswise some way or another, Stovall fired him without saying why.

The next election—sheriffs were limited to one four-year term— he ran again. This time he won. And now, only nine months after his swearing in, Hughey and Stovall were poised to enter another personal face-off, in the matter of the most famous homicide ever to occur in Washington County.

. . . .

Before he left Greenville, the sheriff had made two more phone calls: one to the Mississippi State Penitentiary and one to the Greenville chief of police, Clarence Alton Hollingsworth, who was in court and couldn't leave immediately but said he'd make it to Leland as soon as he could get loose. The call to the penitentiary, known as Parchman Penal Farm, was to order up Nick and Red, a pair of trained bloodhounds. Kenneled at the prison, the dogs were well known all over the state and, according to one former sheriff, were beloved by the public. People naturally liked dogs, he explained. They got a kick out of watching Nick and Red snuffle through the grass, looking for a bloody trail, even though he'd never known them to actually solve a case.

Pink Gorman was dispatched to fetch Nick and Red along with their trainer, Edgar "Dog-Boy" Ballard, a prison trusty. The trip from Leland to Parchman would take an hour or so to get there, same thing coming back.

. . . .

High school kids drove out Highway 82 from Greenville to Leland all the time, past where there used to be a drive-in movie theater called the Anne and a little farther on, to Mink's Dine and Dance, where, weekend nights, they could drink and dance and sometimes eat steak or spaghetti. Once they'd liquored up, boys often squared off in fistfights in the parking lot, while girls who weren't used to drinking barfed up the bourbon their dates had bought at one of the bootleggers' shacks nearby. I didn't go to Mink's often, but I remember it. Once you drove past it and got to the Leland city limits, you came to a sign on your left directing you to Deer Creek Drive and soon after, on your right, Lillo's Supper Club, which as far as I know was the first restaurant in the Delta to serve pizza and is still in business.

. . . .

As Sheriff Foote was making his way to Mrs. Thompson's house, Frank Aldridge and Doc Witte were poking around on the back porch, looking for something that might reveal a clue to the identity of the killer, who, unless he was still on the property hiding in the garage, clearly must have escaped by running through the porch and out that screen door, down the back steps, and over the brick wall behind the garage. They found blood smears on the interior porch walls, the woodwork, and the door into the house. There was also a dark red scrape across the porch floor indicating the dragging of the dead or near-dead woman's body into the bathroom perhaps by using the small rug her body now rested on as a kind of sled.

But there was no blood on the back steps, no footprints, handprints, sprinkles, spatters or drops, no sign of a man's torn clothing. They tried the yard. Nothing there as well. The brick wall was four or five feet high and would have been a substantial challenge even for a skilled high jumper. There were gates that opened to Second Street, which ran parallel to the wall, but they were locked. On the other side of the street there were a few houses, some empty lots, and beyond that but in the near distance the imposing, steam-operated Leland Compress, where ginned cotton was pressed into bales held together by steel bands. Adjacent to the compress was a warehouse where the bales were stored. Together, the buildings took up some seven acres of land. Beyond the compress was a neighborhood where Black people lived in small, closely packed wooden houses.

Aldridge wasn't up to much traipsing. After only a short walk around the backyard he went back inside to check for signs of a robbery, anything indicating larcenous intent. Nothing seemed to be disturbed. The house was stone quiet. Immaculate. It held its secrets.

The investigating team was running out of daylight, maybe an hour before the sun would start to set. Mrs. Thompson's body was still on the bathroom floor. The highway patrol had rolled in, but there was no sign of the dogs. Finally Pink Gorman called. He, Ballard, Nick, and Red had gotten only twenty miles down the road from Parchman when his car broke down, a problem with the fuel pump, he thought; he was waiting for it to be fixed. They still had forty miles to go, no telling how long the car repair would take. They needed somebody to come get Ballard and the dogs right away.

The sheriff arrived only half an hour or so after Aldridge and Gorman, about 4:00 p.m., maybe 4:10. By then more than a few local folk had heard the news, some of them more than likely having noted the police siren screaming by. Neighbors went outside to find out what was going on and where those police and highway patrol cars were heading and what might have happened to necessitate use of that hellish sound in their tranquil neighborhood.

Even more significantly, the switchboard operator of the Southern Bell Telephone Company—housed in downtown Leland in a room above the popular Azlin Drugstore, where people gathered to drink coffee and gossip—was fifty-year-old Myrtle Dyess, who'd been chief manager and switchboard operator for almost thirty years. In which time she'd become decidedly local. Not only had Dyess seen Mrs. Dickins in the drugstore that day, drinking coffee with her nephew, but she'd also listened in to the calls Ruth made later, to the Witte Hospital and Clinic as well as the one Doc made to Frank Aldridge and then Aldridge's call to Hughey Foote. And after that, the call Ruth made to her big sister, Mildred, who'd been at their mother's house earlier but had gone home for lunch and hadn't returned.

Once the news hit the telephone wires, it spread through various channels, from Leland to nearby Stoneville, Elizabeth, Arcola . . . all over Washington County. In no time, the press showed up. First on the scene was the *Delta Democrat-Times* reporter Dave Brown, who happened to be driving around the Leland area when he heard the sirens and went to see what was up. Other reporters who'd heard bits and pieces of the news soon appeared as well, as did a commercial photographer connected to a number of newspapers. In no time, more curious residents set out to see for themselves what was going on and if what they'd heard could possibly be true. By the time Sheriff Foote arrived, a crowd of neighbors and curiosity seekers had gathered in Mrs. Thompson's front yard and along the driveway, a hundred or more people, he guessed. The Drive so jammed with cars and pedestrians he had to honk them out of his way.

Clarification: *white* residents gathered. Even before Ruth's accusation had made the rounds, Black residents took note and stayed home. Those who were at work left.

Go home, one white man told a respected Black employee. *Stay.*

A short, round-bellied bespectacled man, Foote hustled into the Thompson house, leaving the door open behind him the same as Doc, Frank Aldridge, and Pink Gorman. After giving the dead woman's body a quick look, he asked where he might find his only eyewitness. But Ruth wasn't there. Frank Aldridge had told her nephew, Wood Thompson "Thompsie" Hood, the son of her sister, Mildred, to take her to the Witte Clinic to get her injuries seen to. Wasn't that what he should have done?

This will be the first of several occasions when Sheriff Foote got the feeling other people were taking over his job, either by giving orders that were rightfully his to come up with or shutting him out of certain important procedures. He made no bones about needing help on this particular case and was eager for the Greenville police chief, Hollingsworth—who'd been trained in evidence collection at the FBI Academy in Washington—to get to the crime scene and offer his expertise.

Still and all. He was sheriff and the case was his. In order to get the investigation up and running and prepare himself to make a statement to the press, he needed to ask his own damn questions, especially concerning the intruder. Size, exact skin color, clothes, shoes; where he was when Ruth first saw him, which way he went when he left.

But he didn't say anything to Aldridge. He simply went back out to his car and headed to the clinic, once again leaving the front door the way it had been when he got there, wide open.

Soon, the more brazen among the onlookers took that as an invitation to go in and take a look. When nobody stopped them, they wandered down the hall to see for themselves if what they'd heard was true and, if it was, maybe get a peek at the body. Frank Aldridge was still in the house and so was Doc and some other cops and highway patrolmen, but nobody cordoned the crime scene or ordered the gawkers out. Nobody even thought to close the front door. The people who should have been in charge seemed to float like cottonwood fluff in a state of pure disbelief and uncertainty. Which naturally served to roil the chaos way beyond where it had or should have been.

When the sheriff got to the clinic, Doc Witte's son and partner, Dr. W. S. (Wallace or Wallis Stovall) Witte, known locally as Dr. Bunt, was already treating Ruth's wounds, but he waved Hughey on in. An hour or so later, the sheriff hushed the crowd in order to read her description of the killer to the reporters.

. . . .

The next day, every printed account in the country assumed that what Ruth said was what had happened: she'd brought her mother home from the hospital only that morning and that afternoon had been surprised by "a Negro" who'd been hiding in the bathroom, after, in the words of the Jackson *Clarion-Ledger*, "slash[ing] her mother's head and face to a bloody pulp."

Hughey made the same assumption. "If you want to know the truth," he later explained to the DA, "I was looking for a Negro. Mrs. Dickins [said] it was a Negro who did it and I thought nothing else but that it was a Negro."

To a lot of people, this made sense.

. . . .

Later that same day, an armed posse of white men mounted up, preparing to ride horseback past Second Street and the cotton compress, over to "colored town." Their mission, to see if they could find anybody who looked like the man Ruth described or maybe somebody who remembered seeing such a man streak through the neighborhood in bloody clothes. But before they went, the men rounded up the women and children who lived on the Drive and took them to nearby Stoneville for their protection.

When a sixteen-year-old girl who lived on Second Street directly across from Idella Thompson's garage was warned that a murdering Negro was running loose and might even have torn through her own yard to escape, she closed her bedroom door, curled up on her bed, and cried all night. Even on the day I met her, in 2018 when she was in her upper eighties and slightly out of touch with the forward march of everyday life, her face curled into a terrified pinch when reminded of that night.

"It was *awful*," she says and stops to remember, as if envisioning herself closed up in the dark, weeping. After a pause, she repeats herself. "*Awful*."

By nightfall, once the slapping rain set in, the last of the curiosity seekers had gone home. State and county highway patrols had set up a network of roadblocks throughout the area, stopping all vehicles driven by Black men. The patrolmen flagged down a few pickup trucks, but everybody they questioned had an alibi and none fit Ruth's description. A couple of local men were hauled into the Leland City Jail, but they were released the next day.

. . . .

The posse returned later that night, shortly before the rain cooked up so high they couldn't see where they were going. A woman who lived on the creek told me her father had been one of the men riding horseback.

After he brought his wife and daughters home from Stoneville, he said, "There's no Negro. It's somebody in the family."

She's pretty sure he never said that to anybody else.

By the next morning, the Drive had been closed to traffic. The rain hadn't stopped. A lot of the locals who'd tromped through the Thompson house and yard the day before gathered together under dripping store awnings downtown, exchanging rumors and keeping an eye on city hall and any police cars that came and went, just to be in on things, not saying much. Just standing there.

WHITENESS AND
THE MISSISSIPPI DELTA

The first thing to remember about the region in which all of this happened is, it's not a delta. It's a fat, juicy floodplain of mostly buckshot dirt. A real river delta on the other hand is a vaguely triangle-shaped landform born at a river's mouth when it empties into slow-moving or stagnant water. Say, an ocean. A lake. The Gulf of Mexico.

In addition to which even if the "Delta" designation has become sacrosanct and is too melodious to let go of, its full title should be The *Yazoo*-Mississippi Delta, because, geographically speaking, our—those of us who lived there and called it home—piece of the Deep South lies between those two rivers, the bully-boy Mississippi on the west and the winding Yazoo on the east.

It's a lesser river, the Yazoo, in every way. Shorter, narrower, tamer. To find its source, you'd need to make your way some seventy-five miles south of Memphis to Lula, then go east toward Moon Lake to the bayou at Yazoo Pass, which feeds into the first contributing river, the narrow, twisty Coldwater. Follow it for two hundred plus miles, past Tutwiler and Sumner, and you merge into the Tallahatchie, which, right about at Greenwood, swallows up the Yalobusha. And there, the multiple water-ways start life again as the wider, deeper, more significant Yazoo. Which follows the high ridges of the Loess Bluff to just above Vicksburg, where it curves westward and empties into the Mississippi, headed for the Gulf of Mexico, at the mouth of which is an actual, honest-to-God river delta.

Between those rivers and as a result of their constant overflow, there developed, over centuries, an egg-shaped floodwater plain of pure moneymaking alluvium two hundred miles in length and seventy across at its widest point. Nobody called it a delta in the antebellum days. Back then, because of its abundance of trees, vines, canebrakes, mosquitoes, rats, and malaria, it was known as the Swamp. There were bears. Alligators. Snakes. Feral hogs. By the time the state seceded from the Union, only one-tenth of the land had been cleared.

Every spring, the Mississippi rose, overlapping its banks, rolling its way east and south from its Minnesota headwaters, taking in the excess of other major rivers as it went, gathering strength and power. South of St. Louis, the land pancaked, making it easier for the water to demolish curves and pitifully ineffective sandbag levees as it raced on through, dumping whole towns into its maw. When the first two Washington County seats—Princeton and then New Mexico—became victims of this seasonal theft, they were said to have "caved into" the river. Once the original push had moved on, the overflow stood. Wallowed. Grew rank, turning whatever had been growing beneath it into sediment; invaluable rot. Until at last, having deposited its wastes, the water moved on, groaning and slow, twisting its way to the Gulf, creating at its mouth an authentic river delta.

And so the question remains: When did Swamp become Delta? In 1861, when the Twenty-Second Infantry departed from Washington County to fight for the Confederacy, it marched as the Swamp Rangers. Eighty years later, Greenville's softball team revived the label, calling itself the Swamp Angels. In his folksy column in *The Delta Democrat-Times*, Brodie Crump wondered in print "just when the Chamber of Commerce folks began to urge usage of the Delta label rather than Swamp."

He invited readers to contribute an answer. None was forthcoming.

Whenever the name switch occurred, its topographical boundaries were set down forever in 1935 by the Greenville writer David Cohn. "The Mississippi Delta," he wrote, "begins in the lobby of the Peabody Hotel in Memphis and ends on Catfish Row in Vicksburg," a splendid, oft-repeated turn of phrase William Faulkner royally flubbed when struggling to claim it as his own in his Nobel Prize acceptance speech.

Once established, the name stuck, and in time residents of the Delta, formerly known as "swampers," became instant planter aristocrats, as if the lushness of the land itself gave them reason to lord it over other southerners, including Mississippians from the hills and piney woods.

And in the end, call the region what you will, its major asset was and still is its dirt.

Another relevant geographical fact to keep in mind is that the Mississippi Delta has no bedrock. It is all topsoil and squish. When the original bridge was built, connecting Mississippi to Arkansas, the caissons had to be set some 225 feet *below* the river bottom, through the muck and beyond it, to get to soil of a consistency to hold the weight of its towers. From the bottom of the caissons to the top of the towers of the bridge is a total of 843 feet.

In one of his books about the American South, the historian James C. Cobb called the Mississippi Delta "the most Southern place on earth" and quoted the sociologist Rupert Vance's description of the region as "cotton-obsessed, Negro-obsessed," the poorest, blackest region in the country, a crescent of bottomlands where, even in 1938, antebellum conditions had nearly been preserved. The persistence of this helped reinforce a "widespread perception of the Delta as not just a region but a world and a way of life apart." Having extolled the virtues of that world—civility, gentility, manners—David Cohn worried that the current, pre–World War II influx of lower-class whites might wipe out the "flickering dreams of a better way of life," including the vaunted noblesse oblige of the planter aristocracy.

As for Greenville, Queen City of the Delta is one of those fanciful slogans local chambers of commerce like to dream up to enhance a town's appeal. But unlike a lot of others, this one had some validity. Greenville was known for its citified self-image as well as its literary heritage—William Alexander Percy, poet and author of *Lanterns on the Levee: Recollections of a Planter's Son*, about his life and the 1927 flood that devastated much of the Delta; his cousin the erudite philosopher and novelist Walker Percy (*The Moviegoer*); Shelby Foote, known in those days as a novelist and in years to come both as the author of a Pulitzer Prize–winning narrative history of the Civil War and as the most appealing talking head in Ken Burns's documentary series about it; the memoirist and essayist David Cohn; Josephine Haxton, who as Ellen Douglas wrote very fine novels about her native Natchez. With its upscale shopping and proud architecture, our downtown was the pride of the Delta.

As for those of us who grew up there? We certainly weren't *crackers*.

We studied Latin. Read books. Never listened to hillbilly music but danced to early rhythm and blues and, when our proms and cotillions were held in venues not owned by the city, we rocked to the music of all-Black bands from Vicksburg, the Rebops, followed by the Red Tops. Plus we had Hodding Carter Jr., editor of *The Delta Democrat-Times* and winner of a 1946 Pulitzer Prize for editorials "on the subject of racial, religious and economic intolerance."

We bragged on ourselves and managed to stay mostly ignorant about the rest of the state. I don't remember ever visiting Jackson, the state capital. Jackson was boring; we preferred the soulfulness, the food, and the shopping of Memphis. Jackson offered little we couldn't come by on our own. For vacations within the state, we went straight to the coast, Biloxi and Gulfport. Everything else was nonstop drive-through.

By "we," I am speaking here of white people of course. Exclusively.

. . . .

What do we gain from this information? Why does every story written about the murder of Idella Thompson refer to her as a society matron, her daughter a socialite? Both terms are fluid within various contexts (most dictionaries seem somewhat flummoxed by the situational possibilities and employ some form of "social" in the definition, such as "socially prominent," "socially important," or "social climber"; others go out on a modern limb with "jet-setter"), but we know what's implied and why, as a result, the story merited such a big play, not just within state boundaries, but all over the country.

Idella's parents were among the second-generation planter aristocracy, having arrived there in the late 1890s, well after Reconstruction had collapsed, when the Yankees were gone and life was settling back to what it had been with only one difference: no slaves. The period southerners called the Redemption.

The second wave was to some extent an educated one. Doctors, lawyers, bankers. People who sent their offspring to prep school, boarding school, eastern colleges. Not that lawyers and doctors didn't supplement their professional practices with the purchase of large tracts of land to cultivate. On the contrary. Cashing in was the draw; dirt the magic ingredient. By the late 1890s, Leland had added the final necessity: a quicker means of transport than waterways provided. By then it was, in essence, a buzzing railroad town.

The Dean family arrived. The McGees. The family of Idella Elizabeth Stovall Long.

. . . .

I have found two photographs of a newly married Idella Thompson, both shot in New Orleans on the same day in May 1899 at the Canal Street studio of the photographer Eugene Simon. She is nineteen and a half years old and dressed to the Victorian nines, as is her husband, Joseph Wood Thompson, called Wood, who is eight years her senior. In one of the portraits, they are joined by the newlyweds they are traveling with: thirty-year-old William Klingman and Mary Clementine "Clemmie" Turner Klingman, who is twenty-four and Idella's first cousin. The brides share a maternal grandfather, William Tatum Stovall, a doctor, and are honeymooning together.

Idella and Clemmie were born in Tate County, a good bit north of Leland, just east of the Yazoo—territory that may be thought of as on the threshold of the Delta but not quite in it. Idella's father had been living in that part of Mississippi since his family left their farm in North Carolina and settled there in 1852. After acquiring a medical degree from the University of Louisville, Dr. John Ausbin Long married Virginia "Jennie" Stovall, and in December 1879 the couple had their first baby, a daughter they named Idella.

By the time the Longs arrived in Leland in 1888, Idella, age nine, had at least three siblings, sisters Birdie, Addie, and two-month-old Johnie Ruth. By then the town had been incorporated by the state legislature and was prospering big-time. Railroads were operating; cotton was thriving; mercantile and grocery stores had opened; there was a need for doctors. After John Long established a medical practice and opened a drugstore, he—like pretty much everybody who had enough if not hard cash, then credit—bought acreage a little east of downtown near a railroad stop. His parents had farmed, and so he'd grown up with agricultural know-how. He named his plantation Longswitch.

In 1948, when Idella is murdered, her oldest child, Mildred, will be living at Longswitch with her husband and son.

Dr. John Ausbin Long became an alderman, joined the First Baptist Church of Leland, known locally as the church of upscale Social Baptists. Within a few years, Idella's grandfather on the Stovall side arrived with his second wife. They too joined the First Baptist Church and stayed.

The Stovall name was golden. Many others of them settled in the Delta. There's a town called Stovall in Leflore County. Families reproduced with gusto. A Stovall couple in Greenville had eighteen children. When the boys grew up, they ran for office, started businesses, established a large presence. The girls made their debut and, more often than not, married well. Not all of the Stovalls were wealthy or lived a particularly high-toned life. But in the end, the cousinhood provided what they needed: votes when they ran for office, reliable backup, jobs, and a certain swagger. Many are there to this day. They know their ancestry: who served in which war, which cousin died of what, and who married whom. All of the ones I knew had deep brown eyes, dark hair, a quick sense of humor, and a solid sense of family. They always seemed to be in on a joke the rest of us would never be privy to, I expect because they only pretended to be standing on the same ground as the rest of us when really they were off enjoying private conversations within the family. Even the thinnest genetic link to the Stovall cousinhood counted.

Joseph Wood Thompson was twenty-seven when he married into the cousinhood. He'd moved to Leland from Tallahatchie County eight years earlier. From the notices he received in the local papers, he seems to have quickly become quite the young squire about town, at the ready with a witty comment when a *Leland Progress* gossip columnist asked about his marital prospects.

And here, in a full-blown formal portrait, is his answer: New Orleans, 1899. Married into a top-tier family.

. . . .

Murder-story descriptions of Idella Thompson focus on her temperament, health, age, and size. Her doctor spoke of how small she was, how little she weighed, so tiny her daughter called her Bit. Friends and family describe her as "fragile" or "frail." As for temperament, descriptions range from "right difficult" to "high-tempered" to "arrogant," "a bitch from hell," and "plain mean." A pint-sized hothead, ever on the threshold of popping off.

But in 1899 at nineteen she was soft and pretty, a saucy girl in a big hat, on her face a slightly smug expression and why not: she's the daughter of a Stovall mother and a prosperous planter/doctor father, and she couldn't be more stylishly attired or properly married.

Her chin's high, cranked somewhat to her right. She's at ease, comfortable in her finery, used to it. She has a classy nose with a small bulb at the tip and a generous mouth. Her cheeks are a little plump perhaps with baby fat that will soon drop away. She's not smiling—the fashion then was to strike a serious pose and hold it—but her lips are pressed gently together. Behind her dark eyes, cut sharply to her right, lie the kinds of secrets most nineteen-year-old girls harbor. The things she knows that she's not supposed to. The things she wishes she knew or wishes she didn't. Her real desires.

She is very pretty and confident beyond her years.

The bodice of her dress is fashioned from soft material, perhaps silk, with a high collar, a large bow at her throat, and a V-shaped inset of embroidered squares and a handkerchief-sized bit of lace at the point of the V. Her sleeves are wide at the top with a decorative flap over the gathers, and perhaps they end at the wrists in a mutton-leg shape, narrow down the forearm. Her shoulders are quite narrow. She's wearing drop earrings, perhaps of a single pearl.

To top all of this off is the hat, one of those tiered wedding-cake creations stylish ladies wore at that time. The base is round, flat, and about as big as a serving plate, like a man's straw boater. She has set it in an ever so slight tilt to the left, just enough to give her a judiciously flirtatious air. Atop the brim and encircling it is a froth of whipped-cream flounces and flowers, from the middle of which rises a swirl of more lush frippery, atop which is majestically perched a bird in flight. A whole bird, beak, eyes, feet, wings raised high.

Her husband stands behind her. The top of her head reaches just to his shoulder. But her hat rises from there on up past his chin, nose, and eyes, until the tips of the bird's wings graze the swoopy wave he likes to affect at the hairline. He's in dark frock coat and white dress shirt with soft black bow tie and stiff collar to his chin.

They are quite the prosperous couple. Idella is, in a word, splendid. And Wood Thompson knows it. His rather sensuous and clean-shaven features are set, determined, and looking directly into the camera lens, he seems to be defying those who would see him any way other than a man who will make his mark, succeed, take care of his family, rise in the community he's chosen, impress the powers that be with his intelligence and determination, and do well.

Eugene Simon took at least one more picture that same day, of Idella and Wood alone, seated side by side, and if she's not propped on a booster pillow, they appear to be close to the same height, his waved blond forelock rising only slightly higher than the top of her head. She's taken off her hat for this one. Her hair's parted dead center, then pulled in soft waves over the tips of her ears to the back of her neck, where she's affixed a chignon. Wood looks stern and much more serious than in the group shot, but Idella has a kind of winsome look, mouth slightly open, eyes soft, as if she were about to ask a question.

· · · ·

Having returned to Leland, the Klingmans moved in with Clemmie's father on the Drive. By spring of the next year, Wood and Idella had rented the house next door, with Wood's young cousin Foster as a boarder. As young marrieds, the neighboring couples socialized together, traveling to Greenville to go to the theater, attending parties. Klingman would become a traveling salesman for a wholesale grocery company, but Wood Thompson used his connections and whatever inheritance he'd come by from his Tallahatchie County family to establish himself as an entrepreneur and a planter. Within a year of his marriage, he'd rented a thousand-acre plot of land east of town, close to his father-in-law's property. Within a couple more years he'd taken on another thousand-acre farm in that same part of the county, fortuitously located near the Southern Railway line. He and his cousin Foster were also employed at the Leland Mercantile Company, which had been incorporated in 1894 and was said to carry "every necessity of the home and plantation, everything to clothe and nourish the human family . . . the best of everything that can be found in the large trade centers."

By 1902, Wood had done well enough to begin overseeing the construction of a grand home for his family on some 1.7 acres he'd bought at 111 North Deer Creek Drive West. Designed in the popular, ornate Queen Anne style, it had the requisite two and a half stories, the dormers, and turrets, the gingerbread touches, and the porches on two floors that wrapped three-quarters of the way around the house. Within another two years, he'd be president of the mercantile company and the father of two children: Mildred Elizabeth, born in 1900, and James "Jimmy" Wynn, in 1904. Another son, John Wood Thompson, born in 1902, died a year later. He is buried in the Greenville Cemetery.

Asked by a local publication how he felt about Leland, Wood said, "I travel around a great deal, but I always return home satisfied." As for his farmland, like everybody else, he depended on cotton as his money crop, but he'd also been experimenting with diversified farming as the wave of the future and said he didn't think there was a reason in the world why everything consumed by man and beast should not be raised in the Delta.

. . . .

Idella gave birth to her third child, Ruth Idella, on June 9, 1906, and six years later, to their fourth and last, William Wood. Three months later, in what was deemed perhaps the worst overflow in the history of the state, the Mississippi River broke through levees in both Louisiana and Mississippi, leaving an estimated twelve thousand people on the Mississippi side and seventeen thousand in Louisiana homeless. In Mississippi, some of the most intense suffering occurred just outside Leland, where some two million acres of farmland, including Wood Thompson's two thousand, were under four to eighteen feet of water, most of which stayed for more than a month, ruining that year's crop.

When the governor of Mississippi created emergency relief stations for the collection of clothes, food, bedding, and other necessities to be distributed to people stranded and in need, he thought highly enough of Wood Thompson to choose him as the man in charge of the Washington County station. The government sent burlap bags, foodstuffs, tents, and sleeping mats to the Thompsons' big house on the Drive.

. . . .

The next spring, a photographer came to snap a portrait of the Thompson children in their Easter finery. The picture is not dated and Easter's a guess, but everybody's in white and their clothes look crisp and spanking new, the kind of exaggerated finery young children dressed up in to attend Sunday school and church on that sacred Christian morning.

The three youngest are seated on what seems to be a velvet settee: Jimmy on one end, Ruth on the other, the baby between. Mildred, who'd be about twelve or thirteen, is standing behind them. She's wearing a lacy dress with an attached kind of capelet at the shoulders. The fabric is handkerchief thin and frothy. There's a slim bracelet on her left arm, a delicate chain around her neck, and, circling her head, a white satin band adorned with flat bows, one over each ear. Her hands are clasped below her waist, she's tucked her chin fetchingly to one side, and she's smiling away, clearly enjoying the fire out of having her picture made. A big girl, perhaps, though in the dress it's hard to tell.

Jimmy's about ten, and as, presumably, the future man of the family, he's been dressed like one: white starched dress shirt two sizes too big, complete with French cuffs, fastened in place by shiny round cuff links, and a narrow tie, white with light-colored horizontal stripes, held in place by a tie clip. His hands are in his lap and they seem, even in a still photo, fidgety, thumb and forefinger of one hand basketed with the same digits of the other. Darkish skin, hair parted low, combed flat. He's a sweet-looking boy, but his expression is one of suspicion, perhaps even fear, as if he were on the lookout for an ominous turn of events, lurking nearby and bound to show up soon. His mouth is turned down, his dark eyes cut sharply to the right. And you have to wonder, what's over there? Or who? His mother? Father?

Plump-cheeked baby William Wood, who must be about eighteen months old, is in a white cotton frock, either a baby dress or an early version of a onesie, with a kind of sailor's tie at the neck. He's been given a toy to hold, and he is, in contrast to his brother, the model of a happy child. His mouth is open in a rosy O, revealing pearly baby teeth. He's completely huggable, the only one who's not either posing like Mildred or wishing they were someplace else like the other two. By the time he gets to be eighteen, he'll be known as Wood, like his father, and sometimes, in the southern manner, as Little Wood.

Beside him, Ruth. She and her brothers have the same nose, medium-sized with a turned-up tip. All four children have their mother's mouth. The other three have dark eyes like both of their parents, but Ruth's are crystalline and radiate a kind of magnetic shine. When she became an adult, newspaper reporters sometimes commented on her swarthy skin and dark blue eyes, an odd combination difficult to visualize. Her skin color might have something to do with the amount of time she spent working in her garden. But dark blue eyes are rare, and nobody else in the family seems to have them. Unlike her brothers and sister, she has fixed them with great, perhaps, we might say, even challenging, intensity straight into the camera lens.

They've dressed her in a lacy, loose-fitting dress made even more shapeless by the restless, forward-thrusting hunch of her shoulders. She's dropped her hands down out of camera range and is perhaps sitting on them. A delicate chain circles her neck with something like a locket hanging from it. But the most dramatic part of her costume is the bow they've put in her hair. It's not attached to a band or flat like Mildred's but perched on its own, a big puffy explosion of satin, swirled one way and then the other and stuck straight down on the top of her head. Beneath it, her dark hair is straight, short—clipped just shy of her earlobes—and has a kind of flyaway uncontrollable look.

Her posture is one of movement, head forward, body ready to shoot up and go. If I had to imagine her thoughts at that moment, I'd say what young Ruth Thompson wanted more than anything she could think of was to get out of that outfit, get rid of the ridiculous bow, and get on with her life, doing something if not challenging or physical, then at least interesting.

Athletic and brainy, dressed like a Victorian sweetie pie, she represents the coming mid-century version of American womanhood. Not altogether realized yet. On the cusp of a full flowering.

. . . .

Drawing on photographs as a predictor of the future may be misguided. But there are enough times when you can—or think you can—actually *see* the probable outcome of what seems to be clearly pictured there to encourage us to keep doing it.

As for us at this time, the Feys, our ancestors lag far behind the Thompsons in terms of births, marriages, and offspring. My grandparents on my father's side, Walter and Cora Bryant Fey, had married late. A second-generation German immigrant, he was thirty-seven, had lived in Cincinnati with his parents his whole life, and was a railroad inspector. Cora was a thirty-six-year-old milliner who with her sister ran her own hat shop in Lawrenceburg, Indiana. Soon after they were wed, they took the train across the Midwest to the Mississippi River, then down the Mississippi to Helena, Arkansas, where Walter's sister lived.

There, they made a life. Walter bought land, began to farm. In 1912, about four months after the Thompson children were photographed in their Easter finery, Cora gave birth to the first of three sons. Four years later, when she was nearing forty, she bore her third and final child, my father, David Leonard Fey.

My mother was also the youngest of three. As was true with my father, her siblings were both boys. There was another son, the first, who lived only a year. My grandparents Terry Pauline "Polly" Miller and William Bryant "Billie" Smith were craftspeople. He was a leather worker, harness making his specialty. She was a skilled seamstress. At this time, they lived in a small town in eastern Arkansas called Wheatley. When a shoemaker died one town over in Marvell, my grandfather took over his shop. My mother was born at home in 1919, in Wheatley. Her mother was about twenty years old; her father, thirty.

Orphaned at two, my grandmother—Polly—quickly earned a reputation as a handful. Sent with her sister to live with relatives who often passed her on to others, she had an unsettled and grinding childhood. Possibly as a result, she grew into a balky young woman, a hellion who needed to be married off as soon as possible. In personality and temperament she might even be likened to the murdered Idella Thompson, as "fiery," a woman who was willing to give "unshirted hell" to those who crossed her or meddled in her life.

Their upbringings, however, could not have been more different. Nor could any other part of their lives.

The year Idella Thompson was murdered on Deer Creek Drive, the widowed Polly was living in Bakersfield, California, with her second

husband, making fur coats from scratch for movie stars like Linda Dar-
nell, who was also a friend. Or anyway that's what she told us.

. . . .

When my family moved to the Mississippi Delta, Jim Crow rule was
still holding on all over the South. Nobody thought that would change,
ever. It was 1942. I was three. My brother, David junior, was nine months
old. Like me, he'd been born in Memphis.

We had no family in Mississippi, no kin to offer a welcome or give us
the occasional leg up when we needed it. My father had earned a degree
at the University of Tennessee School of Pharmacy in Memphis, but
it didn't take him long to figure out that pushing pills behind a drugstore counter was way too slow. And so he'd taken a job as a traveling
"detail man" for a prescription drug company. Parke-Davis & Company
assigned him to a territory spanning a sizable portion of northwest Mississippi: his job, to drive from one doctor's office to the next, providing
samples of his company's newest products, touting their efficacy. The
company paid expenses and basic salary, but mostly he worked on commission. A natural salesman, he envisioned himself and us sitting top
of the heap in no time. Maybe not rich. But close. Because Greenville
was the biggest town in his territory, he rented a house for us there. My
mother felt safe there; settled.

"I thought," she wrote in her journal, "we would live there"—meaning,
I think, Greenville, not necessarily that particular house—"for ever."

. . . .

The population of the Mississippi Delta has always been, and still is,
predominantly Black. When it came to racial or ethnic designation,
we never spoke of "the minority." The minority was us. *They* had the
numbers. We had the money, the power, the opportunities; we got better schoolhouses, newer books and desks, brick churches. Police officers.
Judges. We could try on clothes in downtown stores and swim in the city
pool. Hold office. Eat at Jim's Café. Vote without fear of reprisals. Live
anywhere we liked. Define the boundaries. Make the rules.

Aristocrat or latecomer, whiteness gave us a pass. We didn't think
about this much. Like hot summer nights and mosquitoes, it just *was*.

We moved in to a nice bungalow at the foot of an important street, Washington Avenue, straight across from the town cemetery. Once we were settled in, Daddy hit the road, often gone for four nights a week, to towns like Drew, Ruleville, Rosedale, Rolling Fork, Cleveland, Clarksdale, even Mound Bayou, an all-Black town in the heart of the Delta. He soon knew all the doctors in every town in his territory. Even more important, they knew him.

· · · ·

World War II was raging. Mama and I prayed nightly for the starving children overseas. I imagined Europe as a bare white rock on which raggedy orphans knelt and lifted their arms to the heavens, begging. We made friends in the neighborhood. The bungalow was sweet and we liked it. But within two years of our occupancy, the landlord's wife called. We had to move, immediately. Her husband, an engineer, had been doing war-related work in another town. Now that his work was done, they were coming back. They needed their house.

Three days before our eviction deadline, my father placed a sizable ad in the paper asking property owners for help finding something for us—even a vacant garage or tent, he joked. To attract attention to the ad, he'd had it outlined in black, but nothing turned up. My mother, brother, and I moved to West Helena, Arkansas, to live with my Fey grandparents until Daddy found us another house. I started school there. But by Christmas, we were back, living in another bungalow in another part of Greenville, on the corner of Cedar and Manilla Streets. We were still living there in the fall of 1948 when, a week before Thanksgiving, *The Delta Democrat-Times* arrived broadcasting the news of the murder of the society matron Idella Stovall Long Thompson.

RUTH'S TURN

Shortly after noon on Friday, November 19, two days after the murder, five men and one woman pulled up at the home of John and Ruth Dickins. When the doorbell rang, John ushered the visitors through the living room and down a short hall into his wife's bedroom. Recovering from her wounds, Ruth lay in bed, propped up on pillows, her swollen left forearm now a robust purplish-blue from the Wednesday afternoon confrontation.

John had arranged seven chairs around the foot of Ruth's bed. One by one, the visiting squad entered: Washington County sheriff Hughey Foote; Leland police chief Frank Aldridge; Greenville chief C. A. Hollingsworth; from Jackson, special investigator and private eye A. E. Crawford; Mississippi Highway Patrol fingerprint expert and former FBI agent Ed Blue; and Washington County court reporter Clara Wing. The men removed their hats and took their seats. Clara Wing gathered up her shorthand notebook and pens.

The inquest had been held at city hall the night before. Among those attending were Ruth's two brothers, her sister-in-law, and her nephew, Thompsie Hood. Sheriff Foote called only one witness, the man who'd called about the crime, Doc Witte. At the end of his testimony, the sheriff declared a recess until the next day, after Mrs. Thompson's funeral. He'd been asking to talk further with Ruth ever since the afternoon of the murder, but the family wouldn't let him come close. She was injured, they said. She wasn't up to talking. Because he'd known Ruth most of his life and was on a first-name basis with her, he didn't push it.

Idella's last rites had taken place that morning at ten in the living room of the murder house, within sight of the original assault. Two ministers spoke, a Baptist and a Presbyterian. After the service, a funeral procession drove to the Greenville Cemetery, where Idella was buried in the Thompson family plot beside her husband. The funeral director and Idella's second cousin, the former sheriff John A. Stovall, made the arrangements and served as one of the pallbearers.

. . . .

John took the remaining chair, there as always to protect and support his wife. They'd been married since 1929, after they'd both graduated from college. Ruth had gone to Hollins, a prestigious girls' school in Virginia where she studied Latin, joined a sorority, and played on the field hockey and baseball teams. No surprise in any of that. Ruth was smart and she was athletic. A Leland woman of some years told me, "It was considered a good thing back then to send girls to college in Virginia." In the Hollins yearbook, *The Spinster,* Ruth's class photos show an unsmiling girl with downward-leaning eyebrows, a distinctly unfussy blunt haircut, and a look of bone-deep unhappiness . . . or perhaps a simple unwillingness to put on a fake happy front for the camera.

Once she got her degree and came home, she hit the road, flitting about the Delta visiting fellow Hollins graduates, making car trips to Greenwood, Clarksdale, and Indianola, often accompanied by her brother Jimmy, who had left the University of Virginia after three years and was living at home, working for his father. Together, they attended cotillions, proms, and Leap Year Dances. Ruth went to card parties, attended a road tour of the *Ziegfeld Follies,* served as bridesmaid in several weddings, participated in whatever social event came along to serve as an excuse for a party. In return, she'd throw her own luncheons, bridge and Rook parties, and special soirees when girlfriends came to Leland to attend weddings, parties, and the wild, well-known "Delta dances" at the Greenville Elks and Elysian Clubs.

The capacious Thompson house could easily accommodate Ruth's guests. A few years earlier, Ruth's father had gotten rid of the wraparound porch and lacy Queen Anne geegaws and had the house enlarged and restyled in the less ornate, neoclassical fashion of the day, columned and stately, not unlike the Greek Revival style of the antebellum South but with more windows and wider spaces, even a sunporch on both ends of the ground floor.

Ruth had almost certainly met her future husband there when, after moving to Leland, John found lodging with the Thompsons. Outgoing and popular, he was handsome and something of a catch. By the time they met, he was working for two of the top cotton brokers in town, both members of a second-wave founding family. The son of a respected Greenwood doctor, called Dick by fellow students, John Dickins is listed in his Mississippi College yearbook as six feet and one-half inch tall and 165 pounds. Captain of the baseball team, member of the football squad and the Senior Honor Society, president of the student body, he's described as "old reliable . . . unfaltering in his trusts, always looking forward, and willing and glad to do his part, or more, in anything that maybe [*sic*] asked of him."

A prophetic assessment.

Announcing the upcoming nuptials, *The Clarksdale Press Register* called the Thompson-Dickins wedding one of the brilliant events of January. Describing John as "one of the state's finest young men," the *Greenwood Commonwealth* predicted that his wedding would "doubtless enlist much interest among his many friends." Somewhat inexplicably, however, no parties in Ruth's honor were listed in any Delta society pages.

For her bridal costume she wore a tan and brown "traveling costume" with matching accessories and carried a fan-shaped bouquet of newly patented Georges Pernet roses—French hybrid teas with tissue-thin petals of delicate shades of pale orange and yellow—mixed with ostrich feathers. No way to know who came up with Ruth's wedding attire, but given her unconventional fashion tastes, I expect she picked it out herself, insisting on the practicality of a neutral-toned travel outfit, offset by an unlikely bouquet featuring ostrich feathers. At any rate, safe to say she was honeymoon ready. Once she and John were man and wife, they could head straight for his car and a three-week driving trip to New Orleans and Florida.

Upon their return, the couple began married life as lodgers on the

Drive. Quick-minded, reliable, willing to gamble, John progressed in no time from cleaner to the kind of cotton buyer who was often asked his opinion of that year's crop yield and quality.

The Dickinses had been married for six years when, in 1935, they bought a vacant lot two blocks from her parents. By then, their first child, a daughter they named Dell, probably after her grandmother's nickname, had been born. By the time they moved in to the modest English-cottage-style house they built in 1940, they'd seen fit to add another half lot to the property, perhaps because Ruth wanted distance between her family and neighbors she might not know or like. And she needed extra room for the lavish flower beds she had in mind. By then, their second daughter, Dorothy Jane, had been born.

Made of brick painted white with dark green shutters, the house was topped by a Gothic-style roof swooping to a point above its bay windows. Asymmetry being in fashion, the formal front door sat to the left of the windows, near the western edge of the house, and led into a tiny foyer and then the living room. But the screen door used by everybody who knew Ruth and John was on the right-hand wall of the house. It opened onto a small porch with a door that leads to what might have been called the den but had become primarily John's reading room, where, evenings, he put his feet up, lit his cigar, and read the papers.

Ruth and John had separate bedrooms. Located pretty much in the middle of the house, hers lay within easy earshot of her daughters' room and had windows overlooking her garden. From her bed, all she had to do was twist her head slightly to the left and, if the curtains were pulled, there it was. Like a painting. Her horticultural creation.

· · · ·

The man from Jackson spoke first. "My name," he said, "is A. E. Crawford and I was brought up by Mr. Wynn and at the request of the sheriff, trying to help as best we can."

Ordinarily, an outsider would not launch a formal police inquiry. Officially, the case was Hughey's. He should have taken the lead. During the trial, when asked by the prosecution if he'd known Crawford would be the man conducting the examination, Foote bristled.

"No, sir," he testified, "I think *I* was the man conducting it."

Asked why, then, he allowed Crawford—a private eye from another city—to take charge, he stumbled. "Well," he said, "he was in on it." Without making clear what he meant by "it."

As a matter of some interest to all, Hughey himself had tried to hire Crawford, based on a recommendation from the Memphis investigator who turned down the job because of a prior commitment. But when the sheriff called Crawford's office, he was told the investigator had not only been hired by the Thompsons' family lawyer and financial adviser; he'd been in Leland since a little after midnight on the morning after the murder and was there now, combing Mrs. Thompson's house for clues and snapping crime scene photographs, working side by side with the sheriff's own officers. Something nobody bothered to tell Hughey.

Later that morning, Crawford helped the local cops find two torn fingernails, a bloody handkerchief, and a small, pearl-like button with thread still attached, as if torn from an article of lady's clothing. That afternoon he worked with the police chief, Hollingsworth, to prepare forensic materials—fingerprints, blood swabs, hair samples—to send airmail special delivery to the FBI labs in Washington.

They'd looked for bloody footprints left by a fleeing killer and for "Negroid" hair. They found neither. The tracking dogs also came up empty.

. . . .

"I know you were hurt," Crawford assured Ruth, "but in trying to arrive at a solution and you being the only eye witness naturally we want to talk to you."

"Ask me anything you want to," she replied. "Maybe I can help you."

A promising start.

Forty-seven-year-old Aldus Elmer Crawford was a small man, unprepossessing in appearance: pale skin, a receding hairline, a pointy nose, thin lips. He wore wide ties and an oversized fedora arranged in a jaunty tilt on his slim pate. But his eyes were beady, and a clever criminal knew better than to underestimate his expertise. He'd been known as a fearless law enforcement officer in the Jackson Police Department, first as a detective and then as Hinds County chief criminal deputy sheriff. He left police work in 1944 to open his own firm, Crawford & Company.

Only eight months prior to coming to Leland, he'd solved a twenty-month-old murder case, a feat that landed his photo on the front page of the Jackson *Clarion-Ledger*. According to the paper, he'd knit together a "measly supply of clues" to nail the killer in Clovis, New Mexico.

. . . .

The PI responded to Ruth's opening challenge with a gentle suggestion.

"Suppose you tell us," he said, "where you were and what was going on when you went to the house. When did you last see your mother alive?"

In some instances, "Suppose you tell us" might well serve as the come-on of an investigator wishing to soothe his subject into a false sense of security. But in this instance the request appears to have been, for the most part, sympathetic. Ruth, after all, was, as Crawford pointed out, a witness, not a suspect. And Crawford was working for, being paid by, her family.

Ruth began her story in the middle of things. "When I came back from Greenville, I went on by the house, that is why I came back, to see about Mother and my little girl was sick. I stopped by the house and Thompsie was there and we sat and talked and fooled around and Thompsie got up to go and said he had about six bits he could spend before going to get his Negro out of the hospital and for me to come with him to Azlin's for a cup of coffee and . . ."

She ran on.

In Clara Wing's transcription, Ruth's story slides barely punctuated along the page, as if emerging faster than even a skilled shorthand practitioner can keep up with. Full sentences follow hard on top of one another, creating a nonstop, unbounded narrative style, words and names tumbling ahead, knocking into previous statements, scattering them like thumbed marbles in a boys' game.

Crawford interrupted the flow. Will she give them the time?

Ruth hardly took a breath before continuing as before. She was sure, she said, it was after one when she left Jim in Greenville and she'd seen Billy (longtime family lawyer and financial adviser Billy Wynn) in the bank and, yes, she was sure that was right, she knew it was after one, but back to when she was at her mother's house, she followed her nephew

Thompsie (son of her sister, Mildred) to the drugstore and drank a cup of coffee with him and talked to Mrs. Azlin (drugstore owner), and then Thompsie went on his way to the clinic and she came back to the house here (*her* house) and got those durn shears because her mother had told her the other day at the hospital she wanted her to cut back some shrubs, she had been fixing a flower bed, that was about a week ago and she wanted to finish it (the bed) but it commenced raining and she (Ruth) found her there and said she shouldn't be doing that and for her to come on in the house and wait and let her do it when she could. So she (Ruth) came on here (to her house) and went to the garage and got the snips and went on back down to do what her mother wanted her to do and be done before she went for her little girl at school, she goes for her every afternoon at 3:45.

She had a gravelly voice, I'm told, the deepest southern accent and the lowest voice anybody ever heard in a woman (even friends and relatives who speak with a decidedly pronounced drawl comment on hers: *oh,* they say, *way more southern than mine*), and a rhythmical, lilting way of speaking, in something like musical waves, which she often punctuated with a brisk, almost staccato "don'tcha know?" in consciously witty, full-stop contrast to the liquid swing, like the slap of a drumstick on the rim of a snare drum indicating the end of a musical phrase. In this she was something of a language performer and more than likely would be a pleasure to listen to as long as you weren't on the lookout for hard information, rationally, even chronologically organized.

If by telling her story in this way she was hoping to catch hold of and control the drift of the interview, she was succeeding. Her free-form recitation proceeded with few interruptions or the request for details commonly used in police interviews as a way of dislodging the subject's certainty and reminding her of the track she should be on. But then, she was a witness, not a suspect. Her murdered mother had been buried only hours ago. The situation was delicate.

And so, she said, it was well past 2:30 that afternoon when she'd gone by her mother's house and talked to Bit and Thompsie, then went with him to the drugstore . . .

Wait. The PI finally stopped her. Did she go to Greenville *after* she left with Thompsie?

Crawford himself either seems to have lost track or is working to urge his client to pull herself together and straighten out her story.

No, Ruth said, answering the question she assumed Crawford was asking. She came straight home (after the trip to Greenville) and went back to the garage and got the snips and took them to her mother's and while Thompsie and she were sitting there (*before* going to Azlin's for coffee) her mother had another request. She said because she (Ruth) fussed at her all the time about being in the garage alone, afraid she'd hurt herself or that the swinging doors would knock her down, she wanted Ruth to take her out there to see about the baby kitty cats her Persian cat Duffy had just had.

Ruth, of course, had it in her mind that she needed to get to the schoolhouse in time to fetch Dell but her mother said, "I hate to bother you, hon" (which was what her mother always said when she wanted Ruth to do something for her), "but . . ." and she added yet another request, "I am afraid it will rain and will you bring me that box of paper shavings Mrs. Azlin gave me?" Her mother loved to fool with her cats, and because she didn't like straw and hay for the babies' bed, her friend Mrs. Azlin had given Ruth a box of paper shavings for her to use instead. Ruth had put the box in her hall closet. That's what Idella wanted her to go get. Ruth knew if she got the kitties fixed up even if it did rain, her mother wouldn't worry about them anymore, which is why she went back to her house for the shavings because, well, even though she said she hated to bother her, her mother thought nothing of asking her to go back and forth between their houses. Which was really all right with her because she petted her mother like a baby and spoiled her. And they lived close enough to make the trips quick and easy.

Crawford let Ruth's disquisition about the cats drone on without asking for clarification or trying to move her in a different direction, even though her narrative was often contradictory, muddled, or both. But the sheriff might well have given orders to go easy on her, considering who she was and what she'd been through as well as the certainty of who the culprit was, if not his full identity, then at least his race, size, and clothes.

Given the PI's silence, Ruth continued.

Anyway she hadn't seen to Dorothy Jane since about a quarter to twelve before she took her mother her dinner and drove Jim to Greenville, so when she went to get the shavings she also took her daughter's temperature and fooled around with her a little and talked to Beatrice Smith, the cook, about supper and made a list of embroidery thread colors Dorothy Jane wanted from the dime store, she remembered that. She thought she put the list in her purse. She then looked for the shavings, but Bea had moved them, so she went on back to Idella's and this time parked in the driveway at the back door, which she didn't usually do, she always parked out front, but as she was leaving, her mother had said to park out back when she returned and that even if she (Idella) was still lying on her resting couch, she'd get up and let her in.

Which, as everybody in the room had to be thinking, meant that door would be locked when Ruth got there; otherwise why would Mrs. Thompson have to get up to let her in?

And if the door was locked, how did the intruder get in?

If anybody on either legal team was wondering about that—and surely somebody was—nobody said so. Or referred to the whiff of inconsistency in Ruth's recall, so dazzled and distracted were they, it would seem, by the drawling depths of her voice, the relentless circularity of her recitation.

So.

She continued.

She went on back down there (*there* being her mother's house; *here*, hers) in the car and parked in the driveway and when she got to the back door the first thing that caught her eye was some blood on the back porch. And some on the door into the house. When she saw that, she felt certain she knew what had happened and hurried into the house as fast as she could go. But even before she got to the bathroom and saw her mother on the floor, a thought had occurred to her.

"As I was going in the bathroom I am sure the first thing that crossed my mind was that mother had killed herself because Papa had killed himself."

Pause. Nobody said anything.

There are many more questions nobody asked, one of which was, how much time exactly or even approximately passed between the moment she drove two or three doors down the Drive to give Dorothy Jane her medicine, chat with Bea about supper, and look for the paper shavings and the time she got back when, after parking in the driveway, she opened the back door, saw the blood and her mother's feet, and immediately assumed Idella had committed suicide? Ten minutes? Twelve? To make up your mind to kill yourself, figure out the means to do it—with what, considering all the blood?—and carry it out?

Of course, they had to give their eyewitness some slack. She'd been through a grievous shock. Ruth would make the point later when, struggling to explain her own behavior, she said, "You can't walk in a room and see blood and have any sense."

Right.

Silence. She rolled on.

As she rushed into the bathroom, someone jumped her from over by the toilet and swung at her and she thinks she ducked and he slammed at her and she commenced wrestling with him and got the snips away and he was twisting her hand and she was fighting with the other one and what was in her mind was to get this thing away from him so he could not kill her too and she slipped in the blood or he hit her and she fell face forward to the floor, which was covered in blood, and he ran out the back door. And while she would "hate to have the responsibility of this," she was sure it was "a Negro but not a yellow Negro," and she was positive in her recollection of the tussle that "it wasn't a big man," he wasn't much taller, she didn't believe, than she was. And he was dark-skinned.

The fingerprint expert Ed Blue stepped in. Would she remind him once again, when she left her mother's house the *second* time, to get the shavings, did she leave by the back door or front?

The front. Her car was out front. She never parked in the driveway unless she was going to her mother's garage or to meet her at the back door, which is what happened that day when, as she said before, Idella told her to park out back when she returned, she would get up from her resting couch and "meet you back there."

Blue moved to the appropriate follow-up: Did she know if the back door was locked when she got back?

A dangerous assumption lay beneath the query and Ruth knew it.

She began, "I believe Mother went back there," and then she switched directions. "I have thought about this." And switched again: "He could have knocked on the door," meaning, of course, the intruder because what Ed Blue was asking is, if Ruth went out the *front door,* leaving Idella lying on the couch toward the *back* of the house where she'd be within sight of the back porch and the screen door leading outside and vulnerable to people who might sneak into her backyard, wouldn't the back door have been locked? Especially since Ruth herself had told them about her mother's obsession with pecan thieves?

Ruth knew that was the root of his question. Everybody in that room also knew that while white people in this part of the country often left their front door unlatched, they always locked the back for the very reason being considered at this moment: because no Black person dared even to knock at the front door of a white person's house. And you didn't want them having free access through the back door.

Ruth spun out a convoluted and distracting tale involving a pitcher of ice water she took from the icebox and poured in a glass *before* she left out the front door the second time when she went to the drugstore and to get the shavings, and a distinct memory of putting the snips on the back porch heater *while* she drank the water, where they, the snips, stayed, in plain sight of the back porch door. So that, and she's thought about this from every angle, when the intruder entered—however he managed to get inside—he could have seen them through the screen and then grabbed them as he came inside, because she's sure that's where they were.

Also. Her mother had gotten old and "fussy with children." Ruth had seen her bless out the little boy next door for doing nothing but playing football in his own yard.

Crawford stepped in. Where exactly in the bathroom was Ruth, he asked, when she fell and bloodied her clothes?

When Ruth answered, saying she "sprawled across" the tile floor, Crawford asked if she fell on her mother and she said no, the floor was "covered with blood" and she fell into it and when she got up from slipping or being pushed she checked to make sure the man was gone and that's when she went to the phone in her mother's bedroom and called the hospital number—162—and asked for Dr. Bunt Witte specifically, because he was Idella's main doctor. But the receptionist, Mrs. Mason, said Dr. Bunt was operating and, according to Ruth, abruptly hung up the phone. And so a few minutes later she called again and asked for "old Dr. Witte," who came to the phone right away. But because he'd become a little hard of hearing he couldn't make out exactly what Ruth was saying except "something [was] wrong with Mother," which he assumed meant she'd had a stroke. He said he'd be right there.

Once again, Ruth circled back. She wasn't finished describing the bathroom, where her mother was lying "up and down" on the tile floor, she thinks facedown. After the man was gone, she tried to see "what was the matter" with her mother. In an effort to roll her over, she "picked her head up and got her by the arms and couldn't do a thing. She felt like a sack of concrete."

Sack of concrete? To describe the weight of your slaughtered dead mother? And could she really stand there either holding or looking at the murder weapon and still wonder what the matter was with Idella when her skull had been split wide open and by the coroner's estimate she had been struck some 150 or more times?

Asked how long Ruth thought her mother had been dead when she entered the bathroom, Ruth again said she believed her mother was "still gurgling and breathing" when she "bolted" through the bathroom door, right before the man jumped her. And once again she referred to the death of her father and, despite her earlier observation that she'd been in Greenville when he died, said she remembered how he had "gurgled." She turned to her husband. "I guess you remember that, Dickins," she said, "you were in there with him, he gurgled."

John didn't directly respond but took advantage of the opening to steer the conversation in a different direction. When nobody interrupted to remind him that as a member of the family perhaps he should let others ask the questions, he returned to his wife's scuffle with the assailant and her heroic recovery of the pruning shears.

It was about here that Ruth began turning questions back on the investigators.

What was the killer's condition? Crawford asked. "Were his face and hands bloody?"

They were bound to have been, she reckoned, "don't you imagine?"

He thought so, yes.

Where was the killer when he swung at her?

"He must have backed up there when he heard the door open, don't you think so?"

He did.

And she wasn't sure whether, after taking the shears from the man and striking at him, she'd bloodied his face, but surely she did, didn't Crawford think so?

He let that one pass.

Asked for specifics about the man's appearance—his size, his clothes, the color of his skin—Ruth said he was small, wore black pants, had dark skin, and was unknown to her.

And might he have had some kind of a "smell about him"?

She responded with a long story about a possible gas leak outside at her mother's house. Idella had mentioned it that same day. And if there was a leak and the man had been hiding in the backyard, mightn't he have had an odor about him, didn't Crawford think so? From the escaping gas?

Crawford did think so, yes.

And when she went out in the hall after she'd gotten hold of the shears and saw that the back porch door was open she's sure the main thing in her mind was that the man was gone, didn't Crawford imagine that was what she must have been thinking?

And wasn't the first thing she'd have done when she found she was loose from him was to call Bunt? Didn't he suppose that was right?

When no one answered, she continued.

After finally reaching Doc, she "went back to see about mother," and because by then it was obvious she was dead, she "petted her little hands" and tried to love her up a little, then went into the bedroom and sat on the radiator to wait for Doc.

· · · ·

Sheriff Foote, who up to this point had remained mum, finally joined in to ask if at any point in the day Ruth had gone out to Idella's garage, a point that will be widely commented on in the days to come, as a distinct example of Ruth's ability to remain unnaturally—even criminally—calm despite the ungodly state of her dead mother's body.

Yes, Ruth replied. By that time Thompsie had arrived, and before leaving for her house (Thompsie would drive her there) so that she could change clothes, and then going to the clinic, as Frank Aldridge had suggested, the two of them went out there to take care of the mama cat and her babies, to make sure the kitties stayed warm and safe. Because her mother loved them so. Ruth thought they should do that right away, even though she'd been injured and needed to be seen to and her mother was lying dead on the bathroom floor. Because she didn't know when she'd make it back.

Afterward, Thompsie drove her to her house and after Beatrice Smith helped her take off her bloody clothes, Ruth told her for God's sake not to let the children see them. And so Bea took the clothes away and Ruth put on a clean outfit. Thompsie left and Mrs. Azlin—who'd heard the news—showed up and took her to the clinic. Doc had left the Thompson house by then and was back at the clinic to clip the hair around the scratch on her forehead but, eager to get home to console his wife, who was Idella's sister, asked his son Bunt to clean the wounds and sew up the one on her head.

. . . .

There are two reasons to make special note of Ruth's casual mention of her father's suicide nine years earlier. One is that while pretty much everybody in Leland and a whole lot of people in Greenville knew that Joseph Wood Thompson had died at home as a result of a gunshot wound to the head and not in the Greenville King's Daughters Hospital after a long illness as reported on the front page of *The Delta Democrat-Times,* people didn't speak of it. The family had managed to transport Thompson to the hospital that morning, where he was declared dead. There'd been an autopsy, but they'd managed to keep the true manner of his death out of the public eye. And so once all of that was taken care of, they shut down the conversation and kept the details to themselves. There was no inquest, no police investigation. For the privileged, death sometimes remained, may still remain, a private affair, for an example of which one has only to note the stark refusal of certain Lelanders to discuss the violent death of Idella Thompson, even now, seventy-plus years after its occurrence.

Stovall Funeral Home took care of Wood Thompson's last rites and burial, just as it would for his wife.

And here Ruth was, tossing the carefully concealed nature of her father's death into a bedside interview with a roomful of men and a court scribe recording her every word. Perhaps even more unnerving is her use of the blatantly graphic term *gurgling* to describe her parents' labored breathing as they lay on the floor of their home in a pool of blood struggling to stay alive.

But Ruth was known to be plainspoken. If her mother and father both *gurgled,* then why not say so? In modern terminology she was known for an unladylike tendency to *tell it like it is.* If people were shocked, so be it.

· · · ·

The *Delta Democrat-Times* obit paid Wood Thompson the standard, upstanding white citizen tribute, listing church, family, boards served on, and—especially important in the Mississippi Delta—numbers of plantation acres owned or managed. Thompson had certainly earned his place on that roster, but he was a far more interesting man than history or local commendations have left us with, and was certainly the linchpin of his family.

He was born in Tallahatchie County just outside the town of Charleston, Mississippi. Eighty miles northeast of Leland and east of the Tallahatchie River, Charleston lies just outside the official boundary of the Yazoo-Mississippi alluvial plain. Hoping to cash in on Delta mythos, tourist brochures and chamber of commerce signs label it the "Gateway to the Delta." Driving east from the Mississippi River toward Alabama, through Tutwiler and Sumner and across the Tallahatchie bridge, a traveler will quickly note a shift in the landscape as the great black-dirt flatness of the Delta splits into hills and crags. Runoff steals topsoil, making for lower crop yields, longer work hours, less leisure time, something closer to a hill-country point of view: churchified, work oriented, and gritty.

Like a lot of other farmers hoping to prosper and even perhaps grow rich growing cotton, the first Thompsons to settle in Mississippi came from South Carolina by way of Georgia in the early 1840s. The brothers Joseph and Foster did fairly well. By 1850, Foster had four children and sixty-one slaves, while Joseph, unmarried, owned forty acres of land worth $10,000. In all likelihood, the brothers farmed together, sharing slaves, land, payouts, and income. Early that same year, Foster contracted pneumonia and, as he lay dying, voiced his last wishes, naming his brother as executor. Joseph took his brother's family into his home and, after his widow remarried, continued to raise his sons. When he died in 1860, the federal census estimated the value of his real estate holdings at $50,000; his personal estate, $153,990, all of which he left to his niece and his three nephews, including Wood Thompson's father, who by the next year was serving in the Confederate infantry. After being discharged at Appomattox, he returned to Tallahatchie County, farmed his portion of his uncle's land, and married.

Idella Stovall Long's future husband, Joseph Wood Thompson, was born in 1871. By 1876, he had a brother and a sister. Two years after that, his baby sister, Lottie, was born. But within weeks of Lottie's birth, yellow fever had begun to gnaw its way through the state. The 1878 epidemic lasted through August and September, until the first frost of the year. By then it had taken the lives of more than four thousand Mississippians, including both of Joseph's parents and two of his siblings, leaving only Joseph, seven, and his two-month-old sister as survivors.

Joseph and Lottie were taken in by Thompson relatives. They remained close throughout their lives. But Lottie was spared the experience of watching her family suffer and die. Her brother was the child with memories.

At nineteen, he was still living in Tallahatchie County, but by then he'd taken to going by his middle name and soon showed up in a newspaper gossip column as "Thompson of Leland." In 1894, a Greenville columnist tagged him as "Bro. J. Wood Thompson," a man who had "only one thing to keep him from getting married and that is the contrariness of the old men with marriageable daughters." A month later, there was another friendly dig: "Wood Thompson says he will be glad when the marrying season closes for he has been worried enough with the matrimonial candidates, and is no longer taking part in such a race himself."

Not long after that, he married into the Stovall-Long family and soon established himself as an upstanding citizen of the Delta. Following the Thompson tradition, he took in family members throughout his life, lodging them, hiring them, seeing to the christening of their babies.

To many, suicide didn't make sense. To this day, people refuse to believe Wood Thompson killed himself, leaving no note and, even more improbably, no will. Somebody shot him, they think. And many of them have a theory about who did.

· · · ·

After Ruth called the clinic but before Doc got there, she tried once more to roll Idella over and lift her by her arms, but, she told the investigators yet again, her mother felt like a sack of concrete and she "couldn't do a thing." So she gave up and returned to the bedroom to wait.

The PI returned to the question of the back doors: Were both screen and inside doors closed when she came in?

Yes. Both were closed.

He repeated himself: Both were closed? Yes.

A lapse on the crack investigator's part: doors open or closed mattered not at all. What counted was the question of *locked* or *unlocked*.

And when Crawford asked if when she came in the house her mother was on the bathroom floor, she returned to the gurgling sound that made her think her mother was still alive, then again asked what *he* thought about that.

Didn't he agree? Didn't it make sense she would think that?

And didn't Crawford imagine when she got loose from the man and he ran, the first thing that entered her head was to try to get Dr. Bunt?

Crawford agreed that, yes, it seemed a reasonable supposition.

And did the murderer say anything?

"I don't believe he opened his mouth."

When the questioning returned to the tussle, she happily supplied details: She grabbed at the snips with one hand and he got hold of the other one and twisted it. And then he somehow grasped her head probably with his other hand. Which is how she got the scratches and bruises. And while she wasn't exactly sure whether or not the man was injured or bloody after their fray, she thought he was bound to have been, didn't they imagine? She couldn't see how he wouldn't have been.

And after he turned her loose and went out the bathroom door, didn't Crawford imagine the main thing in her mind was that he was gone, especially after she saw that the back door was open?

Crawford didn't respond this time but instead handed her pictures of convicts who'd recently escaped from Parchman and asked if she recognized them. Ruth simply repeated what she'd said earlier, that the man was small and young and she believes he was a "black Negro" who must have worn dark clothes because if he'd worn light-colored ones or denim pants she would have remembered.

As for why Idella's maid wasn't in the house that afternoon (Crawford had asked the question), Martha Prewitt had been out picking cotton all fall and didn't come to work except on Saturday and Sunday to help out. Martha was married to Dan Prewitt, a "crazy Negro," and if Ruth hadn't known better, she would have thought he was the one who'd done this, but he definitely was not. And yes, Jimmy Banks, her mother's handyman, was out in his room in the garage when it happened but he was old and deaf as a post, he wouldn't have heard anything. And as to the possibility of the intruder's intention to rob the house, Ruth couldn't say but she swore her mother was the worst person in the world about keeping money at home; her brothers would tell you the same thing.

She got insurance checks in the mail three times a month. After her father died, Ruth had the checks fixed so they'd come that way. Sometimes when they arrived, her mother sent Jimmy Banks or Martha to the bank to cash them. And they would be walking around town with those checks and everybody knew it and she and her siblings had tried to persuade their mother not to do that but she kept on. She also stored dollars inside the pages of books and had a little crocheted bag the size of a tobacco sack she put money in and fastened inside her dress. And while Ruth was positive that neither Jimmy Banks nor Martha Prewitt would have stolen even $1 from her mother, there were others who might. Those people knew full well that "Mrs. Thompson's Negroes" went to the bank with her checks, then walked back home with cash money in their pocket or purse.

Ruth then drifted to another money-related topic. On her way to the hospital the morning of the murder, she had stopped at her mother's house to take an insurance check for $63 out of the lockbox Idella kept to pay the hospital bill. She'd cashed it at the bank on her way. But the bill, it turned out, was $66, so Ruth had to add $3 of her own money. But before she did that, she'd jokingly said to her mother, "What are you going to do about it, old lady? This is not enough money to get you out."

Her mother said that, well, Ruth would just have to put some of her own in, and Ruth agreed, and did what she had to, as she always did in the case of her mother's requests: she made up the $3 difference.

When the sheriff stepped in and asked if the intruder wore a cap or hat, she addressed him by his nickname. "Hughey," she said. "Didn't you ask me that?"

And the sheriff says he thought he did.

And Ruth believed she told him the man had something on his head, and Hughey said it must have been either a cap or a hat because if it had been a rag she'd have remembered and she agreed but didn't want to say if she wasn't sure. "You know me, Hughey. You know that."

When others asked questions, she often directed her answer to the sheriff, the man who knew her best. As for instance when she wondered if a "Negro" might have seen her drive off and, thinking there was no one at home, had gone into her mother's backyard to pick up pecans when Idella saw him and because Idella would "go in a tantrum over those pecans," maybe she opened that back door and started giving the "crazy young Negro" a lot of talk and reached over and picked up the snips and told the man if he didn't get out of her yard she'd run him out.

But did she think her mother would actually strike at a Negro? Yes, Ruth said. She believed she would.

"Mr. Frank," she turned to Chief of Police Aldridge, "don't you believe she would?"

Yes, Aldridge said, he thought she would.

Given his response, Ruth expanded on the possibility that her mother might well have brought the whole thing on herself and if she hadn't been so hotheaded it never would have happened. She thought maybe her mother had struck at the man first, and once she did, the two of them got into it and lost their heads. So that once the intruder came into possession of the snips, that was it; the rest of it was bound to happen.

Idella was just that fiery, and even though she was the sweetest, quietest, dearest thing in the world to her family, she would "light into a Negro in two minutes and give them unshirted hell."

Even her own trusted servants? Yes. "She stayed on their necks all the time."

The interview was clearly losing steam. But Crawford took one last opportunity to remind her of the pictures he'd given her. Had she recognized any one of the men?

She addressed her answer to Frank Aldridge.

"I was lying here this morning thinking about this, you know, Mr. Frank, I know the Negroes in Leland, I have some good Negro friends and I know what an ordeal it would be if I ran into some Negro and it flashed through my mind that he looked like the Negro who did this."

She turned to the sheriff. "You know what I mean, Hughey, and there would be nothing for me to do in that case but get Mr. Frank. Now as well as I remember the looks of that Negro it looks more like," pointing to a photograph, "I am not saying it is this Negro, but it looks more like one with a face like that."

Crawford took note.

By then, Thompsie Hood had entered the room and was allowed to stay and to confirm a couple of Ruth's statements. Running out of questions, the investigators returned to her description of her attacker, which she repeated, adding only that she didn't think he'd been a "brute-looking Negro," if he had been, she'd have noticed.

At least she thinks so, didn't they imagine she would?

The Greenville chief of police, Hollingsworth, said he would think so, yes.

After one last attempt to jog Ruth's memory about the man's clothes, Crawford thanked her and ended the interview.

Clara Wing closed her notebook and stored her pens. The men rose. Presumably John Dickins saw them out. As for what Ruth's nephew, Thompsie, did, I say he stayed with her. He'd been at the inquest. He knew where Doc's thinking was headed and Ruth was a pal. He needed to stay on top of things to protect her.

THE RUN-UP

Sometimes in a family history there's a line separating *before* from *after*, a sudden chop in the night, jagging the ancestral forward motion, sending it in a new and unexpected direction. Often, members of the family, busily realigning themselves and assuring others they are *fine*, fail to immediately understand the import of the event. Others sense it right away. *Nothing was the same after that* becomes something like a mantra.

The violent death of Joseph Wood Thompson served as an example of that.

As for the Mississippi Delta itself during this same period of time, generally speaking everything remained the same in terms of race, class, power, language, and the overall drift of everyday life. The "planter aristocracy" held its firm grip on its identity and worth and though the extent of their privilege was profoundly different, the Feys and the Dickinses/ Thompsons continued to benefit from their mutual whiteness.

When J. W. Thompson was found dead in his library, the fallout could be controlled, the official account orchestrated. A parallel track for the Feys and families like them, on the other hand, made sharp turns in other, more public directions. When the rent was overdue, they could be evicted and left to fend for themselves. When men took their own lives, the local newspaper reported it, often on the front page. As for Black families, the fates of those who had survived rested, so far, on the whims of white people, who had managed to ensure the resolute continuation of their supremacist status and to remain solidly Dixiefied—even Deltafied—in terms of race and class.

But they remained vigilant and in this they had it right: change would not come easily or overnight, but it was in the works.

. . . .

To zoom in on the lives of our primary families, the Feys and Thompsons/Dickinses: surely nothing happens without forewarning, a signal of some kind. The run-up to an event—a consideration of previous circumstances—provides historical context and even potential understanding. To search for which, we back up and blaze through the years preceding Idella Thompson's murder, beginning a few years prior to October 1939, when Joseph Wood Thompson died.

1934–1935

John and Ruth Dickins's first child is born, a daughter they name Dell Thompson Dickins. Because her father's position at work has risen from cotton cleaner to buyer, Dell's parents' financial situation has improved. Within a year of her birth, they purchase a lot on Deer Creek Drive a few houses away from her grandparents.

Accompanied by her sister-in-law, Lottie Thompson Cossar, Idella Thompson and her son James (Jimmy) motor all the way to Los Angeles to watch the underdog University of Alabama beat Stanford in the annual New Year's Day Rose Bowl, 29–13. The trip is lengthy but not unusual. Southerners love college football. More than anything they love bowl games involving southern teams.

They drive home happy.

As for the Feys, David senior has graduated from Helena High School. Called Fats in his senior yearbook, he was involved in such activities as Senior Play—his role was "Sue, a colored maid"—Glee Club, Cheerleader; in the class Who's Who he is rated Peppiest Boy. He enrolls in medical school in Memphis. A princess of the Helena Cotton Festival, his future bride, Dora Lee Smith, from Marvell rides through downtown Helena streets on an ornate white float shaped like a Viking ship. Leaning casually back on her hands like a girl at the beach getting a suntan, she's wearing a formfitting white gown and toque hat, carrying a muff. She has tilted her hat roguishly to one side. Both the float and her outfit are adorned with cotton bolls. Her float wins the grand prize.

In *Human Geography of the South*, the sociologist Rupert Vance identifies the "cotton obsessed, Negro obsessed" Mississippi Delta as the "deepest South," a region where he found "the highest economic range in the South" and was struck by the contrasts there, the mansions and manners of the planter aristocracy, "affable and courteous with equals, commanding and forceful with inferiors," while "the Negro" was "to be found at [the] lowest level in America."

At this time, the Black population in the Mississippi Delta still outnumbers the white population by some two and a half to one.

1936

June 4. Joseph Wood Thompson's sister, Lottie, is called to his bedside after he undergoes surgery at Greenville's King's Daughters Hospital. His condition is said to be serious.

Dora Lee Smith graduates from Marvell High School. She is awarded a Music Prize Card for Excellence in Piano.

1937–1938

When the Greenville Cotton Exchange holds its annual fundraiser at the Hotel Greenville, John Dickins, now thirty-six, is chosen to preside. They raise $750.

Dora Smith marries David Fey during a double date with another couple. They keep the wedding secret until it is announced in the Memphis *Commercial Appeal* several months later. They move to Memphis, where David is in medical school, but when Dora becomes pregnant, in order to get out of school faster, he switches to pharmacy. He goes to work at various drugstores, supplementing his income with gigs playing four-string banjo with visiting orchestras on the roof of the Peabody hotel.

In a runoff election for police chief and marshal of Leland, Frank Aldridge beats out the incumbent.

August 10, 1938, Beverly Lee Fey is born in Memphis. Her mother names her for a debutante whose photo she has seen in the newspaper.

Two and a half months later, on October 28, the Dickinses' second daughter, Dorothy Jane, is born in Greenwood, the home of her father's family.

After David finds work in Ruston, Louisiana, the Feys buy a car and move to Ruston. Beverly is four months old.

1939

Within a couple of months, David has a beef with the owner of the Ruston store. The Feys move to Clarksdale, Mississippi. But by August 10, when Beverly's first birthday rolls around, they have returned to David's birthplace, Helena, Arkansas, where he has somehow "taken ownership of" a downtown drugstore and changed its name from King's to Fey's Pharmacy. The local newspaper features an interview with him, accompanied by a headshot. He exudes confidence. Beverly's mother throws a birthday party for her at their rental on Perry Street and invites a number of small children. There's a cake. Beverly's little terrier dog attends. His name is Jack, which is her first spoken word. At one year, she has lived in four states.

. . . .

Some time before nine o'clock on the morning of October 23 in Leland, Mississippi, five days before Dorothy Jane Dickins celebrates her first birthday, a shot is heard throughout the 100 block of North Deer Creek Drive West and beyond. Minutes later, Dell and Dorothy Jane's grandfather Joseph Wood Thompson is found lying near the fireplace in the library of the house he'd had built for himself and his family when he was in his early thirties, bleeding heavily from a head wound. The family manages to transport him to the King's Daughters Hospital in Greenville.

Nobody set much store by the obituary in the next day's *Delta Democrat-Times*, headlined "Illness Fatal for Prominent Leland Planter and Former Official." Too many people heard the shot. Some even said there were two shots, only one of which hit home. Illness might have been the reason behind J. W. Thompson's death, but it wasn't the cause.

Issued by the Department of Commerce, his death certificate—Standard Certificate of Death No. 18037—lists the deceased as Joseph Wood Thompson, a white married male planter and merchant, age sixty-seven years, nine days, and twenty-six months. Date and time of death, October 23, 1939, 9:00 a.m. Place of death, King's Daughters Hospital, Greenville, Mississippi. Immediate cause, gunshot wound of head. Site of injury, home, Leland, Mississippi.

To the question of *how* death occurred, whether by homicide, suicide, or accident, the attending physician, Dr. Paul G. Gamble, wrote, "Don't know." The "informant"—a close friend or member of the family who signs off on the deceased person's identity—is Thompson's little sister, Lottie Cossar, now the lone survivor of the scourge that killed the other five members of their family. He is buried the following day in the Greenville Cemetery.

. . . .

The death certificate is filed away in the monster archives of the Commerce Department, eventually to be microfilmed and sent to libraries all over the country as well as the Mississippi Department of Archives and History in Jackson.

Four days after the burial, on Dorothy Jane Dickins's first birthday, *The Delta Democrat-Times* runs a "Notice to Creditors" advising anyone holding a claim against the J. W. Thompson estate to file it at the chancery court within six months of his death; otherwise it will be dismissed. Because Thompson has left nothing behind to indicate his wishes as to the disposition of his estate, there will be no executor. Instead, the courts have appointed Idella L. Thompson and her lawyer, W. T. "Billy" Wynn, co-administrators. Their names are on the notice, which runs daily for three weeks. It gives claimants until April 23, 1940, to file.

Because probate will consume most of the following year, Billy Wynn suggests to the family that they plan to meet with him toward the end of 1940 to sort things out, he presumes in a peaceable manner. In the meantime they might want to give some thought to their interest, or lack of, in landownership and farming. As for the Deer Creek house, it remains in Idella's hands.

On December 22, less than two months after her husband's death, on her sixty-first birthday, Idella, in a sense, takes control of her life as a widow by co-signing a deed with a well-heeled neighboring couple agreeing to a house swap: her Greek Revival mansion for their stately, if far smaller, one-story dwelling, with an added $3,000 bonus to cover the greater value of her house and large corner lot. Rabun and Josie Jones's house is located about a block and a half down the Drive from Idella's toward her daughter Ruth's house, now under construction.

She moves, taking her family—sons Jimmy and Wood, daughter-in-law Demetra, her late husband's nephew Lee Cossar—with her to what is then 311 Deer Creek Drive but in the coming years will change to 313 due to the building of a new house in a currently empty lot. Her servants, Jimmy Banks and Martha Prewitt, remain in her employ. Banks is given a room over the garage where he will spend his daytime hours. A wired system is installed, connecting his room to the house with a bell that alerts him when he is needed.

Idella and her entourage settle in to wait until probate ends and they can meet with Billy Wynn in December.

In Mississippi, the assets of a person who dies without a will, or intestate, are distributed in accordance with a default system known as Mississippi laws of intestacy, or intestate succession, which mandates that assets of the deceased be divided equally among his immediate blood relatives: living spouse and children. The law applies, however, only to assets that would have passed through a will, had the deceased left one, which usually comes down to properties owned exclusively by the deceased, in his, or her, name only.

That the farmland of J. W. Thompson was to be divided equally among Idella and her four children strongly indicates that title to the acreage he left was held by him alone, despite a great part of it having originally belonged to his wife's father. In the ensuing years, Thompson purchased adjacent land and eventually renamed the plantation Dellwood, for his wife and himself, a nice touch. On the other hand, he made no move to include his wife's name on the title.

Husbands created the laws of intestacy to keep their property out of the hands of in-laws and second husbands. But Thompson's failure to write a will is puzzling. If the obits had it right and at the time of his death Thompson had indeed been ill for two years or more—confirmed by the June 1936 report that his sister had been called to his bedside after serious surgery in Greenville's King's Daughters Hospital—wouldn't he have wanted to set his house in order ahead of his passing? Mightn't Mr. Billy Wynn have made the suggestion?

Hard to figure.

1940

The U.S. census, taken in April, lists Idella as owner of 311 North Deer Creek Drive, estimated worth, $7,000. Living with her are James Thompson (incorrectly called Jessie), thirty-five, listed as a wageworker; Wood Thompson, twenty-eight, farmer; his wife, Demetra Thompson, twenty-six, unemployed; and Lee Cossar, twenty-nine, insurance agent. Ruth and John's house, at 403, is estimated to be worth $8,000, while Rabun and Josie's comes in at $17,500, a nice gain for the Joneses.

The Feys are listed as renters on Perry Street in West Helena. He is the proprietor of a drugstore who worked every week of the previous year and sixty hours the week before the census was taken. His income comes from "other sources," but currently is zero.

All four houses still stand. Both Thompson houses are in fine shape, while the Dickinses' and Feys' have deteriorated considerably. When Beverly visited her house in Helena for the first time since she lived there, it was uninhabited and shabby. Two curious young Black children playing in their own yards came close to find out why she was poking around their neighborhood, looking at an empty, falling-down house. When she told them she'd lived there as a baby way back maybe before their grandparents were born, they were amazed, probably because they couldn't imagine a person of her years ever having been a baby.

In 2018, the Dickinses' house retained a more substantial appearance but was in great need of repairs and a face-lift. Deer Creek Drive–ers consider it an eyesore. At one point, a representative from the Leland Historical Foundation asked the new owner if he'd mind if they cleared away mangy scrub bushes and carted off an old refrigerator lying on its side in the backyard. He agreed without hesitation.

By the time Billy Wynn meets with the Thompson heirs, the war in Europe has grown more intense, and the U.S. government has enacted the first peacetime-conscription act in its history. A month later, William Wood Thompson, twenty-eight—five feet seven, 155 pounds, with a light complexion, hazel eyes, and brown hair—registers for the draft, giving an office at 512 West Second Street as his home address and the J. W. Thompson Estate, 108 Fourth Street, as the address of his employer.

Four months later, his older brother, Jim—at five feet nine and 170 pounds—registers as well, giving his address as North Deer Creek Drive; his age, thirty-seven, complexion ruddy, hair black, eyes brown. As the person who'll always know where he is, he lists his mother, Idella. He will serve in the army for only a few months. No reason is given for his early discharge. Wood escapes the draft maybe because of his inherited family responsibilities.

Hodding Carter Jr., editor and publisher of *The Delta Democrat-Times* and a member of the National Guard, leaves Greenville for military service but returns home soon afterward, having developed serious eye problems. He and his influential wife, Betty, become interested in issues involving racial inequality, which she terms "the Negro problem." He begins running editorials decrying discriminatory practices in the Delta, causing agitation among many of his readers.

Hoping to get a leg up and save enough money to educate their children, a lot of Delta poor white and Black men sign up to serve in the army. Many of those who are rejected because of illiteracy find ways to slide in. Farms languish as labor becomes increasingly hard to come by.

In December, Billy Wynn gathers the Thompson clan together in his office. The first thing he needs to know is whether anybody in the family has an interest in farming. Other options are to rent out all or part of the land or even to sell it.

Nobody wants to sell. In the Mississippi Delta, as in most parts of rural America, land is sacrosanct. *Never sell the land,* parents tell their children and their children's children. *They're not making any more of it.* J. W. Thompson wasn't the biggest landowner in the Delta by any means, but he owned enough to call his holdings a plantation. His wife and children have no intention of letting some other family take that from them.

As for actually going into farming, however . . .

Jimmy has no interest. For one thing, he's no kind of a farmer and never will be. For another, he's felt even more off-kilter than usual since his father's death and prefers to opt for a smaller plot than he's rightfully due and rent it out. Mildred feels the same way, what with her husband having enough farmland to manage already and her son about to go off to college. She too will take a cut in acreage and rent. Jim and Mildred agree to settle for five hundred acres each, leaving the other eighteen hundred to two thousand far richer acres for Wood, Ruth, and Idella to manage.

Since her father's death, Ruth has been showing up regularly at Billy Wynn's office to learn the business end of the operation. She has a head for figures and, as her husband says, has always liked having a little business of her own. Because Wood has worked with his father, he knows something about farming. And so brother and sister agree to become partners: Ruth handling the money, Wood—sometimes still known as Little Wood—acting as "dirt man." For extra income, they'll rent out a portion of the land. Idella will stay on the sidelines. Watching. Asking questions. Keeping an eye out.

Once the partnership is official, Billy Wynn opens an administrators' account with the Bank of Leland allowing Ruth to sign checks without his co-sign. To enable Ruth and Wood to get going by planting time in late winter, he also arranges for the Southern Credit Corporation to furnish 1941 production credits. The loan is easy enough for Wynn to set up. He holds an interest in the company.

As encouragement, John Dickins buys Wood and Ruth a tractor so that they can join the current move from mule and plow to mechanized farming. Other than that, he butts out. His wife is perfectly capable of running her own show. And he has enough on his plate dealing with cotton prices and trading, especially now that he has to keep up with the war's influence in addition to the ordinary volatility of market swings.

1941

War. Labor shortage. Thompson land suffers. Ruth and Wood incur bigger debts than either of them expected.

Three days after Beverly's third birthday, after giving birth to David L. Fey Jr., Dora Fey contracts polio, probably in the recovery room of the Baptist Hospital, where she remembers shivering with relentless chills despite the many layers of blankets nurses covered her with. Because her husband is out drinking with friends, celebrating the birth of a son, she manages to engage a hospital ambulance to take her home. The Helena drugstore deal having fallen through, the family has moved back to Memphis, but they stay only a short while before returning to Clarksdale for a bit, then back to Memphis. Dora's condition remains improperly diagnosed for weeks. When the pain in her right leg becomes unbearable, a dentist removes a bad tooth. A doctor suggests milk leg as the problem; another, postpartum depression.

By the time she sees a Memphis specialist at what she calls the "crippled person's hospital," the damage has long settled in: the muscles of her right calf and foot have atrophied; her spine is less than straight. By then the Feys have moved in to a duplex in midtown Memphis, their half of which they've actually managed to buy.

Ruth—undeterred by rising debts and her brother's inability to teach his workers how to operate the tractor—stays busy no matter what. She plays in golf tournaments, does civic, church, and garden club work, plays bridge. In August, she and her daughters drive to Manitou Springs, Colorado, where they join her mother and brother Jimmy, who regularly spend one or two summer months there, vacationing and escaping the polio epidemic, like other people of means.

She and the girls are home in time to invite thirty-four children to a third birthday party for Dorothy Jane.

December, Pearl Harbor. Ruth joins other Leland women, rolling bandages and sending packages to the Red Cross. As far as anyone can tell, or so it seems, her partnership with her brother is faring as well as anybody else's in this difficult time. But then, liking to have her own little business doubtless entails a good bit of discretion and nondisclosure on Ruth's part, whatever the truth.

1942

Given Ruth and Wood's inexperience and the national situation, the farm doesn't take long to deteriorate alarmingly in terms of both dirt and money. A lot of their dependable workers have left for the armed service; many who stay are new to mechanized farming and have to be taught, and Wood can't seem to get a handle on it either. Progress is hard to come by. Clouds of boll weevils descend upon the South. No sooner does Wood get a cotton crop going than the big-snouted beetles hit, overnight it seems, to feed on the plants' tender buds and flowers and decimate a whole field.

Although Billy Wynn sees to it that the SCC continues to supply production credit, by early 1942, Ruth, Wood, and by extension Idella are $20,000 in debt. Wood is beginning to despair while Ruth, determined to stay the course, clamps down. She manages to snag a federal land bank loan of some $35 to $40 an acre and negotiates another loan from a Memphis bank that neither Wynn nor John nor anybody else in the family knows about. Idella drops out of active participation.

Envisioning a lifetime of an hourly wage standing behind a counter measuring out prescription pills, David Fey, twenty-three, begins to look for a way to use his pharmacy degree and his knowledge of medicine to make more money faster. He is soon hired by Parke-Davis & Company and given a Mississippi Delta territory as traveling detail man. The company pays expenses and a small salary, but primarily he works on commission, a dream job for a hotshot salesman. By June he and his family have moved to Greenville, their eighth residence. They now live in the Washington Avenue bungalow, nine miles from the Drive, the Thompsons, the Dickinses. While there, he becomes involved in a scheme that has him trafficking in sporty used cars from an unknown source. Beverly clearly remembers a mention of "the black market" when her mother parks too close to another car at the downtown post office and puts a scratch on a snappy two-door yellow convertible that disappears the following day.

Dora Fey's father, William Bryant Smith, dies the next month, possibly of cancer. His wife, Beverly's grandmother Polly, buries him not in Brinkley, where he died, or Marvell, where they lived most of their lives, but in Helena, a city he despised.

In 1992, Beverly traveled to the Maple Hill Cemetery with her uncle Jess and aunt Frances Smith to find her grandfather's grave. Jess and Frances had never been there, nor had William Bryant Smith's other children or grandchildren. When the grave was located, Beverly asked her uncle why Polly had had her husband buried in a city he hated. Jess said he didn't know but thought maybe it was because she knew he wouldn't want to be there and nobody would come see him, a revenge for no telling what. Probably nothing. Probably, Jess reckoned, just pure damn meanness. "Mama was like that," he quipped.

1943–1944

As Wood and Ruth's debts increase, they rent out bigger pieces of land to other farmers. The property is mortgaged, the land grown rank with weeds. Maintaining her usual busy life, Ruth attends bridge parties, plays golf, throws parties, motors often to Memphis with women friends, to Greenville to conduct banking business. Her life is her own business.

The Feys are kicked out of their first Greenville house. They fight eviction, lose. Dora throws the polio boot she's supposed to wear the rest of her life in the trash, buys wedgies with ankle straps, moves back to Helena with her two children to live with David's parents. Beverly starts school there.

Hugh W. "Hughey" Foote runs for Washington County sheriff, as do two Stovall brothers, John A. and Jody. By then, the Mississippi state legislature has passed a 10 percent tax on the retail and wholesale sale and distribution of "commodities prohibited by law," specifically alcohol. Mississippi being a "dry" state, they justify the taxation of illegal products by calling it a "black market tax," designed to "discourage black markets by imposing a tax on them." Because county sheriffs also act as tax collectors, bootleggers depend on their goodwill. Sheriffs profit hugely. Limited to one term in office, they hit the ground running upon inauguration.

John A. Stovall beats out both Hughey Foote and his own brother in the sheriff's election. Once in office, he chooses Foote as his chief deputy but within the next year fires him.

1945

By January, the Feys are together again in a two-bedroom Greenville bungalow at the corner of Cedar and Manilla Streets. They get a Chow dog named Mink. Dora hangs the reproductions she loves, Gainsborough's *Blue Boy* and Erich Correns's *Southern Belle*, images of a time and place far beyond the imaginative possibilities of eastern Arkansas.

Elected president of the Washington County National Farm Loan Association, John Dickins chairs the organization's annual meeting; at night he plays fast-moving money games with his eleven-year-old whiz-kid daughter, Dell.

In late May, an unseasonal hailstorm wipes out Ruth and Wood's crops. They manage to find a way to hang tough through the rest of the season, but by December, Wood is finished. His situation is different from Ruth's. She has John, which means she doesn't depend on what rent and crop money they can bring in, as he does. And he can't see how they'll ever work out from under the debts they've accumulated. He suggests talking to John. Ruth resists but her brother has lost heart and so she gives in.

At war's end, Black soldiers from the Delta return home with a new sense of national citizenship and rights beyond the limits previously imposed on them by economic oppression and threats of violence. White men like Speaker of the Mississippi House Walter Sillers Jr., a Mississippi Delta planter and staunch segregationist, begin to issue dire warnings to their constituents: the federal government is out to bring the South to its knees by forcing its people to accept racial equality and "non-segregation."

It takes John Dickins no time to assess the situation. Ruth and Wood can last no more than a year before turning over the land to the boll weevils. They owe the SCC $65,000, the federal land bank another $58,000. When the bills come in, it turns out they owe another $22,000 to various merchants and suppliers.

Wood suggests a deal. "Dickins," he said, "how about giving me my equipment and my house and I will try fighting grass and rent Jim's land."

John bails them out. At a price. The Thompson place becomes the Dickins place.

1946

Mink chews up a poodle and is taken away by Beverly and David junior's father, who returns alone. They get a small fat friendly cocker spaniel, Taffy, who quickly becomes Beverly's first love; as a family they join the Presbyterian church and the Greenville Country Club, which is only two blocks from their house. Dora and David play in golf tournaments there. In addition to his Parke-Davis job, David and two other druggists purchase an interest in a Rexall drugstore downtown. He becomes Greenville's favorite Santa Claus, wins a jitterbug prize, emcees all over town, performs in blackface minstrel shows, becomes a lovable presence wherever he goes. Summers, Beverly and David spend long afternoons in the country-club swimming pool, which has a custodian but no lifeguard.

When the *Delta Democrat-Times* editor, Hodding Carter, wins the 1946 Pulitzer Prize for editorial commentary attacking Mississippi U.S. senator Theodore Bilbo and upbraiding the U.S. government for its treatment of Japanese Americans, the lifelong white supremacist and Ku Kluxer Bilbo lashes back. "No self-respecting Southern white man," he shouts in a speech, "would accept a prize given by a bunch of nigger-loving Yankeefied Communists for editorials advocating the mongrelization of the races." Within the next year Bilbo will oppose antilynching legislation, filibuster against the Fair Employment Practices Committee, and publish a book: *Take Your Choice, Separation or Mongrelization.*

In July, the decomposing body of a Black man named Leon McTatie is discovered in a Delta bayou. Although six white men are arrested for whipping the tenant farmer to death—allegedly for stealing a saddle—and two of them have confessed to the theft, an all-white grand jury deliberates for less than three minutes before setting all six men free. Protest marches and meetings of organizations like the National Association of Colored Women, the NAACP, and the National Lawyers Guild demand a federal response. Truman makes a speech expressing sympathy to the McTatie family and sends representatives from the Justice Department to Mississippi, but nothing is done.

1947

January 1. Freezing weather spreads across the country from Texas to Michigan and east into the New England states, dipping down into the South to wallop the Mississippi Delta with the worst ice storm in its history.

The Dickinses skip their usual New Year's Day trip to New Orleans to attend the Sugar Bowl with a gang of Leland friends—mostly Ole Miss fans—possibly because of the weather or maybe because no Mississippi team is playing.

David Fey's parents are spending the holidays in Greenville, their first visit to the home of their youngest son. On Sunday after church, they all go for a noonday meal at the Magnolia Lounge, a short-lived restaurant with high-flown culinary aspirations and an over-the-top state flower decor. Soon after they are served, Beverly and David junior's proudly overweight grandfather stands, white linen napkin tucked in his shirt collar, choking on a piece of meat he can't get down or bring up. This is long before knowledge of the Heimlich maneuver became a restaurant employee requirement. He somehow recovers but a day later suffers chest pains and is taken to King's Daughters Hospital, which is jammed due to the weather. There have been fires, wrecks, power outages, respiratory illnesses. Though diagnosed with heart failure, the Fey grandfather is assigned to a hallway bed with only a screen to protect him from contagion and the chill air. During surgery, doctors discover fat tough as gristle around his heart, which put it at risk long before the choking incident further weakened it. He dies. The family drives to Helena for the funeral. Because David is the youngest and the least stable son, his brothers hold him somewhat responsible. He blames bad doctors, the cold hallway, the fat, and inevitably himself.

David Fey and John Dickins compete in a thirty-six-hole golf tournament. David shoots 160; John, 181.

Ruth keeps her social life going despite the money troubles, attending bridal showers and weddings, giving parties, taking jaunts out of town while continuing to seek outside money to keep the farm going, keeping her efforts secret from her husband.

Hugh W. "Hughey" Foote again runs for sheriff. Stanny Sanders enters the race for district attorney; Willard McIlwain for Washington County prosecuting attorney. The former district attorney Arthur Jordan is elected district judge. In the coming year, all four of these men will become major players in the biggest murder investigation and trial ever conducted in the county, if not the entire state of Mississippi.

When John A. Stovall announces his intention to run for the county board of supervisors, Hodding Carter pens a scathing editorial attack on his record as sheriff. Stovall loses. He returns to his original job as undertaker in his own funeral home.

Ruth wins booby prize at one of the many bridge parties she attends and throws a hot tamale supper honoring the young girls and women in the Sunday school class she teaches. She spends a Saturday in Octo-

ber traveling with her sister-in-law and Ann Finch, a young teacher
and girls' basketball coach at the Leland white high school. In November, she'll make another trip with Finch, spending a Friday night with
Stovall relatives before driving to Baton Rouge to attend the LSU–
Ole Miss football game.

"She liked young women," a woman who knew Ruth told me in a
phone conversation, a certain undertone to her voice leaving no doubt
what kind of "liked" she meant. After a pause to catch her breath and
decide if she should continue, she added, "Like Ann Finch."

Others wave the whiff of scandal away. *She liked lively people,* is their
take. *People who felt free to go off and do things.* Like *the unmarried young
schoolteachers who boarded in a house just down the Drive. They were just
there.*

David Fey switches from Parke-Davis to Merck pharmaceuticals and
places enough drugs in doctors' offices to make the Millionaires' Club
celebration, a drunken blowout the company stages in Chicago at the
Palmer House. A few months later, the Feys take a driving trip through
the Smokies in the Buick Roadmaster David purchased, surprising his
family by simply pulling the two-toned green beauty up in the side yard
and parking there while pressing on the horn without letup to alert the
neighbors. After stops in Gatlinburg, Natural Bridge, and Williamsburg,
they drive to Norfolk, where Dora's least favorite brother, Robert, and
his family live, a less than successful visit. But the trip thrilled David
junior and Beverly. Taking a long-distance break from home meant
home would still be there when they got back.

December 20, 1947, in Leland. Doc and Bunt Witte celebrate the
opening of the Witte Clinic and Hospital, complete with, in the clinic,
examination rooms and pharmacy and, in the hospital, full X-ray equipment, two operating rooms, a lab, three private rooms for white people
and two for "colored," also racially segregated wards, waiting rooms, and
dentist's offices. At 3:00 the next morning, the first baby is born. He is
white.

Dr. Dorothy Dickins, John's sister, head of the Mississippi State College Home Economics Department, conducts a study sponsored by the
college's Agricultural Experiment Station in Stoneville, in which she
focuses on the educational and occupational experience of the Black

population in Bolivar County. Her survey finds that 84 percent of the population of that county is Black and that nearly half of the adults have less than a fifth-grade education. As mechanization is swiftly replacing them in the fields and they've neither been taught nor urged to develop skills or education other than farmwork, the survey chronicles the current hopelessness of the African American population all over the Mississippi Delta. This survey is covered at length in *The Delta Democrat-Times,* and if for the modern reader it can be both shocking and unspeakably bleak, it's far less so for Delta white and Black people of this time.

Ruth makes three more trips with Ann Finch. When they drive to Memphis for the day, Idella goes with them.

For some Deltans, including the *Delta Democrat-Times* editor, Carter, the most anticipated event of the year takes place between Christmas and New Year's Day. Founded in 1942 by the Daughter of the Confederacy Mrs. Judge Rabun Jones, mother of the man who now inhabits the original J. W. Thompson mansion, the Delta Debutante Club invites some twenty or so girls from Greenville and surrounding towns to dress up in hoopskirts and white evening gowns and bring their daddies to present them formally to society at a grand ball, a ritual dating back to the time when a daughter's "presentation" was a kind of meat market for prospective grooms.

The girls are white. None is Jewish.

After this year's event in the Hotel Greenville ballroom, Carter praises Mrs. Jones for her tireless work on an event that, in his opinion, makes Greenville "the social capital of the Delta." But, he wonders, isn't the hotel ballroom too small for the "huge throng" attending? He lobbies for a move to a city auditorium where the event might be more comfortably staged, say the one in Clarksdale. Civic leaders from that town eagerly accept the offer, but Mrs. Rabun Jones firmly rejects the suggestion. The club is hers.

1948

New Year's Day. While the University of Texas is walloping Alabama in the Sugar Bowl, Ruth and John have elected to go to Memphis instead, to watch Ole Miss's star quarterback, Charlie Conerly, make two touchdown passes in the fourth quarter to beat Texas Christian 13–9 in the first ever Delta Bowl. They are there with about thirty other Ole Miss fans from Leland, including a number of Stovalls.

Two days later, as Hugh W. Foote takes office as sheriff of Washington County, Stanny Sanders and Willard McIlwain are swearing in as, respectively, DA and county attorney. Later that month a front-page *Delta Democrat-Times* article headlined "12 Sentenced; Circuit Court Term Adjourned" reports that the newly elected county circuit court judge Arthur Jordan has imposed sentences on twelve convicted defendants: "six white men, one white woman, four colored men and a colored woman."

Ruth and Idella take Dell to a Gulf Coast girls' camp where she excels at tennis. Beverly and four of her friends attend a weeklong camp in Hardy, Arkansas, where the swim teacher corrects the stroke they'd invented thinking it made them look like Esther Williams. They make lariats. Beverly gets a tick.

In July, in an effort to pressure the national Democratic Party to give up its support for President Truman's civil rights program, the Mississippi and Alabama delegations walk out of the national convention and, with other southern states, form a splinter group they name first the States' Rights Democrats, then the True White Jeffersonian Democrats, and finally the Dixiecrats. After condemning a number of administration proposals, including a law against lynching and another banning the poll tax, they nominate the South Carolinian Strom Thurmond for president and Mississippi's governor, Fielding Wright—a native Deltan—as his running mate.

Dora Fey beats Ruth Dickins in a nine-hole golf tournament when she shoots a respectable 39 and wins the runner-up prize, a major victory for a woman whose polio foot was supposed to keep her in a corrective boot for life.

The U.S. Department of Agriculture predicts a very big Mississippi cotton crop ahead. Two months later, an agent from the Delta Experiment Station tells Greenville Kiwanians the South is on the threshold of moving into farm mechanization for more production and higher income. And the state tax collector announces record-high revenues from the October black-market tax on bootlegged whiskey.

November 2, in the presidential elections, white Mississippians vote in record numbers for the Dixiecrats Thurmond and Wright, who win 87.17 percent of the state's popular vote and all nine electoral votes.

Big cotton harvest. Pecans coming on strong. Bunt Witte hospitalizes Idella Thompson for high blood pressure, manages to keep her there for a week.

. . . .

November 16. The night is clear, the weather pleasantly cool. Clear skies. A full moon. Idella Thompson is safely tucked into her hospital bed, her blood pressure normal following a week of bed rest. Known to be energetic and controlling, Mrs. Thompson is a hard one to keep down. As the whole family knows, her younger daughter, Ruth, is the only one of her children who knows how to handle her.

And so it is Ruth who arrives the next morning, November 17, 1948, to take her mother home. After she sees to Idella's discharge and adds an extra $3 of her own money to pay the hospital bill in full, she drives her home, to 311 Deer Creek Drive.

She parks out front.

Ruth's two brothers, Jimmy and Wood, are there. As is her sister, Mildred. They pitch in, helping settle their mother, making sure she's comfortable.

The day begins.

. . . .

The run-up having chronologically crested, we move ahead.

HUGHEY'S PLIGHT

On Wednesday, November 24, exactly one week after the murder, Frank Aldridge called the Dickinses' number. John picked up. It was morning, not much past eight fifteen. He and Ruth hadn't yet eaten breakfast. Aldridge minced no words. They needed John to bring Ruth to the courthouse by nine o'clock. When John asked the police chief what the hell was the matter with him, Aldridge shot back with an equally hotheaded "What the hell's the matter with *her*?"

John slammed down the phone. But Billy Wynn had advised the family to cooperate with the investigation in every way possible, and so he and Ruth skipped breakfast, jumped in their Chevy, and headed to Greenville.

After a week of coming up with nothing much, the sheriff had begun to think he'd reached the end of something. Call it a phase. Ordinarily, by now he'd have some kind of idea of what happened and who the assailant was or might be, especially in a crime that had, at first, seemed open-and-shut: Ruth told them who did it; all they had to do was go find him. They'd combed the relevant neighborhoods and roads. Hughey had interviewed more than fifty suspects; Crawford, close to that many. But the thing wouldn't come clear.

Maybe, the sheriff began to think, it was because they were looking in the wrong direction. Maybe they had what cops call tunnel vision or were simply turning a blind eye toward a possibility they didn't care for.

At the courthouse, the Dickinses found most of the same crew waiting for them: Crawford, Foote, Blue, Hollingsworth, and Aldridge. When Hughey gently asked Ruth if she would join them in his office and indicated he meant her only, John went outside and sat on the steps.

Inside, after a brief discussion, when Crawford asked if she would agree to a lie detector test, Ruth said of course, she'd be happy to. She wanted to do anything that might help. They all headed to the office where Crawford had set up the machine he'd brought from Jackson, but when they got there, Crawford said he wanted only one witness with him and that was Ed Blue.

With that, according to Hughey, he ushered Ruth and Blue into the office and slammed the door.

Hughey didn't like it, but he didn't know what else to do but go on back to his own office and wait.

Four hours later, when Ruth emerged from the courthouse, Hughey was with her.

Would John, he asked, mind taking his wife to Gamble Brothers Clinic for a physical exam, this time by a Greenville doctor who wasn't kin or directly involved in the investigation? John wasn't keen on that either, but he bit his tongue. This was how things had been done the whole way through. Whoever called to ask something of Ruth asked first for John's permission.

By then, her bruises had faded and the swelling in her left arm had gone down, but the clinic's report indicated some heretofore undetected small yellowing bruises low on her shins, an injury that might well follow a barrage of quick, sharp kicks. Defense wounds, almost certainly.

. . . .

A couple of days later, Crawford announced that Ruth had passed the lie detector test with flying colors. But the next news somebody turned up was that Crawford's machine was defective and had to be sent out for repairs immediately following her test. In addition to which, who cared about a lie detector test if it couldn't be used in a trial?

There were other indications of disarray.

In one newspaper interview, the sheriff had admitted that the bathroom floor "on which Mrs. Thompson's hacked body was discovered" had been mopped before the investigation was complete and crime scene photos taken. And yes, the clothes Ruth wore that day had been found soaking in a washtub at her home. And Mrs. Thompson's clothing, he hated to report, had been burned to ashes at the funeral home.

As for forensic evidence at the scene, they were, he repeated, still waiting for the FBI report.

When Hodding Carter, editor and publisher of *The Delta Democrat-Times,* wrote an editorial asking why no reward had been offered for information leading to the conviction of Mrs. Thompson's killer, he cited the "many rumors arising from the slaying," which had, he said, "hurt more than one person." One way to stanch gossip, he quipped, was to find the killer, and the offer of a substantial sum of money might well move that process along. That was how things were usually done.

A subsequent *Delta Democrat-Times* article wondered if the sheriff and the cops were actually doing all they could to solve the case.

By the end of November, the *Clarion-Ledger* had joined the fray. Needing a new angle, a reporter proposed a fairly arcane possibility.

"One need not be very superstitious," the front-page story suggested, "to be impressed by the record showing that this murder was the third violent death in that family in recent years." One was of course that of J. W. Thompson. Another was "a son-in-law, ambushed in his home and assassinated." And then, of course, Mrs. Thompson. Was this ribbon of violence the result of sheer coincidence, the paper asked, or could it be a *family curse?*

The possibility of a third killing, that of a son-in-law shot in his own home, was often cited; the man's name was usually given as Meadors; the date of occurrence, "during the last big flood in this area." One story declared unequivocally that Meadors was shot by his wife, a Thompson daughter. That would have to be Ruth's sister, Mildred, who was listed in the 1920 census as nineteen years old, living at home, and divorced. There's no official record of an early marriage, and I've found no death certificate or obit for a man named Meadors who might have been murdered during that period, whether in Mississippi or Tennessee, where Mildred went to school for a short while. The claim may well be hogwash; nonetheless, it has persisted.

In early December, the sheriff dropped a bombshell. After admitting that the search for a killer matching Ruth's description had been a failure, he went on to say that actually he and his officers had "almost entirely discounted the probability that a Negro committed the crime." Not that they weren't still seeking evidence to support that assertion. But . . .

This was huge. If "a Negro" didn't do it, who else was there? Rumors ran wild and morphed into *known facts*. Hadn't there been money issues? Betrayals? Idella, it was said, didn't like the women Ruth hung around with. Plus, Ruth was money hungry. She was strange. So was that brother of hers; didn't he tell people certain things about his father's death; wasn't he off his rocker? The family was hexed, nuts, plain weird. Why did Ruth dress like that and chop her hair off in a way that made her look like a man? What kind of woman did that?

It was Ruth, some said. Had to be.

Not Ruth, others swore. And not Jimmy Thompson either but somebody else. A white man who knew things he threatened to spread through town if Idella didn't pay up. Information about Jimmy, his secret life. As everybody knew, Jimmy was Idella's favorite of her children, so when the blackmailer made the threat—according to this particular theory—she flamed up and grabbed the shears as if to attack. The man snatched them away and went after her; Ruth walked in, the man came at her, she got the shears back, he escaped.

And there was Jimmy himself. Maybe he quarreled with his mother, who knew what about, but something his mother said set him off; she was good at that. When Ruth discovered her big brother attacking their mother, she stepped in. Discovering that Idella was dead, she told Jimmy to get out and wait for an hour or so to come back, then figured out a way to cover for him, the same way the family did when—a lot of people still believe this—he shot his father. What if, once the Negro theory had been discounted, the Thompsons got together and—convinced that no all-white, all-male grand jury would indict a respectable, churchgoing white lady from a family like theirs—decided Ruth should take the hit instead of letting Jimmy plead insanity and be sent to Whitfield when most people considered life in the state insane asylum a worse fate than Parchman prison?

That theory didn't exactly round out to perfection. First off, would

John Dickins agree to such a scheme? Would Ruth risk abandoning her daughters?

. . . .

On December 19, a month and two days after the murder, Idella Thompson's last will and testament was filed, revealing that in July of that year it had been modified to name Ruth her executor. There were no other changes. The reduced size of her estate surprised a lot of people, in that it now consisted of only one fifty-acre tract of land and one sixty-acre tract, plus the residence on Deer Creek Drive. What happened to J. W. Thompson's two to three thousand acres?

Some people knew. Those acres now belonged to John Dickins. Not everybody, though.

A. E. Crawford wrote up his report, made copies for John Dickins and Doc Witte, and went home to Jackson.

Hughey worked on his case. The winter session of the next grand jury meeting was scheduled to begin nine days after Christmas, on Monday, January 3, 1949. Long before then, he needed to have presented the district attorney and the chief prosecutor with a case convincing enough to produce an indictment. Otherwise he'd have to wait for the summer session in June.

He didn't want to wait. Especially now that he'd zeroed in on a suspect.

. . . .

A week before Christmas, Leland's mayor, Bill Caraway, extended an open invitation to people from all over the Delta to come see "the best looking Christmas trees in Washington County." Installed by the city's light plant, three thirty-five-foot trees had been spray-painted silver and draped with colored lights. Once they'd been secured on wooden rafts, they were floated into the waters of Deer Creek and anchored in place between the two pedestrian bridges that spanned it. Each tree had been strung with some seven hundred lights: blue bulbs on trees floating on either side of the bridges, multicolored on the one between. A magical sight that people from all over the Delta drove to Leland to see.

The ritual has continued through the years, growing more complex and Santa-fied in time. Traffic backs up along Deer Creek Drive during the holiday season. Some people sit in idling cars, taking in the colors, the lights, the sparkling creek water, which seems to produce its own stash of lights and color within its ripples and sway. Others park downtown along either Main or Broad Street and walk. They can see the lights as soon as they reach the railroad tracks.

. . . .

In 1948, of course, anyone who chose to take North Deer Creek Drive West, whether on foot or by car, would pass breathtakingly close to what had become the most famous house on the Drive. From the sidewalk, a pedestrian could, with a single sidestep, veer onto the front lawn of the murder house. A policeman might well have been stationed there to make sure no one came any closer. Even so, it's hard to imagine people not stopping to comment and wonder, wasn't that it? The house where it happened? Did Ruth's brothers still live there?

If they kept going in the same direction, within maybe twenty steps they'd also pass the house where Ruth and John Dickins lived with their daughters.

Christmas fell on a Saturday. *The Delta Democrat-Times* didn't publish Saturdays, so at least there'd be no news for the Dickinses to avoid that day. But they couldn't help noticing as cars and pedestrians, people who knew nothing about them, slowed down as they drove by, hoping to catch a glimpse of them. Some five years later, in a letter, John Dickins described the Christmas night of 1948 as the saddest of their lives. He and his family were, he wrote, "most miserable." Knowing the rumors about his wife's connection to the murder and that there was nothing to do to stop them, they had become a "very peculiar family."

. . . .

Nobody much from Leland drove to New Orleans or Memphis to a bowl game that year, possibly because none of their favorite teams had been invited to play. At the Sugar Bowl, the Oklahoma Sooners played the North Carolina Tar Heels, but really, who cared about North Carolina? As for the Delta Bowl, in only its second year of existence, not only was attendance sparse, but the game was lousy: the College of

William & Mary wiped out Oklahoma State, 20–0. The *Delta Democrat-Times* sportswriter Charlie Kerg advised the Memphians that if they were going to call themselves the Delta Bowl, it might be a good idea to invite a team real Deltans would drive 150 miles to watch, like maybe the Ole Miss Rebels?

The next day, a Sunday, the news hit. A Washington County grand jury of twenty white men had been assembled and was likely to review evidence in the Idella Long Thompson murder case during the session coming up the next week.

The person the State of Mississippi was about to accuse hadn't been publicly named, but everybody knew who it was. There was no one else.

GRAND JURY

Grand jury sessions don't ordinarily garner a lot of attention unless and until the jurors issue an indictment. But on Monday, January 3, 1949, in Greenville, reporters and curiosity seekers gathered early at the county courthouse. Not that anything important would necessarily happen that day, but given the heat of the moment a lot of people simply wanted to be in on the beginning of whatever came next, before everybody else got the news. So they showed up. And stood around shifting from one foot to the other, talking about the only thing on their minds.

The Delta Democrat-Times had published the names of the grand jurors, who one by one filed into the courthouse. Most of them were ordinary members of the community, with one big exception: the hometown columnist Brodie Crump. With his wild shock of white hair and white mustache, he was, to say the least, *not* ordinary. He'd also written a tribute to Idella after her death in which he remembered the good old days of parties and dancing in the original Thompson house. He was also friends with John Dickins.

His inclusion on a grand jury that would soon consider the state's case against a Thompson-born woman married to John Dickins seems questionable. But there he went, into the courthouse.

At 9:30, once all twenty men had been ushered into the courtroom, the circuit judge Arthur Jordan entered. A small handsome man, in his trim suit and bow tie and no judicial robe, he came off as an unreconstructed, old-fashioned southern dandy on his way to a social gathering. Sandy hair combed over to one side and pasted flat, at fifty-nine he looked younger. Walking at his usual fast clip, he took the bench, comfortable in the knowledge that somewhere either on his person or in the mysterious pockets of his bench were the cigarettes he'd smoke during the proceedings.

After greeting the men lined up before him and officially impaneling them as grand jurors, he asked them to elect a foreman. To no one's surprise they promptly chose a distinguished member of the planter aristocracy, Andre Worthington from Glen Allan.

The judge reeled off their general duties. They were, he said, strictly an investigating body and would not rule on the matter of guilt or innocence. After conducting a detailed review of the evidence presented to them by the state, they'd first have to decide whether they thought a crime had been committed. If the answer was yes, they'd then vote on whether the person charged with that crime had probably—more than likely—committed it. That was the practical definition of probable cause. An affirmative vote of at least twelve out of the twenty members constituted a formal accusation: an indictment. But, he cautioned the men, they shouldn't hurry. Instead, "take your time and give the county a good going-over." And "don't be so quick to adjourn."

The men retired to the grand jury room, but had other cases to consider before taking on the Thompson murder, including one accusing the previous sheriff, John A. Stovall, of allowing illegal slot machines to operate in the county. They might get to what promised to be a lengthy presentation of the state's case against Ruth Dickins later that day or perhaps the next, but probably not. Courthouse sentries guarded the door while lawyers, witnesses, and various law enforcement officers waited in the corridor, pacing and sometimes whispering privately to one another.

The sheriff had submitted a witness list to the court, which sent it on to the grand jury and, later, the press. Some of the names published in that day's *Delta Democrat-Times* came as no surprise to anyone—the sheriff, chief of police, Bea Smith—while others—bankers, loan officers, farmers—not only were unexpected but offered locals a sense of what the state was up to.

People said right off, so the motive is money? But why would Ruth Dickins need money? Her husband was rolling, her family had all that land, and even if something nobody knew about was going on, what in the world could it be to rile her up to such a state that she'd go at her mother that way? After studying various possibilities, they figured the sheriff and the DA must know something they didn't.

Did they?

A motive had taken Foote and his team some time to come up with, but back in December, while checking subpoenaed bank statements and loans, they found something to work with. And maybe it wasn't the barn burner they were hoping for, but they thought it might work. In addition to which, the bottom line was it was all they had.

. . . .

By the time the prosecutors Stanny Sanders and Willard McIlwain were summoned, it was past three on Wednesday the fifth. After their initial argument, they called their first witness.

Sheriff Hugh W. Foote entered the grand jury room, carrying a large cardboard box filled with evidentiary material: clothes, shoes, bloody garments, the bathroom rug, the pruning shears. Two officers followed, lugging Mrs. Thompson's bloodstained back door.

Over the next three days, jurors would hear testimony from thirteen witnesses, ranging from Doc Witte to the switchboard operator Myrtle Dyess. The former sheriff John A. Stovall had asked to be summoned so that he could explain why Mrs. Thompson's clothes had been burned, even though, having been sheriff himself, he surely knew people didn't get to testify before a grand jury just because they wanted to. Nonetheless, he stuck out the wait for one whole day. To no avail. This part of the show belonged exclusively to the state, and Sanders and McIlwain saw no reason to add the funeral director and ex-sheriff to the witness list or expect him to testify against his cousin.

Outside in the hall, Deputy Sheriff Murray Etheridge killed time by telling stories to anybody who would listen, including the inside tale of the ambush of the Thompson son-in-law. It happened, he declared, in Leland, during the flood of 1927. Most people thought the dead man's wife, the other Thompson sister, shot him. But he didn't know the man's full name. That his last name was Meadors was all he knew.

. . . .

Saturday afternoon, January 8, the foreman, Worthington, called for the bailiff. They were ready. Facing the judge, he announced the grand jury's decision. There was, they believed, probable cause to suspect the accused, Ruth Thompson Dickins, of having "unlawfully, willfully, feloniously and of her malice aforethought . . . kill[ed] and murder[ed] one Idella Long Thompson, a human being."

Once he'd thanked and dismissed the jurors, Judge Jordan ordered the sheriff and his deputy to leave immediately to serve the indictment. Finding Ruth at home in Leland, they arrested her for first-degree murder, took her into custody, and drove back to Greenville. It was four fifteen when they turned in at Courthouse Alley and parked in front of the county jail.

By then, John Dickins had engaged the services of the attorney W. Benjamin "Ben" Wilkes, known as perhaps the best criminal and civil defense lawyer in the state, to conduct Ruth's defense. When Foote and his deputy exited the sheriff's department car with Ruth in tow, Wilkes was waiting.

Also present were the state representative Hilton Waits from Leland, a powerful ally and friend, and Ruth's brother-in-law, Shields Hood.

John, who'd been working in his Greenville office, arrived ten minutes later. Once Ruth had been officially indicted and granted bail, John arranged to cover her $10,000 bond. She was ordered to appear in court nine days later, on Monday, the seventeenth, for her arraignment, at which time she'd be formally charged and asked to enter a plea.

On their way to their cars, John, Ruth, and Ben Wilkes were mobbed by spectators trying to get a closer look at the woman who—most of them believed—had murdered her own mother.

When reporters pressed Wilkes about a plea, he didn't hesitate. Not guilty.

What about a change of venue? He hadn't decided.

And would she testify? Probably.

The next day, in front-page stories all over the state, newspapers ran the first installment of the Ruth Dickins Fashion Report, a ritual that continued throughout the trial. Assuming—rightly, for the most part—the reading public would consist primarily of women and girls eager to know what kind of outfit a socialite wore on her way to be arrested for matricide, periodicals described in detail the manner and style of her clothes, shoes, and general appearance, saving for last her bareheadedness and noteworthy hairstyle.

. . . .

Fifty-seven years earlier, *The Boston Globe* and New York *Sun* devoted the same kind of attention to the attire and demeanor of Lizzie Borden, on trial for the at-home ax murder of her father and stepmother. On her first day in court, Borden wore a *black wool dress trimmed with purple velvet at the cuffs and hems, a black lace hat accented by two blue rosettes and a small feather, and the black gloves that would accessorize every outfit she wore through the trial.* *The Sun* deemed her hat "a model for theatregoers," her dress so perfectly fitted it was as if "she had been measured for it in Paris." Her looks, however, disappointed. "She is, in truth, a very plain-looking old maid."

Ruth chose simpler garb. For her first appearance in court she donned a beige and brown two-piece suit and low-heeled brown oxfords. No makeup, no jewelry other than a slim gold watch. No hat. No gloves. Dark hair combed up and away from her face in a low pompadour, swept behind her ears and cropped at the neck in a style that from this day forward will rarely be called anything but a "mannish bob."

As a potential murderess *and* member of what was still sometimes called the planter aristocracy, she had, like movie stars and members of the British royal family, moved in to the rarefied realm of instant celebrity. That attention would be paid to the wardrobe and grooming of such a woman goes without saying. Implications would be wrung from the puniest detail.

When John and Ruth married, Ruth wore "a tan and brown traveling costume." In less than three weeks from her trial, they'll celebrate their twentieth wedding anniversary. Might she have been paying tribute to the irony of the two near-identical dates by wearing the same outfit on both occasions? No way to know, but she remained trim and muscular throughout her life, and certainly her sly wit might have covered the possibility of that, despite the circumstances.

. . . .

Three people who didn't come to the courthouse the day Ruth was arrested, who wouldn't be around to help take care of her daughters or give her and her family comfort during the coming months, were her brothers, Jimmy and Wood, and Wood's wife, Demetra. They had left the state a day *before* the grand jury was scheduled to meet, heading for various points including Memphis, New Orleans, Little Rock, and McAllen, Texas. From West Texas they even dipped down into Mexico. The only reason they gave for the getaway was to take brother Jim to see a doctor in Memphis. And after that, what? And why? To avoid the rumors? To protect Jimmy?

They stayed away until June, when the attorney Ben Wilkes subpoenaed them to testify in Ruth's defense.

Their January flight went unnoticed in the press. The big news was here at home, in Greenville and Leland, with Ruth.

THE IMPORTANCE
OF BEATRICE SMITH

On Monday, January 17, Ruth layered up for the cool weather. Choosing carefully, she fitted herself out rather more smartly than usual in a gray wool flannel suit with a belted jacket under which she buttoned a "mannish white shirtwaist" and black sweater. But she stuck to her customary low-heeled blocky shoes and combed her hair "in its usual short, straight bob."

When called to Judge Jordan's bench for her arraignment at 9:25, she stood and, flanked by her husband on one side, her attorney on the other, moved purposefully ahead, as instructed.

Advised of the first-degree murder charge against her and asked to enter a plea, she answered "Not guilty" in a "firm, clear voice," then returned to the defense table, where she sat leaning heavily forward, arms folded on the table taking her weight.

The courtroom was standing room only, an overflow crowd jamming the corridor outside the courtroom. People jostled one another to get a better view. All they could see was the judge, who sat high.

Aware that in her case jury selection might take several days, Judge Jordan had planned to get moving right away. But before he could begin, Ben Wilkes motioned for a continuance, a postponement. This came as a surprise to no one. The news that Beatrice Smith, "negro cook of Mrs. Dickins" and her key defense witness, had suffered a nervous breakdown had been reported in several Sunday papers.

To confirm her condition, Wilkes called Smith's personal physician to the stand. He had, he testified, been treating Smith for more than ten years and had never seen her in such a state. When he went to her house a few days before she was scheduled to appear before the grand jury, he found she'd gone "all to pieces." It took, he said, "four or five people to hold her." Her husband said every time a car drove up, she thought police officers were coming to take her to jail. She was having terrible dreams; in one she saw her sisters looking up at her, hanging by her neck from a tree. As if lynched.

Then, when she'd finally pulled herself together enough to show up at the courthouse to testify before the grand jury, she'd had to wait in the hall for four hours, which pumped her agitation even higher. She'd never had anything to do with a trial and was, the doctor said, "just plain scared to death." No mention was made of the fact that as the only Black person called to testify, she might have had cause to be nervous. What if she got things wrong? Who were all of these other people in the hall, every single one of them white, and she had no idea why they were there. Was there some reason she was having to wait so long? How much could she actually remember?

When she'd finally testified and the grand jury foreman said she could leave, she went home and fell apart all over again. She'd even taken too many of the sedatives her doctor had prescribed and gone into a semi-comatose state. Her physician described her condition as "grave."

When the prosecution didn't object, Jordan sustained Wilkes's motion for continuance and rescheduled the trial for the June term of the circuit court. Asked if Beatrice Smith would be up to testifying at that time, her doctor refused to speculate. Her condition, he said, might be permanent. She might end up in the asylum for life.

The disappointed crowd filed out, making plans as they went to return in six months. Meanwhile, Beatrice Smith's husband took his wife to an undisclosed location where she could spend the spring with family and receive proper treatment.

Ruth and John went home. Three days later they mortgaged their house, presumably to help pay legal fees. They then proceeded to go about their lives quietly and without notice. Staying close to family, they consulted with Wilkes and tried to tamp down worry by focusing on their daughters. But Ruth looked bad. She was losing weight, it seemed by the minute. Her husband, sister, and nephew swore to stand behind her no matter what. Her brothers and sister-in-law motored on, heading for their next stop.

WAITING

Adolescent girls like to scare one another, to experiment with emotions. We'd laugh until we couldn't stand up, tears running down our cheeks, faces red with exertion, shaking one another by the shoulders, sometimes in hysteria, other times pure joy. We'd cry until we choked when a dog died in a movie or the March of Dimes fundraiser came on between the cartoon and the feature, showing a small boy learning to walk in thigh-high braces, holding tight to support bars while Gordon MacRae sang "You'll Never Walk Alone." Or was it Howard Keel?

My father used to entertain my friends and me at nighttime cookout parties with scary stories. He'd have bought steaks and marinated them in soy sauce and olive oil. Waiting for the coals to turn from black to screeching red, he'd gather us close, turn out the lights, shine a flashlight under his chin, and squeeze his face into a fright mask. Affecting a Vincent Price *mua-ha-ha-ha* laugh, he'd launch into thrilling stories of evil perpetrated by familiar monsters he made his own by reverse spelling their names. Dracula was Alucard. Frankenstein was Nietsneknarf. And there was my favorite, Lon Chaney's sad-faced Larry Talbot, who under the full moon morphed into hairy, regretful Namflow. But Alucard was everybody's favorite.

Scare us more! we implored. *Take us beyond what we know!*

Mayhem was our turf. Not yet sexual beings but on the verge of we didn't know exactly what, my girlfriends and I went to the picture show every Sunday afternoon, mostly to the Paramount, occasionally to the Delta despite its reputation for a rat infestation, or the boxlike Lake, the last building before the levee. Lusting for whatever would cause us to scream, gasp, weep, or fall apart in laughter, we thought we wanted to see for ourselves what the worst thing imaginable looked and felt like.

Concerning the Thompson murder, *The Delta Democrat-Times* brought us the daily ration we required. Dutifully we combed it, hoping for more than was there. The sheriff said there wasn't "a Negro." Now what? After my mother played in a golf tournament against Ruth Dickins, we joked about how somebody should have told her to stay behind that killer woman to save herself from being whacked with a nine iron.

When we couldn't find what we were looking for, we did the next best thing. We imagined. What had it been like? The shears. The slashes. For years I thought I remembered a detective magazine featuring a terrifying Ruth in glasses on the cover, staring out like the devil we thought she was. And perhaps there was such a magazine, but I'm now convinced the woman I remembered seeing was somebody else.

Now, looking at newspaper and magazine pictures of her, I see only sadness and exhaustion. If she did kill her mother, it seems, the rage came and went.

And if she didn't? If not her, then who?

In Greenville, back then and for the most part now, nobody thought she didn't do it.

. . . .

But the continuance made us restless.

Getting through the six months between Ruth's indictment and her trial felt like waiting for a storm that has either stalled or lost its way somewhere out in the deep blue unknown. All we heard was rumors. Reasons she did it. Reasons to think maybe she didn't. We couldn't help wondering. What kind of person she deep down was. What kind of mother Idella had been. How it felt to stab a person to death.

. . . .

My family and I were still living in the Manilla Street bungalow then, but change was in the works. Daddy had made the Millionaires' Club again. He decided the time was right to fulfill a promise he'd made his wife all those years ago: to build her a home. They'd buy a lot, not just on any street, but one of the best in town. And we'd move in to the posh life we were meant for. Not next year or the next, but now. Because *now* was all there was.

Like other magazines, in those days *Better Homes & Gardens* sold architectural house plans, complete with an illustration of the finished house, drafting information, cost estimates, and a detailed list of required building materials. My mother studied them. "Which one do you like?" she'd ask David and me. And she'd show us one two-story house and another. The one she eventually chose was a three-bedroom, described by the magazine as "A Friendly House," a "trim beauty" with qualities that "make familiarity breed delight." There were special features like two and a half bathrooms, one with a stand-up shower, a real dining room, and a big kitchen tiled all over and with room for a breakfast table. The floors were wood, and in the pictures the whole thing had a look of lightness and shine. Like a dream house.

In no time, she and Daddy had signed off on a loan toward the purchase of the north sixty-five feet of Lot 4, Block 4 in Greenville's Park Addition, at 830 South Washington Avenue, only a block and a half from the house we got kicked out of in 1944. Mama ordered the Friendly House plans. They bought the lot. Hired a construction crew. Work began.

. . . .

As for Idella's house, it went on the market in late winter. Unlike many infamous murder houses—known in real estate circles as stigmatized property—it didn't have to be, in a sense, reimagined beforehand: given a new facade to discourage crime scene tourists or a general cheering up of the exterior to establish what realtors call curb appeal. There are people who specialize in this kind of site renewal. They sometimes even manage to change the main entranceway by shifting it a good quarter or half turn so that it qualifies for a new street address.

The house at 311 North Deer Creek Drive sold in April, only five months after the murder. It went for $16,000, more than double the value placed on it by the U.S. Census Bureau nine years earlier. The sellers—the estate of Idella Long Thompson (Ruth T. Dickins, Grantor)—however, would receive only $9,128.22 cash from the sale, after a deed of trust had been paid. The purchasers, the real estate agent Lester Watson and his wife, Doris, a bookkeeper for the Leland Chevrolet Company, weren't wealthy, and they didn't buy the house to fix up and flip. They moved in. When Lester Watson died in 1953, his widow stayed on until her death in 1994.

By then, the house number had changed from 311 to 313 due to new home construction on the block.

. . . .

Ruth's name hit the front page again on Monday, June 6, 1949, when the summer term of the Washington County Circuit Court was set to open with the second grand jury session of the year, followed by civil and criminal trials. When a reporter recognized Stanny Sanders as he entered the courthouse and asked what day the Ruth Dickins trial would start, the DA said it was inappropriate to comment and hurried away, under his arm the bulging accordion file he was never without. His brush-off nonetheless made the front page.

But the bigger headline was "Grand Jury Goes into Session, Includes First Negro Since Reconstruction."

Walter G. Wilson—a teacher and girls' athletic coach at Leland Negro High and the owner of a downtown drugstore—was clearly qualified to serve on the grand jury. If Judge Jordan tried to find a way to work around the Supreme Court ruling granting him that right, he failed. Wilson was seated. He and the other grand jurors, all of them white men, would consider eight cases of murder, only one of them against a white man. But it was the manslaughter charge that attracted the most attention.

Alex Clark Jr., eighteen, had been known as the Sweet Potato Slayer since he and the Chinese grocer Jeu Sing argued about change and rather than pay up Clark threw the tuber at the grocer. It hit home, the middle of Sing's forehead. He collapsed. Clark took off. A few days later the grocer suffered a brain bleed and died. Clark was arrested and charged. The nature of his weapon made his case the object of barely suppressed hilarity among attorneys and white people who considered their Black brothers either a joke or a menace.

Ruth's trial wouldn't begin until all of the grand jury cases had been cleared.

. . . .

By this time the Fey family had moved from the house at the corner of Cedar and Manilla into their own spanking new two-story on Washington Avenue. It looked exactly like the Friendly House pictures in the magazine. I had my own bedroom and David had his. We thought this was it. We were set for the rest of it. Daddy said because the block we lived on had a boulevard, this meant we were rich. Only rich people lived on a boulevard. Nobody didn't know that.

. . . .

On Thursday, June 16, Judge Jordan held a preliminary session to announce a decision he'd made regarding *State of Mississippi v. Ruth Thompson Dickins*. Because of the wide coverage the case had attracted, in addition to the county's usual practice of calling 36 citizens for jury duty, he had requested the drawing of another 170 names.

Jury selection would begin the following Tuesday. He banged his gavel. Court was adjourned. The session lasted only minutes, but Ruth and John were there. She was said to be calm, gloomy, hatless. Now that the weather had warmed, she'd gone into her summer wardrobe and was wearing a plain cotton dress, sometimes referred to as a simple wash dress, and flat-heeled shoes.

Two days later, she gave an exclusive interview to the longtime Memphis *Commercial Appeal* news reporter Bob Marks. Called "Mrs. Dickins Tells Own Story: Why Should One Who Loved Her Mother as I Did Kill Her?," the lengthy story was accompanied by a large photograph of Ruth at home, sitting in a small rocking chair in John's study. Posed in front of the tiled fireplace, hands folded in her lap, she looked terrible. Dark eyes ringed in shadows, she seemed to be making a feeble attempt to smile, but the natural down drift of her eyebrows and sad eyes belie the effort. Shoulders slumped, chin tucked, she looked lost, as if the person she once was had left and gone someplace else.

Marks described her as five four, with clear, deep blue eyes, her complexion a "hue between olive and swarthy." Thin, having lost, she said, some thirty pounds since her arrest, she'd combed her "thick raven black" hair away from her face in everybody's favorite "mannish bob" and was wearing an uncharacteristic open-necked blue-and-white-striped housedress, topped off by a "flowered pinafore cooking apron."

And why would she be wearing a knee-length, ruffled, and sashed cooking apron for an interview with the biggest newspaper in the mid-South? Was this somebody's idea of strategy, designed to counteract her high-society status as well as her questionable sexual identity? Did it make sense to, say, Ben Wilkes, John, Billy Wynn, her sister, Mildred, to present her instead as a simple homebody whose life centered on the health, happiness, and feeding of her family? Or did Ruth just not care what she was wearing or how she looked?

The interview took place on a Saturday. Hard to know who else was in the house that day, but odds are John was. Probably other members of the family as well. Even so, Ruth would have chosen her own wardrobe. And more than likely had resisted the idea of the interview and had to be convinced, then held out against dressing up for it.

· · · ·

Marks, who'd worked for *The Commercial Appeal* since he was nineteen, in old-school tradition, avoided use of the first-person pronoun by referring to himself as "the reporter." After describing Ruth's appearance, he moved on to the crime itself. Ruth dodged nothing. But she sometimes contradicted previous statements, as, for instance, when Marks asked how her clothes became soaked in blood. That happened, she replied, either when she fell across her mother's body or when she fell on the floor where the "blood from her [Idella's] head had flowed." She thus sidestepped her assertion to the police that she did *not* fall on Idella while also contradicting her family's insistence that blood on the bathroom floor was scant and spotty as a way to explain away why the alleged Negro intruder hadn't left footprints or blood drops. And when asked about the killer's appearance, she said, as best she could recall, he wasn't a big man. He "had a thin face and thin lips" and was "not very black"—contrary to her original description of him as dark-skinned.

Marks devoted a fair amount of space to Ruth's lie detector test, careful to point out that the man who conducted it—Crawford—actually worked for her family and was paid by her husband. Also, he'd been told by the Mississippi attorney general that such a test had never been introduced in a Mississippi trial. And even if the judge allowed it, he might well rule against allowing the jury to consider the results. Did she know that? Ruth didn't respond.

She disputed all anonymous chitchat, including the rumor that while she and Thompsie Hood were having coffee at Azlin's, her nephew told her that Idella was planning to change her will and make Uncle Jim the executor. Which some people were saying was the thing that set Ruth off. Ruth's friends, however, had scoffed at this story and so did she.

And there was the speculation that Idella had struck first, prompting her daughter to retaliate. One possible scenario was that Idella had insulted her, maybe pertaining to her inept handling of the family finances or her friendships with young women. And when Ruth responded angrily, Idella picked up the pruning shears and, reason having morphed into blind rage, lashed out. In self-defense, Ruth grabbed the gardening tool away from her mother, and once she got into returning her blows, something snapped. She kept slashing until Idella was ruined and dead.

"I know people are saying that," Ruth said. "That is terribly unfair and false. I believe you could search the country over and never find a person who could honestly say he saw me in a fit of temper. My mother was hot-tempered because she was sick. But I don't believe you can find anyone, family or friends, who ever heard me speak a cross word to mother or her to me." And furthermore, "How could anyone who loved her mother as I did want to kill her?"

Undeterred, the reporter threw out another unconfirmed report. "People say you shot your father."

Ruth bit her lips, perhaps to tamp down her anger or give herself time to figure out how to avoid answering. Her father, she finally replied, shot himself because he was in bad health. "There was never any question as to the cause of his death."

Either Marks didn't know that indeed there had been a question and it appeared on his official death certificate, or he knew and decided not to pursue it.

As to the criticism about not issuing a reward, that was also untrue;

she and her husband and brother-in-law had privately offered $1,500 to "reliable Negroes," thinking that was the best way to find the killer and that in fact "certain Negroes" were still looking for the culprit.

Marks waited until near the end of the interview to bring up the most sensitive rumor he'd heard: that Ruth was "an expectant mother."

Ruth knew about this one as well and had nothing to say about it except that it was untrue. While the many references to her "mannish" appearance seem to question her sexual preference, this speculation is bizarre. Did someone think hormonal surges could stir up emotions powerful enough to lead a forty-two-year-old woman to hack her mother to ribbons?

Marks wrapped up with questions about the anticipated confrontation between opposing lawyers. On one side there was the veteran Ben Wilkes, thought to be pretty much impossible to hoodwink. He'd be assisted by his Harvard-educated nephew, Burwell Baylor "B.B." Wilkes, twenty-eight. He was young but no slouch himself.

Their adversaries, on the other hand, were fairly new at their jobs, each one having served in office for only eighteen months. And although state law allowed either man to act as lead prosecutor, County Attorney McIlwain from Greenville had yielded to District Attorney Sanders, five years his junior and a resident of Greenwood, some fifty miles away. What did she think? Was that smart?

Ruth stood down on that one. Lawyers were her husband's turf.

· · · ·

The story ran Monday morning. Later that day, prosecutors issued a statement declaring lie detector tests generally unreliable, pointing out that in addition the test was administered by the private detective who'd been paid by the defendant's family and was conducted on an instrument so unsound it had been sent off for repair immediately afterward.

And in the end, nobody cared about the lie detector test one way or the other.

II

TRIAL

Ruth and John Dickins leaving the courthouse. This photo appeared in the *Greenwood Commonwealth* and other newspapers but was taken by an unnamed member of the Associated Press. Ruth is wearing the girlish dress with the white collar and cuffs and is carrying her beaded bag. Over her left arm she's draped a blousy, light-colored raincoat she often wore into the courthouse, despite the June heat. In another photo, taken later, John is carrying the raincoat for her and, as always, is close by her side, making sure she doesn't trip or fall.

THE JURY

Tuesday, June 21, 1949. Courtroom doors would open at eight thirty, proceedings to begin at nine. By seven, spectators had lined up from the courthouse front steps down the main sidewalk, continuing in a ninety-degree left turn to Edison Street and around that corner. There were many more women than men. One woman brought her baby. Some carried lunches in brown paper sacks so that once they'd snagged a seat, they wouldn't have to give it up. A few even brought picnic baskets packed with fried chicken or egg salad sandwiches and thermos bottles of coffee or iced tea. Those who'd had previous courtroom experience brought paper fans.

That early in the day, the humidity was holding off. Somewhere between nine and ten, the air would sink into a mucky, sour-headed sull. By noon, heat would bear down hard, temperatures predicted to peak in the mid-nineties. Anybody who'd been inside knew the courtroom had six ceiling fans, but they moved slow, and that far up in the rafters they didn't do much more than lick the air. Same with the three window fans. They also knew that by the time they'd sat there the whole day, they'd be sticky and rank, the seats of their clothes damp enough to wring out.

Never mind any of that. Turning back was not an option.

Once the doors opened, the half-hour leeway gave them plenty of time to pick out a seat. And so a lot of them bulldozed their way inside without bothering to check to see who they might bump into or run down, causing a slight panic among both spectators and guards. More people might have crammed in if there'd been benches. But Washington County had installed old-fashioned theater chairs made of dark wood with rounded backs, solid armrests, and flip-up seats, connected one to the next by a wrought-iron base.

After hearing about the melee, Judge Jordan ordered the doors locked until only minutes before nine from then on. Nothing changed. Once people heard that, they became even more aggressive, jamming the doorway, pushing, shoving, and bullying their way forward.

By the time Ruth and John entered at a little past 8:45, the courtroom was packed. Dressed in a "pin striped brown and white summer frock trimmed in white piping" and clunky brown-and-white spectator pumps, Ruth carried a small beaded bag big enough to hold her wallet and cigarettes. No makeup, no jewelry other than the gold watch, no hat covering her dark hair. Blue eyes focused straight ahead, she made her way to the defense table in front of the judge's bench, where she collapsed into her chair.

John, her hulking, watchful bear, sat on her right. Wearing a light-colored short-sleeved shirt tucked into baggy, belted gabardines, white shoes, and no tie, he placed his summer straw fedora on the table beside Ruth's bag, carefully setting its brim faceup so as not to get bent out of shape. The lead defense attorney, Ben Wilkes, took a seat on Ruth's left, his nephew B. B. Wilkes at his elbow, while members of Ruth's family were directed to reserved seats, close to the jury box. When on his way into the building Stanny Sanders was asked if he planned to ask for the death penalty, he said he would leave that decision up to the jury. He and Willard McIlwain sat at their own table, perpendicular to the defense, but close.

Of the lawyers, tall, somewhat paunchy Ben Wilkes—dressed in a frumpy, dark suit, his thinning dark hair parted low—seemed to emerge from another time, the others having donned lightweight, crisp summer attire. Sanders, a compact, boyish-looking redhead, came off especially well in terms of appearance, his bright red hair in sharp and stylish contrast to his cream-colored suit. In the hours ahead, all of the lawyers except Wilkes will pare down and work in shirtsleeves.

At nine sharp, the bailiff entered and issued the usual "All rise." Once the courtroom was on its feet, the judge entered and took the bench. He too wore a summer suit—no robes—his striped bow tie adding a final fashion note to his signature upbeat, cavalier look. As a point of privilege, he'd had a court clerk place a small floor fan near his feet and direct its flow toward his face.

After giving the audience permission to sit, the judge quickly got down to the business of calling the first group of prospective jurors.

. . . .

Although it had been more than eighteen months since the U.S. Supreme Court had issued a ruling declaring that disallowing qualified Black members of the community from serving on juries constituted an abrogation of their Fourteenth Amendment rights, few members of the race had been summoned to join a Washington County jury pool, from which the final jury would be selected. Which meant of course that none had been chosen to serve on a criminal jury, ever. As for women, state law banned them from jury service altogether, a sanction that persisted until 1968, when Mississippi became the last state in the country to change it.

In June 1949, nobody paid any of that a shred of attention. Obviously, the fate of Ruth Thompson Dickins would be decided by twelve white men, a circumstance generally considered a gain for her side.

. . . .

An estimated 340 spectators had settled into the second-floor court-room. Most sat level with the lawyers and the defendant in the large auditorium, which was reserved for white people. Seats in the so-called Negro balcony, high on the wall directly opposite the judge's bench, were also full, a small overflow crowd standing in the rear.

Outside on the lawn, a concessionaire hawked hot dogs and soft drinks from coolers. During the lunch break he'd bring his wares into the courtroom, where he'd sell out to those who neglected to bring their own fare and didn't want to risk losing their seats by leaving. The judge had banned the taking of photographs inside the courthouse, but photographers managed. A two-page magazine spread would showcase the presence of mostly young women in flouncy summer dresses and open-toed shoes, holding hot dogs and Cokes, smiling as broadly toward the camera as beauty contestants on parade. A group of high school boys were rumored to have brought wooden Coke cases to balance on end outside the windows, hoping for a glimpse of the woman who killed her own mother. But when they realized the courtroom was on the second floor, they packed up their soft drink cases and left.

Or so the story goes.

Ruth reportedly drank only one Coca-Cola and smoked one cigarette all day. She spoke occasionally to John but for the most part remained silent. Defendants are usually told by their lawyers to do what they can to maintain their dignity and look confident but not arrogant, to try to think of something other than what they're being accused of, especially during the listing of gruesome details and harsh accusations. And not to look at the spectators.

Ruth was good at this. She held steady and strong, making use of what a tabloid out of Chicago would tag her "mannish force." But that, and the way she dressed, her bizarre unconcern with her appearance, confused people and did her no favors with the jury.

One reason Mississippi white men gave for eliminating women from the jury pool was to protect their delicate natures from unnecessary congress with the seamy side of life. By dressing as if unimpressed with such tired thinking, Ruth flaunted many rules in the southern lady's book of rules and behavior.

Nonetheless, she had a lot going for her. Guilt and innocence aside, she was a respectable white woman without so much as a traffic ticket to her name. The biggest question the prosecution faced in making jury selections was, what might persuade twelve Mississippi white men to convict a Sunday school teacher, wife, and devoted mother, a member of the upper echelon of their own established community, of the first-degree murder of her own mother? Nobody thought it would happen, especially considering Ben Wilkes's reputation and the inexperience of the prosecutors. Local gamblers were laying three-to-one odds against.

The parade of prospective jurors, called veniremen, began. In the process known as voir dire, Judge Jordan questioned members of the pool one by one to make sure of each man's eligibility to serve. He summarily dismissed ten of the first sixteen he interviewed when they admitted having already formed an opinion about the identity of the killer. By the end of the day, he'd qualified twenty. Smoking cigarettes, he posed direct questions, listened intently to the answers, leaning into his personal floor fan and concentrating. Were they really against the death penalty?

Were their reasons for being excused valid? So what if a man had bought property from John Dickins, why should that disqualify him?

Once a venireman was qualified, he moved into the jury box for more specific questioning by the opposing attorneys, who'd been making notes about each one. In this particular case, lawyers on both sides focused primarily on matters having to do with conviction and punishment: circumstantial evidence, the death penalty.

By four fifteen, the state had accepted a full jury, but when the defense challenged the inclusion of five of the men, forcing them to step down, that left only seven acceptable to both sides. At five, Jordan called for a recess until the next morning and ordered the call-up of twenty-two additional men from the special jury pool he'd created.

. . . .

On Wednesday, while the crowd waited for the main doors to open, new members of the jury pool entered separately. Among them were two Black men, E. M. Bryant, a schoolteacher from Arcola, and G. B. Brown, the one Black man in Greenville who might actually be seated. Brown's Pastry Shop had been a fixture in Greenville since 1939. Located on Nelson Street in the heart of what was known as colored town, it was especially favored by white people. The ice cream was homemade and so were its many varieties of cookies, cakes, pies, and bread, pineapple upside-down cake a specialty. On Easter and other religious holidays, Brown's sold out early. People considered G. B. Brown a decent man, honest, hardworking, and in no way a troublemaker. His only drawback was that he wasn't white. And the general thinking locally was a Black man had no right to judge a white person, especially not a white woman. (White *lady* would emphasize the point.)

He was also smart. When the judge asked for his position on the death penalty, Brown said he didn't believe in capital punishment under any circumstances. Which got him out of the courthouse and back to the bakery to run his business and oversee the perfect upside-down flip of his pineapple cakes.

The schoolteacher, Bryant, however, passed Jordan's eligibility test, which gave him the distinction of being the first man of his race to sit in the Washington County jury box on a white person's criminal case.

The judge did what he could to get him excused by mutual consent of the lawyers, but when neither side agreed to use a challenge to unseat him, Bryant solved the problem himself. He would not, he told Stanny Sanders, award the death penalty based on circumstantial evidence. Nor could he see himself voting to electrocute a white lady.

Dismissed from further service, he stepped from the jury box and exited the courthouse.

When a headline in the next day's *Delta Democrat-Times* reported that "an Arcola Negro school teacher almost got on the jury," it's the "almost" that resounds. There's a shudder of dread inside the adverb. A feeling of a near miss, the hint of a crack in the wall of resistance. If *almost* today, what about tomorrow and into the future? White people had a responsibility to halt dangerous possibilities ahead of their unfurling. They had to focus. Whatever it took.

Jury selection continued throughout the second day, Ruth somehow managing to look cool while the crowd sat "shirt-sleeved and sweating in the sweltering heat" of the courtroom. As the day groaned on, all those who'd been so crazy to get in, as well as Ruth and her family, grew restless, listening to the DA ask again and again, "Would you send a woman to the electric chair based on circumstantial evidence?" followed by Wilkes's "You wouldn't convict anybody on a bunch of rumors, would you?" The tedium wore everybody down as much as the heat, especially when by five that afternoon only four more jurors had been seated.

. . . .

To explore Ruth's unnatural passivity and check on her health once again, when the trial is over, she'll be examined by two doctors, a personal physician and one chosen by the court. Both will diagnose low blood pressure. Dr. Hugh A. Gamble, brother of the man who signed her father's death certificate, will also find her red blood cell count low enough to qualify her as anemic. Symptoms of these conditions include lack of energy and a slow heartbeat. Which may or may not partially explain why she could attend her own murder trial looking unruffled and placid, needing only one cigarette to get through the day. On the other hand, she might well be just plain exhausted, physically and emotionally. And in truth, her behavior isn't that unusual. People on trial often seem to float far from their own lives, no matter how embarrassing or personal the details on parade before them. It's not their life anymore. It's a *case*. As observers, they've jumped the tracks of their own selfhood and are looking across it.

The juror search ended the next morning when a businessman named R. A. Worthington assured defense attorney Wilkes he would not be prejudiced by the coincidence of his planter brother, Andre, having served as foreman of the grand jury that indicted Ruth. Once he was sworn in, twelve men had been seated. Six were farmers; others included a lumberman, an insurance salesman, a businessman, and three employees of the U.S. Gypsum Company.

They were churchgoers, fathers, members of men's civic clubs and the chamber of commerce. One man was reported to be in the "movie business for Negroes."

Judge Jordan called a recess until 1:30. As Ruth left the building, she told a newsman she was "more than glad" everything was being brought to light. Because "we've got to get it over with, you know." When asked about her children, she said Dorothy Jane was being kept by friends in Leland. Dell had left for summer camp two days earlier. And in fact, in the presence of either or both of her daughters, she said her family tried to talk about the trial as little as possible.

She and John got in their Chevrolet and drove home to Leland for lunch.

OPENING: STANNY

When court resumed at the appointed hour, the judge was startled to look up and see twenty or so white people standing behind the seats in the balcony. Curtly, he reminded the interlopers that the balcony was not for them and asked guards to escort them out of the building immediately. White people invading a space restricted to Black people was not something Jordan or anybody else in town, regardless of race, had experienced, in this courtroom or anyplace else.

The mood downstairs had changed. After two and a half days of tiresome jury selection, the real thing was now about to begin, a dramatic unwinding of the event itself: what really happened. Even Ruth had perked up, her blue eyes "sparkling with lively interest."

Jordan called for the jurors, who filed in. All twelve men wore wide-bodied short-sleeved white shirts and light-colored summer pants. The U.S. Gypsum Company employee Wilson Webb had been chosen as foreman.

After delivering a brief, boilerplate speech explaining the purpose of the opening statements they would soon hear, the judge turned the proceedings over to the state.

Stanny Sanders rose, walked past the defense table, and stood at the far end of the jury box facing the judge. From there, he had a clear view of all twelve men. He addressed them in a loud, clear voice.

All due respect to the judge, he said, the state would *not* be making an opening statement. He would, instead, move straight into the case against Mrs. Dickins. In northern Mississippi, he explained, it was common practice to jump ahead like that, without advancing the theory you hope will sway the jury in your direction. It was also—though he didn't say so—a way to dribble the particulars of a case to the jury bit by bit, giving nothing away until he was ready to use it for his own purposes. Thereby controlling the suspense. And the narrative.

A bold choice. But Sanders was young, relatively new to the job, and just cocky enough to ignore custom and make his own way. A trial, after all, was a kind of sporting event. A lawyer who was unconvinced of his superior skills was probably dead in the water before the judge declared, "Game on."

During the lunch hour, the prosecution had rolled a stand into the courtroom and placed it in the space between the defense table and the jury box, facing the jurors. They set a bulletin board on the stand; tacked to it, an architectural drawing of Idella Thompson's house as it was on the day of the murder. Sanders called Walter Parsons Jr., the civil engineer he'd hired to make the sketch. While Parsons made his way to the witness box, the prosecutor passed out copies of the drawing to the judge and jury.

A standard line of attack. First, set the scene. Sink its dimensions deep into jurors' minds so that they can visualize the setting where the crime transpired, room by room and inch by inch. With the engineer's help, Sanders painted the picture.

State's Exhibit 1. Parsons was excused. Sanders called Frank Aldridge.

The Leland chief's primary job as a prosecution witness was to set up the reading of Ruth's bedside statement to the police. To prepare the jury, Sanders carefully led Aldridge through a recital of his actions on November 17, 1948, beginning with the call from Doc Witte: where he and Officer Pink Gorman were when it came through, what they found when they arrived at Mrs. Thompson's house, the shape he was in physically that day, where Ruth was and who was with her, the location of the shears, stool, heater, bathtub, commode, back door. The body. How much blood there was.

Asked to describe the state of Idella's body, Aldridge told the jury she was "beaten all over, her head and hands all cut up and she was bloody all over and she was lying on her back . . . on the floor and partially on a bathroom rug." As for the shears, he didn't pick them up to examine, but, no, he didn't see any blood on them. He described the neat-as-a-pin condition of the house, buttoned down the location of the telephone, and agreed that, yes, he and Doc had gone out into the backyard to look for footprints and, no, he didn't close the front door after he and Gorman entered.

Sanders then arrived at the moment he'd been aiming at. Was Aldridge present when, two days later, the defendant made a statement "with regard to what happened down there on the afternoon her mother was killed"? After Aldridge answered in the affirmative and was asked to name the others who participated, he struggled. Ed Blue, he said, was there. A. E. Crawford, Sheriff Foote . . . and either his memory went blank or he was too nervous to remember. Flustered, he included Doc Witte, who wasn't present that day, then, when corrected, left off a few who were. Sanders fed him.

Was Miss Clara Wing there? Yes. And who was she?

Gently prodded, Aldridge came through. And once the defense had accepted Ruth's statement as Exhibit A and Sanders had passed copies to the judge and jury, McIlwain stood and, holding his own copy, joined his partner.

While Aldridge waited in the witness box, the two lawyers took turns reading the twenty-five-page statement aloud. McIlwain assumed the role of Ruth, while Sanders took on the various questioners, beginning with Crawford.

. . . .

"*My name is A. E. Crawford,*" he read. "*And I was brought up by Mr. Wynn and the sheriff . . .*"

McIlwain, in turn, read Ruth's answer: "A. *Ask me anything you want to . . .*"

Sanders as Crawford again: "Q. *Suppose you tell us where you were . . .*"

. . . .

This kind of thing would never happen today. The interview would have been audiotaped, digitized, perhaps even videotaped. Jurors and spectators would hear for themselves how Ruth spoke, at what point she stumbled over certain answers, skipped past questions, reversed herself, or came off as entirely credible. But in 1949, the two young lawyers did what amounts to performing a dramatic reading, presumably—they weren't actors after all—without inflection or interpretation. Later that day, the statement reached an even wider local audience when in its evening edition *The Delta Democrat-Times* devoted a good bit of space on page 1 and almost all of page 2 to the interview with Ruth. The whole thing.

When the two men finished, McIlwain returned to his seat and Sanders turned back to the police chief. "Mr. Aldridge," he said, "you said the bathroom was covered with blood?"

It was, Aldridge replied, "as bloody as could be."

"Covered with blood" was important. When Sanders reminded the police chief of his previous description of the bathroom floor, he was pursuing a major point in his case, which came down to how—if the bathroom floor was *covered*—"as bloody as could be," "a mass of blood"— the stone cold killer could hack Mrs. Thompson to death, then *slam* into Mrs. Dickins, tussle violently with her, make his way from the bathroom through the hall and across the back porch, out the back door, down the steps and over the wall, across Second Street, through an empty lot toward the cotton compress and "Negro settlement," without leaving behind one trace of his presence. Not one partial footprint, handprint, or drop of blood.

Sanders didn't ask the entirety of that question, but he implied every word of it. When, after another question or two, he passed the witness, Wilkes conducted a comparatively benign cross-examination, apparently designed to trip Aldridge up further in his recall of the setting and the circumstances of the killing.

The Leland police chief, Aldridge, was not a great witness, either because he was more than a little panicked from nerves—having known Ruth Dickins for twenty years, being himself remotely kin to her and married to a member of one of the founding families of the town—or because he was simply forgetful if not somewhat dim. I've heard stories. Like the time he woke up from a nap at a cowboy movie playing at the local theater and, hearing shots, drew his pistol and blew a hole in the screen. Certainly Sanders and McIlwain would have filled him in on what they'd be asking him, but on the stand he couldn't remember who was there the day Ruth made her statement or who lived next door to Mrs. Thompson even though the Goodloe family had been neighbors for years and he'd been chief even longer.

But when it came to specifics like where the body lay, at what angle, between which bathroom fixtures, and details such as how Ruth looked with her hair down in her face and her dress all bloody, and other concrete details, the police chief did what the state needed him to. By naming the day, the time, and the location and by placing the body, the weapon, and the accused in the house pictured on the scale drawing, he gave Sanders the opening to the story he hoped the jury would buy.

After some minor follow-up back-and-forth between prosecution and defense about the Thompson backyard and the neighborhood beyond it, Aldridge was excused, and Sanders called the longtime Witte Clinic bookkeeper Pauline Mason, who answered the phone when Ruth rang up asking to speak to Dr. Bunt Witte.

When Sanders asked how that conversation went, Mason said when she told Ruth Dr. Witte was in the operating room, she asked for a different doctor's number, and once Mason gave it to her, Ruth hung up.

Did she mention her mother? No. The intruder? No. Did she sound excited or nervous? No, she was calm. She was normal. And yes, Mason recognized her voice right off.

Then what happened? Five minutes later, Ruth called back, still calm, nothing in her voice to indicate trouble of any kind. She had only one question. Was old Dr. Witte there? Within minutes she was talking to him. Excused, Mason stepped down.

Sanders called Doc.

. . . .

At his age—sixty-six at the time of the murder—K. L. Witte admitted, he'd grown hard of hearing, and so he didn't get everything Ruth said, but he got "the Negro part" and the part about Mrs. Thompson being on the floor or maybe it was the bed. Whatever it was, he took it for granted she'd had a stroke of paralysis and that the Black person she mentioned was somebody's cook or yardman, trying to help her up. But even if he didn't catch everything she said, he got the highest spots. He put on his coat and hat, got in his car, and went up there right away. Knowing he'd be asked how long it took him to get from the clinic to Mrs. Thompson's house, he had test run the drive several times on his own. He'd made one in three minutes and one in six. Call it five. Five was about right.

. . . .

When, back around the turn of the century, a young Doc Witte joined in partnership with Leland's then best-known physician, Dr. John Ausbin Long, he had no idea that within three or so years he'd become not only co-owner of Long's drugstore but also Dr. Long's son-in-law, married into the Stovall cousinhood. Or that things would turn out the way they had, him on the witness stand testifying for the state against the granddaughter of his late partner and his niece by marriage, who was on trial for the first-degree murder of his wife's big sister.

A wrought-up set of circumstances to say the least. Aggravating enough to cause some men to hang back and, if not refuse to blurt out what they'd seen, heard, and thought, at least to show some hesitation or even ambivalence.

Not Doc.

Ruth, he said, met him at the front door and led him to the second bathroom. Doc knew right off that Idella Thompson was dead. The wounds on the left side of her head were enough to kill anybody on their own. She was, he declared, "chopped all to pieces." But he did the doctor's standard due diligence, knelt down, and lifted her left hand to check for a pulse. Her wrist and hand were cold. Not rigid yet. But ice cold and beginning to stiffen.

She'd been dead a good piece of time.

He didn't examine her more closely than that, there being no need. Some of the wounds had clearly been administered after death. When Sanders pulled out a photo of Mrs. Thompson lying dead, the defense objected. The photograph didn't give the jury any information about who the killer might have been, nothing to help them decide whether the defendant was guilty. The prosecution, Wilkes argued, was offering it only because of its "gruesomeness" and to prejudice the jurors against the defendant.

But, argued Sanders, weren't photos of dead people always gruesome?

The judge overruled Wilkes's objection. Sanders proffered the photograph. Doc confirmed the state's supposition. The photograph was indeed a true and correct representation of the body of Idella Thompson as he had seen her on November 17, 1948.

Sanders feigned mild surprise.

Did she look *exactly* as she did when Doc saw her?

Yes, except for one thing: she'd been cleaned up. Washed, he thought.

After passing the photograph to the jury, Sanders returned to the matter of the blood. What about the bathroom itself, was the photograph an accurate representation of the scene as Witte observed it? Not altogether, he said. By the time the photographer came and took the pictures, the bathroom had also been cleaned up. There was a whole lot more blood when he first got there. Not just on the bathroom floor. Spattered all up the side of the tub and outside the bathroom in the hall and up on the wall. Even a little on the bathroom ceiling. Blood was everywhere. As for Ruth's clothing it wasn't merely stained; it was *saturated*.

Sanders passed three more photographs of Mrs. Thompson to Witte and then—after Wilkes had again objected and the judge overruled—to the jury. Each time, Witte remarked on the cleanup of the body.

He'd seen no footprints heading out the back door, no man's cap or torn clothing.

And when he went from the bathroom into Mrs. Thompson's bedroom to use her bedside phone to call the police, did he leave tracks behind him on the wooden floor? Yes. His were the only ones at that time. As for the small rug under Mrs. Thompson's body it seems to have been used to drag her body from the porch into the bathroom.

And the weapon? The shears lay between Mrs. Thompson's head and the bathtub, toward the footstool. There was not much blood on them, if any at all; clearly they'd been wiped clean.

As for Doc's expertise at examining dead bodies, he'd been doing that for forty-two or forty-three years; nonetheless, to make certain his assumptions were correct, he'd made a point of going to his office to research rigor mortis and how long it took for bodies of different sizes—Mrs. Thompson being of such small stature—to grow cold and rigid and eventually to atrophy. He'd even visited an undertaker's shop to observe the process for himself, partly because his own family was involved, which made him eager to get things right before making any kind of statement and partly because he simply wanted to know. He'd come to the conclusion that to the best of his judgment Mrs. Thompson had been dead a minimum of one hour.

Sanders, in the hard-of-hearing *Excuse me?* pretense that lawyers love, asked for a reprise: You would say at least one hour?

Yes, sir.

Disputing Ruth's insistence that she called the Witte Clinic immediately after the killer fled out the back door at 3:30, Witte had estimated the time of Idella Thompson's death as between 2:15 and 2:30. If this was even close to accurate, Ruth had had ample time to wipe the shears clean and get a story straight and ready in her mind to pass on.

Sanders ended his questioning by asking the doctor once again if in his opinion some of Mrs. Thompson's wounds had been inflicted after her death. He not only said yes to that but also said that several of the postmortem cuts were deep enough to have killed her by themselves.

And finally, "She is bound to have been pecked up all over because, though I didn't see all over her, what we saw was enough."

. . . .

Clearly, Doc Witte was used to having his word accepted as gospel. When the defense attorney Wilkes began his cross and asked why he hadn't initially reported his observation that an object, more than likely the victim's body, had been dragged from the back porch to the bathroom, he briskly snapped, "Because I'm a doctor, not a police officer," firmly enough to elicit titters from spectators, followed by a threat from the judge to clear the courtroom.

On the other hand, the sight of his wife's sister dead on the bloody bathroom floor might well have kicked off a feeling of personal outrage he couldn't tamp down. Or maybe he was simply thin-skinned and petulant. He's pretty hard looking. Tight-lipped and wary. Maybe he was the kind of doctor who didn't like his diagnoses questioned. He was Leland's doc after all.

He was not, however, Idella Thompson's regular doctor. His son Bunt was. And he had never been Ruth's personal physician. Matter of fact, Doc was considered elderly at that time; plus he had other interests, including a prizewinning show horse named Miss Leland. Bunt, on the other hand, was a surgeon in addition to his general practice, and so he could cover medical problems his father couldn't. And Bunt—*Doctor*

Bunt—was the one who had examined and discharged Idella that same morning.

Doc's lack of direct personal experience with Ruth and her mother might have served as a testament to his objectivity, but on cross Wilkes poked at his expertise at evaluating time of death especially as it related to the gradual process of a corpse to grow cold and then rigid. The aging doctor didn't back down, but sometimes his hearing problem made him seem uncertain, especially when Wilkes had to repeat himself. Wilkes never let up on the question of where the blood was and how much of it there was. A point of crucial interest to both sides.

At five, Judge Jordan ended the day's testimony and exited the courtroom, followed by Ruth and her family, including her brothers and her sister-in-law, Demetra. Spectators waited quietly before filing out themselves.

The temperature outside was still in the nineties but, compared with the courtroom's swelter and funk, felt cooler, less heavy. Cars moved slowly around the block, windows rolled down, people's heads poked out. Everybody hoping for the same thing: to get a glimpse of Ruth.

. . . .

When it came to motive, readers of that day's *McComb Enterprise-Journal* scored a juicy hint of what might lie ahead. According to an "authoritative source," the paper reported, at the time of her mother's murder, Ruth was operating her late father's eighteen-hundred-acre plantation east of Leland, which she "owned jointly with her husband," who had purchased it from other members of her family. Furthermore, according to the source, "Mrs. Dickins has long been accustomed to borrowing money to finance her seasonal crop making and in previous years had also borrowed to finance real estate interests."

That all Delta farmers lived on year-by-year credit was a given. Nobody didn't know that. More than once, I heard my father tell my brother, "It's not the amount of money you have that matters. It's your line of credit."

What the *Enterprise-Journal* didn't say or even hint at was why Ruth's financial dealings might have led to an argument so red-flaming hot it sowed the seeds of violent matricide.

DAY THREE

By Friday, the onslaught of the curious had grown even larger and more insistent. To keep people from forcing their way through the courtroom door, guards had to string a rope across it. Once again, twenty or so white people who missed out on a seat downstairs managed to sneak into the balcony and were standing in the back, against the wall. There were vacant seats up there, by the way, but no white person considered making a move in their direction.

When the judge took the bench, he once again ordered the trespassers out of his courtroom. Guards made sure they left the building.

Dressed in springlike blue broadcloth, Ruth leaned heavily on the table, rubbed her face, and drank several cups of water. People said she was finally showing some strain.

First up was Sheriff Foote, whose slightly pique-ish tone made it clear he'd been more than a little miffed that not only wasn't he called to the scene until three thirty—which meant by the time he arrived at four, Deer Creek Drive was already jammed with people—but Ruth wasn't even there, having been given permission to leave the crime scene to go home to change her clothes and then go to the Witte Clinic to have her injuries seen to. He did walk through the Thompson house as soon as he got there, but if he wanted a description of the man Ruth said killed Mrs. Thompson, he had to maneuver his way back through the crowd and drive to the clinic and get it from her there.

And he certainly did want it. Because, the sheriff explained, "we thought of nothing else then but that a Negro did it." And if they were going to find the right Black man, they had to know, or at least get a good idea of, what he looked like. Which only one person knew.

There were other things that irked the sheriff. Probably the one that got him most was the high-handedness of the PI from Jackson, A. E. Crawford. Not that he wasn't perfectly willing for the man to do whatever he could to further the investigation. As a matter of fact he'd tried to hire Crawford himself, only to find that Billy Wynn had beat him to the punch. From the beginning, Foote had been more than happy to acknowledge the greater expertise of other men, especially in the areas of evidence collection and identification. That was why he placed a lot of faith in the only two local officers who'd had FBI training, Chief of Police C. A. Hollingsworth and the Mississippi Highway Patrol identification officer Ed Blue.

But in the end he was, after all, the sheriff. Like it or not, the case was *his*. A fact he thought some people found ways to ignore.

After talking to Ruth at the clinic, he'd gone on back to the Thompson house to search for evidence: prints, hair, clothes, a shoelace, a button, anything the killer might have left behind. Making his way straight into the bathroom to take a closer look, he found Mrs. Thompson lying on her back half on a small rug and half on the white tile floor, which he described as covered with blood. Wearing a green wool dress hiked up above her knees, a ripped hairnet buried in her scalp from the blows she sustained, one shoe on and one off, she was a terrible sight. Somebody had at least draped the bathroom rug partially across her thighs, but for a white woman of that age and size to be so exposed, right arm broken, two fingers connected to her hand only by strings of skin, well, it was perfectly awful. It was hard for him and everybody else who saw her to imagine the savagery it took for a man to do such a thing to a tiny old woman, only hours out of the hospital.

When Sanders presented a shot of the bathroom and asked about the difference in the condition of the floor as shown in the picture and what the sheriff had seen when he first arrived, he was returning to a question he'd asked both Doc and Frank Aldridge, one that would resound throughout the trial.

Foote came out with it. The bathroom floors weren't, he said, as bloody as they had been and for a good reason. By the time the picture was taken, they'd been mopped. And then he dropped a bombshell.

"I had the floors cleaned myself," he admitted. "Because they [people] were tracking blood all over the house and I didn't see what difference the floors would make. But the walls and tub and everything else wasn't touched."

Sanders let that sink in. The sheriff of Washington County had admitted having a crime scene prematurely altered.

He then moved on.

"I hand you another picture." Keeping the procession of images going, with each one he asked several related questions. The blood smears on the outside of the bathtub, in the washbasin, and on the walls, the one blood spot up on the ceiling. Had Foote seen them? What did he think? Had he noticed them right away or later?

Finished with the bathroom photographs, he moved to the back porch, the back door, the screen door, the yard, the brick wall across the back of the lot, the barbecue pit, gates, garage, step by step. Any blood on the doors? The wall? On the gates? Any footprints? Fingerprints?

To each question, Hughey gave the same answer. No. No. No.

Once the photographs had been proffered to the jury, Sanders turned to other pieces of evidence.

First, the brown-edged lady's linen handkerchief found soaked in blood and crumpled, as if wadded up and forgotten, in the bathtub. The sheriff himself had collected and wrapped it in brown paper and given it to Chief Hollingsworth for inclusion in the package they'd be sending to the FBI. Same thing with the bathroom rug.

It was still morning when the prosecutor quietly asked Mr. Foote if he'd seen any shears in the bathroom.

Yes, Foote replied, he did.

Where?

On the bathroom floor between Mrs. Thompson and the footstool.

And the condition of the bathroom floor was . . . ?

Bloody.

The condition of the shears?

No blood on top of them that he could see.

When Sanders reached for his next exhibit, Ruth buried her face in her arms and did not lift it until after the weapon had been exhibited, identified, and passed around the jury box. The shears gleamed. Spectators strained to see the metal handles, the hawk's-beak blades.

"Mr. Foote," Sanders asked, "what is this I hand you?"

Pruning shears.

Had he seen them before?

Yes. In Mrs. Thompson's bathroom.

Were they in the same condition as when he found them? Except for FBI identification marks, yes. As for blood, there'd been a little on the underside but none that he could see on top.

Sanders didn't ask Foote how this could be possible, given the state of the room and everything in it, as testified to by previous witnesses as well as himself. First, because Wilkes would object and the judge would sustain; second, because he didn't have to. The statement spoke for itself.

Once the bathroom rug and the weapon were officially offered as evidence, the prosecutor asked about the failed search for a suspect matching Ruth's description and then made his first move toward a possible motive. Did the sheriff know anything about a $600 rent check made out to Mrs. Thompson, which Ruth might have had in her possession? Yes, Foote said, there were two checks, one of which Ruth and her brother Jimmy had gone over to Greenville to cash.

Stanny Sanders yielded the floor to Ben Wilkes without pursuing the matter further.

Ruth straightened her spine and sat up.

. . . .

Wilkes spent a good-sized block of time on the sheriff's opinion of A. E. Crawford, presumably to rile Foote up enough to get him to acknowledge his own lack of experience at homicide investigation, especially as compared with the well-known private eye from Jackson. Regarding Ruth's original statement to the police, for instance, which they were both in on, he wondered if Foote had understood in advance that Mr. Crawford would be the man conducting the examination.

Foote bristled. "No, *sir*," he said. "I thought *I* was the man conducting it."

Wilkes rolled on. That being the case, why did he let Crawford do most of the questioning at "this girl's" house—gesturing toward Ruth— on the very day, by the way, of her mother's funeral?

The best the sheriff could come up with was, "Because he was in on it and everybody else was asking questions too." As a matter of fact, he went on, Crawford had been in on everything since late that first night when he arrived in Leland from Jackson in time to help a news photographer take crime scene photos. And Sheriff Foote wasn't against that; he welcomed whatever help he could get. But things went beyond what he expected.

For instance, after Crawford finished his report, he handed out copies, one to Billy Wynn, one to Doc, and one to himself, and went back to Jackson. Foote thought that was it. He'd gone home for good. Then, after only about a week, "he come back and done some more work on it that I didn't even know he was doing." In fact, the only reason Foote knew Crawford was back in town was that Frank Aldridge told him, and Frank only knew it because a police officer driving by the Hotel Greenville saw him out front talking to somebody. But even that was all right. Anybody could have made an investigation who wanted to. But there was the other thing.

Foote went back over the day soon after the murder when they asked John Dickins to bring Ruth down to the courthouse. Aldridge was there. So were Pink Gorman, Ed Blue, and Crawford. After Ruth agreed to take a test on the lie detector machine Crawford had brought from Jackson, he wouldn't let anybody except Ed Blue in the room with him when he gave it. He said he wanted only one witness in there and shut the door in their faces. It wasn't until later they found out the machine was broken and had to be sent off for repairs.

Wilkes made no comment. He moved on.

When he asked about the issue of the bathroom floor, Foote repeated what he'd said before: people were walking through the rooms, making tracks, and messing up the rugs, and when somebody in the Thompson family said she wanted the floor mopped, he'd agreed to let the handyman, Jimmy Banks, come inside and take care of that.

And, Wilkes wondered, what about pictures showing drag marks from the rug allegedly used to move Mrs. Thompson's body across the porch floor to the bathroom?

Foote squirmed in his seat as he admitted having also ordered the porch floor cleaned before the pictures were made.

Wilkes feigned surprise. "*Before*," he echoed Foote, "any pictures were made?"

"Yes, sir." Noting the defense attorney's sarcastic tone, Foote tried to explain. "If you want to know the truth, Mr. Wilkes," he added, "at that time I was looking for a Negro. Mrs. Dickins told me it was a Negro who did it and I thought nothing else but that it was a Negro."

That was why, he said, he never attached any significance to the drag marks.

Wilkes seemed to wind up his cross by rhetorically asking if the Dickinses had been willing to cooperate with his investigation and comply with his requests. With this, the sheriff agreed unreservedly.

That being the case, Wilkes wondered why the sheriff saw fit to question Ruth on the very day of her mother's funeral.

Foote protested: he *wanted* to interview her right away, he *tried* to do that, but her family had isolated her. She was injured, they said. She wasn't in any condition to talk. And besides, he couldn't swear it was the same day her mother was buried or not; he just went as soon as they let him.

Wilkes passed the witness.

The picture you get is of a distraught sheriff on the defensive, working to save face and protect his reputation.

· · · ·

The Greenville chief of police, C. A. Hollingsworth, confirmed the statements of Aldridge and Foote as to the circumstances he discovered at the Thompson house a little later that afternoon. A dependable, articulate witness, he supplied vivid, detailed descriptions of the porch, hall, and bathroom walls and floor. He also seemed more confident than the others that the wide blood smears started on the porch floor and ran like a line of tire tracks down the hall into the bathroom, where they ended in a rumple under Mrs. Thompson's lower body.

"This rug," he said, "was dragged through the door where Mrs. Thompson's body was lying. [It] had been dragged around the door. And Mrs. Thompson's body was partially lying on [it]."

He also confirmed the earlier testimony regarding the absence of bloody footprints and the failure to find a blood-spattered Black man anywhere in the vicinity. And presented evidence he was personally responsible for locating: hair samples and the broken tips of three fingernails. Each piece of evidence was contained in its own envelope. As Hollingsworth carefully opened one small brown envelope after the other and identified each as he went, he held the courtroom's attention. The Jackson *Clarion-Ledger* described the moment: "The only sound in the packed courtroom during the presentation of the hair was the crackling of paper as Hollingsworth, a strapping big man with horned rimmed glasses, opened the paper packages and envelopes of evidence."

After marching out a long string of other material evidence, he withstood Wilkes's cross-examination and stepped down, having credibly managed to create the possibility of a murderer who—wishing to move Mrs. Thompson's body from the openness of the back porch where the fight began, lacking the strength to do that on her own—had used the rug to help her slide the body through the hall into the bathroom.

The judge called for a brief recess.

At the end of which, the Parchman Farm trusty and dog handler Edgar Ballard recounted how on the afternoon of the murder, Officer Pink Gorman had picked him and the bloodhounds up at Parchman, but on their way to Leland the car broke down. They still had a forty- or forty-five-minute trip ahead of them and in addition had to wait that same amount of time for another officer to come get them. Being as how it was November, by the time they got to Leland, the sun was starting to set and rain clouds were piling in. The backyard was already damp, but according to Ballard, Nick and Red liked to work in moist grass. So they got down to business right away and pretty quickly struck a trail from the back door to the garage and back to the house again. He thought maybe they had something, but the killer wasn't in the garage and certainly he wouldn't have gone back to the house knowing Ruth was in there. He had to have left either by leaping over the back wall or through the gate, and there were no prints or tracks back there.

Sanders pointed out that, as everybody knew, the Thompson handyman, Jimmy Banks, spent daytimes in a room over the garage. Could the scent, he wondered, be his?

Ballard said yes, that was the thinking, and because Banks wasn't considered a suspect, he went on and carried Nick and Red down the driveway and all over the back and front yards and out into Second Street and beyond, through that cotton field over there, but they couldn't pick up another trail. No blood. Nothing. He'd stuck around for another hour or two before hitching a ride for himself and the dogs back to the state prison, where, he told Wilkes on cross, he'd been incarcerated for nine years.

Middle of the afternoon, Sanders called the court-ordered doctor who examined Ruth a week after the murder, when she'd been asked to come to the sheriff's courthouse office for a second interview and ended up taking a lie detector test. He wasn't Mrs. Dickins's doctor and didn't personally know her, but he was the person who'd found the bruises Ruth hadn't mentioned: one above her right knee about the size of a silver dollar and five below her left knee, varying in size from a silver dollar to a quarter. These seem to have come from a blow of some kind.

A kick perhaps?

Yes.

The prosecution didn't spell out the obvious implication: that a kick to the shins was far more than likely to be a lady's defensive move than a man's.

The Stovall Funeral Home employee W. J. Boone Jr. testified that he, his boss, John A. Stovall, and other members of the funeral home staff arrived at the Thompson house around four that afternoon and within two hours had moved Mrs. Thompson's body from the crime scene into the other bathroom where they disrobed her and washed her body. At around seven or so, they took her to the funeral home.

One by one, Sanders then handed Boone the same four photographs Doc Witte had identified as showing a true picture of Mrs. Thompson's body. Boone verified that, yes, he was present when the pictures were taken.

And what time was that?

About three.

In the morning?

Yes.

This meant the official photographs of Mrs. Thompson's body were taken *after* she'd been cleaned up and moved from the crime scene to the funeral home, where presumably she lay on a stainless steel table waiting to be embalmed.

Sanders, oddly enough, didn't follow up on this and neither did Wilkes, who during his cross-examination might have used the fact that Foote failed to have pictures of the victim taken at the crime scene to cast doubt on the sheriff's investigation.

But Sanders couldn't afford to open the door to any more disparagement of the sheriff's actions than had already come up, and because Ruth's defense team was out to make the case that Idella Thompson hadn't lost as much blood as Doc Witte, Aldridge, Hughey, and the whole prosecution crew were asserting, the best thing for the prosecution to do was to let this one go by as well.

To finish with Boone, Sanders asked about the number of cuts Mrs. Thompson suffered to her head.

"She was," he replied, "so mutilated you couldn't count the number of cuts. All I can say is there were so many cuts you couldn't count them." And as if that didn't quite do it, he said it again. "It was just mutilated that is all."

Nobody in the Delta other than somebody determined to believe Ruth's story gave a minute's credence to the idea that a Black man would stick around inside a white lady's Deer Creek house in the middle of an afternoon long enough to stab her that many times even after she was dead, no matter what she'd said or done to set him off.

Those twelve jurors sitting in the box listening knew that as well as everybody else.

· · · ·

Dr. W. S. "Bunt" Witte had been Idella Thompson's personal physician since he returned to Leland from an internship in the army in 1942 and began to practice medicine in partnership with his father. After signing off on Mrs. Thompson's discharge from the hospital on the morning of November 17, he'd gone into surgery and was still at work there when he heard about the murder, which he figured must have been around four o'clock. Ten minutes later, while he was still in the OR, somebody told him his first cousin Ruth was in the clinic needing attention. So he asked a colleague to finish sewing up so he could go see about her. He found Ruth sitting in a chair with her head being shaved where she had two wounds. One didn't amount to much; he and an assistant put maybe four stitches in the other one, which didn't go to the bone, only down to the fatty tissue. She had bruises and a swollen hand and arm. Once he'd finished—she was not charged one penny for the procedure by the way—and she'd gone home, he went to Idella's house, arriving at about 4:45.

On the stand, Bunt Witte seemed a good bit calmer than his father, less agitated, more professional. He said nothing about the shock he surely felt when, having discharged a patient in the morning, he found her lying in a river of her own blood, mutilated beyond comprehension, some six hours later that same afternoon.

As for vital statistics, Idella was five feet tall and weighed about ninety pounds. Her blood pressure was a little over 200 diastolic when she entered the hospital but had come down to a normal 140 by the time she left a week later. Unfortunately, however, that would last only if she stayed in bed.

"Aunt Dell," he explained, "was very active. It was very hard for her to stay in bed." Which is why they kept her in the hospital for a week, so she'd be well rested by the time she went home.

As to her general health, she complained of pain in her left shoulder and arm, and while the doctor thought it was from arthritis, she worried about angina, mainly because "she was a Stovall and most Stovalls died of angina." She also had a slight enlargement of the stomach and colon, a condition she thought was more serious than did Witte or a Memphis specialist she'd gone to see. Witte described her gastric symptoms as only "a little annoying." Some stomachache and a disturbance in the bowel movements. But she talked about it a lot, he recalled.

By the time Bunt got to Mrs. Thompson's, the house and yard were mobbed and he had to park down the street. Ruth's brother-in-law, Shields Hood, said there were so many people it looked like a place that was giving away nylon hose. By then the sheriff had banned entrance to the bathroom, and so Bunt wasn't allowed to examine the body at that time but only glanced at it through the bathroom door. The first he was able to examine her closely was almost two hours later, after the funeral home staff had taken her to the other bathroom to disrobe her and wash her body. That happened at 6:30. By then, rigor mortis had begun to set in.

And did he examine her wounds at that time?

Aunt Dell's wounds?

Yes.

He took out his notes. The first thing he couldn't help noticing was multiple wounds on her head, concentrated mostly but not exclusively on the left side. Most of the hair on that side was gone. She wore a hairnet, which had been shoved down into her head by the blows, and when he picked it up, skin and hair came off with it. It was, he said, nothing but gruesome. There was no criminal (sexual) assault. She had a fractured skull over her right ear about two inches long and about three-quarters of an inch wide. From the cuts on her head it looked as if she'd been hit 150 or 200 times around her head and her left eye. Her right elbow was broken. The middle finger of her right hand was practically severed. The left ring finger was hanging by a flap of skin. There were multiple scratches on her right forearm, which was broken.

Could she have sustained that many wounds and still lived?

He thinks a good 40 to 60 percent of the blows were inflicted after she was dead. And so, no. She could not have. No chance.

. . . .

Under Wilkes's scrutiny, Dr. Bunt acknowledged his cousin Ruth's devotion to her mother. She was, he agreed, certainly the only one in the family who looked after Idella while she was in the hospital. The other daughter, Mildred, came maybe once, but Ruth came every day, several times a day. She was the one who waited on Aunt Dell.

Wilkes: And was their relationship everything it should be between a mother and a daughter?

Bunt said it was. On the other hand, it had to be said that Idella was crazy about her son Jimmy. She'd told Bunt "he was the only one of her children who wasn't mean to her."

Wilkes quickly stepped in. But she didn't mean that, did she?

Bunt couldn't say. He'd told his aunt in no uncertain terms he was *her* doctor and he didn't want to talk about family.

What about the injuries Ruth sustained on her hands?

She had swelling on the dorsal part of her left hand that ran from a ring on her finger to her wrist. It was bruised. Her right hand and arm were swollen. And two of the fingernails on that hand were torn off, not the whole nail, just the white part, known as the top edge, maybe one thirty-second of an inch wide. If she had bruises on her shins from something like a kick or a blow, he didn't see them.

On rebuttal, after determining that Bunt Witte knew Mrs. Thompson as well as or better than anybody else in the family, Sanders asked if, when attacked, she was capable of putting up a stiff fight for her life.

About this, the doctor had no doubts.

"From the looks of the bathroom where we found her body," he said, "she was bound to have put up a devil of a stiff fight and, knowing her as I did, I know she fought to the death."

And how did he know that?

"Because she is a Stovall and made of the same kind of stuff I am."

. . . .

The state's final Friday witness, H. E. Campbell, the Washington County deputy sheriff assigned by Foote to lead the search for the suspect Ruth described, told of law officers walking up and down the creek banks and through the cotton compress—searching between and behind some seventeen hundred bales of cotton waiting for transport—while another group of both policemen and volunteers rode horseback into the residential sections looking for a man who resembled the one described by Mrs. Dickins or somebody who'd seen a man like that or knew who might have done such a thing, somebody who had some kind of beef or other with Mrs. Thompson, or anything else.

They also combed the area for shoes and bloody clothes the fleeing killer might have shed. They stayed on the job that first night until four or five the next morning and kept looking for several days and nights afterward. "I did all I could in the investigation," Campbell said, "trying to locate a Negro."

Wilkes took Campbell through a number of photographs of the territory beyond Mrs. Thompson's back fence, in an effort to validate the defense theory of the killer's escape through a vacant lot on the other side of Second Street toward the cotton compress and into the colored neighborhood.

When the witness was excused, Judge Jordan called a recess until the next morning.

. . . .

All in all, Friday the twenty-fourth was a long and lousy day for the Dickins-Thompson-Stovall clan. The front-page *Delta Democrat-Times* story, banner headlined "DEATH SCENE DESCRIBED," followed by the too-many-cuts-to-count description, also included many direct quotations from Doc Witte's damaging testimony and ended with the observation that "much of the defendant's calm ebbed as she frequently buried her head in her hands and looked anxiously at her husband and attorneys."

On his way to his car, Stanny Sanders told newsmen the prosecution expected to conclude its case the next day.

SATURDAY MORNING

For the state's finale, Ruth wore springlike aqua, perhaps in an effort to cheer herself up. Clearly the previous four days had taken a toll. She looked tired to her bones. Soon after taking her seat, she put her head down in her arms and didn't lift it except occasionally, to say something to her husband. Even then, she kept wiping her face with her hands as if to rid herself of the bad news coming at her. John was, as always, right there, hovering, attentive, and supportive, but he too seemed tense and weary.

There were, at this point, a number of lingering whys hanging over the courtroom. One was, why so many of the trial's female attendees chose Saturday to dress up in far finer garb than usual. Some possibilities come to mind. Was it perhaps to celebrate the onset of the weekend so as to be properly attired for that night's parties? Or could it be because they'd heard Stanny Sanders announce that the prosecution would rest its case today and they wanted to celebrate his almost certain victory in advance by upgrading their wardrobes? This particular segment of the audience was overwhelmingly biased in his favor, partly because they favored his prosecutorial position, but also because of a drop-dead bad-boy charm he exuded that, combined with his ferocious intensity, gave him a certain energetic appeal to a lot of women.

When the judge called for the state to continue its case, Sanders began by recalling the Greenville police chief, Hollingsworth, and asking him to specifically identify and enumerate the articles he'd sealed in small envelopes and sent to the FBI for analysis. A slow-going process. As in:

Sanders to Hollingsworth: "What do you have in your hand?"

Hollingsworth: "A hair found in the bathroom over the bathtub identified as Q-22."

Sanders: "We offer that as Exhibit A15 to this witness's testimony."

Sanders: "What is this you have in your hand, Mr. Hollingsworth?"

Hollingsworth: "Hair found on . . ." And so on.

Once he'd established the identification number and original location
of each piece of evidence, the DA shifted to the analysis they'd received
from the FBI. Hair by hair.

The process was, if anything, even more tedious than Hollingsworth's
earlier testimony, and yet the audience was rapt. No whispers, no cough-
ing. Were they waiting? If so, for what?

As if sensing a dip in the jury's attention, before turning to one particular envelope, Sanders took a sharp turn in a new direction.

How long, he asked, as if suddenly coming upon the thought, had
Hollingsworth been with the Greenville Police Department?

Since, Hollingsworth said, March 1931.

And, Sanders wondered, had he had an occasion during those years
to see "Negro hair"?

The answer might well have been *of course,* being as how a policeman
in Greenville or any other Mississippi Delta town dealt far more often
with Black victims and suspects than with white. But Hollingsworth
simply said yes, after which Sanders asked him to tell the jury, based on
his long experience, whether any of the hair he found was "Negro hair."

"No, sir," the resolute chief declared. "It was not."

Sanders then returned to the envelopes. Calmly. As if the break in
the flow of questions hadn't been intentional. What did the next one
contain?

Hollingsworth described the small nest of light-colored hair taken
from Idella Thompson's fist.

After hair samples came torn fingernails; after that, the scrap of
bloody material clinging to the bathroom wall; the bloody matter found
near the tub; the blood-soaked linen handkerchief; the blood-spattered
footstool.

Of special significance were the clothes Ruth had on that day, which
Doc Witte described as "saturated with blood." Unfortunately, none of
the investigators had thought to ask Ruth to set her garments aside as

evidence until Thursday morning the eighteenth, the day *after* the murder, when Frank Aldridge asked Hollingsworth to drop by the Dickinses' house and collect them.

In her bedside statement, Ruth had acknowledged that, yes, she'd gone home to change out of her clothes on her way to the clinic to get her wounds seen to, but it wasn't to get rid of evidence. She just didn't want to scare the children. With that in mind, she said, she gave her bloody things to Beatrice Smith and knew nothing about what happened to them afterward.

Hollingsworth had gone to the Dickins house as Aldridge requested. John answered the door, but when Hollingsworth told him why he was there, John turned him over to Beatrice Smith. She, he said, could help him. And he turned and went back into the house.

When the maid brought the clothes to the front door, they were wet. That was the first any of the investigators—including Hollingsworth, Foote, Aldridge, and the rest—knew that Smith had dumped them into a tub of soapy water to soak overnight. She'd taken them from the tub only that morning to hang outside on the clothesline. Whether she did any of that on her own or because Ruth told her to, she didn't say.

When Sanders asked Hollingsworth to describe the clothes, he read from a list: a lady's gray suit jacket and matching skirt, white-polka-dot aqua silk blouse with two missing buttons, a slip, a pair of hose, pair of shoes, and a girdle. But after Sanders proffered the packaged clothes as evidence, Wilkes objected. Because Hollingsworth had no search warrant and no permission from John or Ruth to remove possessions of any kind from their home, the introduction of the clothes would effectively force the defendant to give evidence against herself and therefore should be considered inadmissible as evidence.

The judge took little time to agree.

Sanders's objection went nowhere. Blood soaked or not, as far as a possible jury examination went, the clothes were out.

A point for the defense.

. . . .

As for fingerprints, the investigators had lifted comparatives from everybody connected to the household in any capacity, from Ruth's young children to Idella's elderly employee, Jimmy Banks. The handprint by the back door was useless. It wasn't bloody and besides could have been there for weeks. And in truth, Hollingsworth said, fingerprints didn't always show up all over the place the way people think.

Once the hair, buttons, fingernails, clothes, and fingerprints had been put in order, Hollingsworth and A. E. Crawford delivered them to Sheriff Foote, who with Crawford's help packed them up and sent them to Washington.

Identification Officer Ed Blue, who'd returned to the Thompson house on Friday the nineteenth, after Ruth made her statement, took the stand to add more details. He found a hair on the side of the bathtub and a jagged bit of fingernail under the hall heater. One of the officers with him found another hair on the bottom of the footstool. Only the fingernails were Ruth's. None of the hairs. And none was described as "Negroid."

Sanders then recalled Foote, who acknowledged receiving a gray-streaked, blondish clot of hair from the funeral home employee who discovered it in Mrs. Thompson's fist. When recalled again within the next hour, however, Foote will say *he* took the hair out of Mrs. Thompson's hand himself. In either case, FBI analysis proved it came from the dead woman herself, not Ruth or an unknown source. More than likely, Idella had grabbed at her own head to try to relieve the pain or to fend off another blow and came away with a fistful of her own hair.

. . . .

Sanders devoted the rest of the morning to evidence experts, including two FBI agents whose testimony quickly became hypnotically repetitive: "That is the known hair of Mrs. Thompson ... the known fingerprints of Mrs. Thompson ..." By lunchtime, he'd offset Ruth's claims of a murderous intruder while contributing little hard evidence of her guilt. Other than the fingernails, all forensic materials had come from Idella Thompson. Observing lawyers thought Wilkes should thank the FBI agents for making the case for his client.

And now? The elephant in the courtroom tapped its foot. The biggest question of all—that of *Why?*—awaited its time on the stand. What could possibly cause a middle-aged daughter—a child of privilege and education, a bright, athletic young girl who grew into a civic-minded mother and Sunday school teacher—to turn savagely on the mother she'd spent so much time taking care of?

Motive. There had to be one.

The majority courtroom opinion was that Ruth Dickins was guilty. She killed her own mother. But so far, they'd been given little or nothing in the way of a *motive*.

The judge called for a lunch break.

THE CATALYST

Back in court, after a quick recall of one of the FBI agents to hammer home the bureau's official conclusion that none of the analyzed hairs found in the Thompson house came from "a member of the Negro race," Sanders prepared to pull his case together and then rest it. The plan was to get this done right away, this afternoon, as promised, in order to give the jurors the rest of the weekend to mull over what they'd heard and seen and—if his and McIlwain's hunch was correct—be ready, if not actually *eager*, to dispute the findings of the defense.

Waiting until Monday to dole out essential information constituted a blunder they had no intention of committing.

He called the Leland cotton merchant E. A. Bates. Did he, Sanders asked, know the defendant, Ruth Thompson Dickins?

Bates said yes, he knew her, and, yes, he'd had financial dealings with her. The first time was in August 1946, eight months after John Dickins took over ownership of Dellwood plantation. When Ruth came up to him at that time and asked for a cash loan in the amount of $600, she was very insistent in advance of receiving the money that John Dickins never know she'd asked for it. Bates wasn't concerned about why she needed money or what reason she might have for keeping it secret from her husband, but he thought he remembered her saying something about needing to pay some bills. Whatever she used the $600 for, she hadn't repaid the loan by the time Mrs. Thompson was killed.

And then?

About two months later, she came back and asked for another $400. Once again, Bates didn't ask why she wanted the money or what she needed it for; he just gave it to her. All Ruth said was don't tell John.

Bates didn't set a date for her to pay him back, but she might have mentioned March 1 of the following year, he didn't exactly remember. Anyway, he told Ruth, he wasn't in a hurry to be repaid.

When Sanders asked about a third loan, Bates tried to avoid answering, but the judge said he had no choice. This one had to do with a request Ruth made on October 1, 1948, only a month and two weeks before Mrs. Thompson was killed. Bates was standing on a downtown Leland sidewalk when Ruth drove up and asked if he could lend her some more money. He told her he couldn't this time, he was tied up with tax problems. She didn't say anything else; she just drove off.

Whatever Ruth did or said, Bates wanted to make clear, it made no difference to him whether she paid off the loan or not. And he was pretty sure if he needed the money, he could have gotten it from John. Who, as a matter of fact, he added, had paid him back just recently.

Sanders passed his witness without asking why Bates, whose profession would put him in close business contact with John Dickins, was nonetheless willing to betray a husband's confidence by participating in his wife's surreptitious scheme, no questions asked.

Ben Wilkes for the defense asked only one question: Did Mr. Bates know Ruth to be a devoted wife, mother, and daughter?

Yes, Bates replied. Very devoted.

The witness was excused.

A thousand dollars was a piddling amount of money to get excited about. And a piddling amount for Ruth to keep secret from her husband. What could she be up to that she didn't want him to know about? What could matter enough to convince her that going to men who knew and respected John and asking them to keep a secret from him was acceptable?

The question wasn't asked, perhaps because the prosecutors presupposed the jurors' understanding of the financial shenanigans farmers relied on to get them through a difficult season and that, no matter their own profession or station, the twelve men would consider handshake deals and conspiratorial benevolence among the top-tier families a steadying factor in what they thought of as "our way of life."

Ruth was a Thompson. A Stovall. John on the other hand came from Greenwood. He'd become a major presence in Leland, not through trusted family connections and longtime residency, but marriage to a Stovall descendant and success as a cotton man. Whatever his accomplishments, however, he likely remained—to some—a second-tier Lelander.

. . . .

John Aldridge, a farming member of the Stovall clan, was Sanders's next witness.

He confirmed that, yes, Ruth had also visited him looking for a loan. Aldridge lived eight miles south of Leland in Wilmot. He'd known Ruth practically her whole life. So when she drove out there December 11, 1947, and asked him for a loan of $500 cash to be repaid in a year, he didn't hesitate. He sat down and started to write her a check then and there. When she asked for cash instead, not wanting John or the Bank of Leland to know anything about the loan, Aldridge dug up the bills and paid her. And never thought about it again.

On cross, Aldridge testified he'd known Idella Thompson and her whole family for years and thought Ruth was as sweet to her mother as anybody he ever knew had been with theirs. As to the loan, it had been repaid by John Dickins. After the murder.

When the prosecution declined to ask further questions, Aldridge was replaced by Alice Scott, employee of the Nettles System Incorporated, a loan brokerage company with offices in downtown Greenville.

On August 6, 1948, Scott told the court, three months before Idella's murder, Ruth had entered their office. Asked if she needed help, Ruth said she was hoping to procure a loan for $750. It took Scott little time to work out a deal for that amount whereby Nettles would mortgage Ruth's used car on a fifteen-month payment plan, but in the end, she testified, they charged Ruth interest of 4.762 percent, or—as Scott figured it— $56.47, plus an additional brokerage fee of $152.03.

Sanders asked Scott to clarify that. By her calculation, was he perhaps mistaken or did this mean that Mrs. Dickins would pay Nettles $209.50 on a $750 loan?

The nonplussed Scott confirmed it. That was, she said, how the company did things.

Incredibly enough, Ruth accepted the terms, knowing full well that if she'd gone to the Bank of Leland or the Greenville Bank & Trust, she wouldn't have been out the brokerage fee. But if she did that, John would find out. So she signed the contract and walked out with the money.

Even staid Ben Wilkes waxed slightly sardonic in his opening question to the Nettles employee. "That is," he said, "a right profitable little establishment you all have got?"

Scott didn't deny it. "Yes, sir," she replied.

And this loan Mrs. Dickins was making from you was on a used car? Yes, sir.

On the fifteen-month loan payment plan?

Yes, sir. The rate was set at the main Nettles office and approved by the state. That was how the company established the amount of the fee.

Both Sanders and Wilkes left hanging the question of why a woman of privilege and standing saw fit to go to a place like Nettles to apply for a loan. And anyway, what in the world connection to Idella Thompson's death was Stanny Sanders making, no matter what Ruth was up to?

Two o'clock by now, maybe closer to two thirty.

. . . .

Replacing Sanders, Willard McIlwain called for their next witness.

Twenty-three-year-old Hampton Collier, a young farmer and co-owner of the Leland Gin Company with his brother John, took the stand. The Collier boys had lived in the Leland vicinity their whole lives, so they knew pretty much everybody in the area, including the Thompsons. And since most of the farmers around there came to them to get their cotton ginned, they were well known around town themselves. The Colliers lived at the Dunleith plantation, less than a mile from Dellwood, and like a lot of farmers they owned some of the acreage they farmed and rented some, usually from people who wanted to hold on to their property but not work it. People like Idella Thompson and her son Jimmy.

Every year, Collier testified, he wrote a rent check for $600 to Idella and one to Jimmy for $1,852.50. When Jimmy called him on the morning of November 17, 1948, to "annoy" him about paying the rent he was owed, Collier told him he'd already written the checks and would leave them at the gin office with his manager, L. E. Ware, that day.

He wasn't sure exactly what time it was when he left the checks with Ware, but thought it must have been around noon. Before lunch anyway.

And yes, he said, answering McIlwain's inquiry, he was talking about the day Idella Thompson was killed. November 17, 1948.

McIlwain offered the checks as evidence. James W. Thompson had endorsed his and deposited it at the Greenville Bank & Trust Company the same day Collier left it at the gin office, the seventeenth. Idella's check, however, had to wait until December 20, when Ruth became administratrix of her estate and could endorse and deposit it. That check didn't clear Collier's account until January.

McIlwain passed his witness.

And—this is Wilkes on cross, still plugging away at establishing Ruth's good character—how long did Hampton Collier say he'd known Ruth Dickins and the Thompson family? All his life. And did he know what kind of relationship existed between Mrs. Dickins and her mother? It appeared to be all right, at least that was what he'd gathered from friends.

And was she a loving and devoted daughter? Yes, sir.

Collier stepped down.

· · · ·

L. E. Ware lived on the Collier boys' plantation and worked for them as manager of the gin office and, yes, he was at work the day Mrs. Thompson was killed. And yes, he definitely recalled seeing Ruth Dickins that day. The first time was around ten that morning. He was standing in the gin office door when she came up and told him who she was, then said she needed to know if Mr. Hampton Collier was around. When Ware told her he was not, she said, straight out, "He was supposed to have paid me some rent."

Maybe she said exactly that—"supposed to have paid me some rent," not "supposed to pay," but "have paid," as if the money were overdue—and maybe she didn't. Ware's recall was going back seven months and he had no reason to make a note of exactly what words she used, at least not at that time. Later, however, hearing what happened to Mrs. Thompson might well have sharpened his memory to some extent. Back then nobody thought Ruth had anything to do with the murder, but the coincidence of her showing up out of sorts on that same day did catch Ware's attention. And the fact that he quoted Ruth as if from memory revealed something about his opinion of her, on its own. He clearly didn't like her attitude, and what McIlwain and Sanders knew was that a jury of twelve white southern men would have noted L. E. Ware's dislike as well as the abruptness of Ruth's declaration as quoted on the stand, the bossy bluntness and pure unladylike rudeness of calling out the office manager's boss to his face.

And, McIlwain wondered, did Mrs. Dickins say where Collier was supposed to have been when he paid her that rent?

Ware couldn't remember exactly where they agreed to meet, but he thought she mentioned a place over in Greenville. But according to her, Collier didn't show up. And anyway, although Ware didn't make a point of it, what she was after was none of his business. He was an employee, not the boss, which gave him the privilege of avoiding this kind of touchy confrontation with an uppity woman.

Ruth stood there. Ware waited her out.

Ruth got the message and left.

About an hour later, at around eleven or so, maybe eleven fifteen, eleven thirty, she came back. Ware was standing out on the gin platform facing the highway when she drove up this time. Without getting out of her car, she rolled down her window and shouted up to him.

Had Collier been by?

When Ware said he hadn't, she left again, only to return an hour or an hour and a half later at around one o'clock. This time she didn't say a damn word but just "drove by and blowed her horn."

Ware stepped out.

From the car, she yelled up asking once again if Mr. Collier had been there. This time he told her yes, and he thought he'd left what she wanted.

Still sitting in her car, she asked if he would please bring the checks down to her.

By now Ware was ready to do about anything to get Ruth Dickins out of his life so he could get on with his work and not have to deal with her high-hatted unpleasantness. So he went down to her car and gave her the checks.

She took off. And that was that.

To make certain the jury took in the details, McIlwain repeated several of his questions. Was Ware sure he delivered the two checks on the same day Idella Long Thompson was killed?

He was certain. And yes, she came three times at the times he'd specified. And no, nobody was with her. She was alone.

None of this matched Ruth's statement to the investigators, describing her actions on the day her mother was murdered.

When Wilkes had no questions, the state rested its case.

It was 3:22 p.m. Saturday the twenty-fifth.

. . . .

The prosecution had established giant holes in Ruth's statement, indicating if not a concretely established or even particularly compelling motive, one they hoped was strong enough to convict the woman, if not for murder one, then manslaughter. And they weren't by any means finished. With luck, Ben Wilkes would put Ruth on the stand, setting her up for a cross-examination Sanders and McIlwain figured would prove their case more effectively than anything they'd discovered, suggested, or said.

Judge Jordan recessed the court until Monday morning at 9:00.

To news reporters, Ben Wilkes confirmed that the defense was ready and—he addressed the number one question—yes, the defendant would *more than likely* take the stand.

Lawyers thought "more than likely" was a trumped-up public statement of confidence Wilkes hoped would translate as *I am so convinced of my client's innocence I will let her speak for herself in her own defense.*

A move he had no intention of carrying out.

. . . .

The courtroom emptied. John and Ruth drove to Leland.

WEEKEND

Every evening, while jurors were taken to another part of the building for their dinner, maintenance workers cleaned the courtroom floor of crumbs, spilled coffee, lemonade, Coke, cigarette butts, and whatever other trash spectators, lawyers, and clerks might have left behind. That done, they brought in twelve iron bed frames, each with its own single mattress, pillow, and linens, and set them up around the courtroom as a kind of communal bedroom. Finished with their meal, the men cleaned up, changed, and went to bed looking up at the same ceiling fans they'd labored under all day. Nobody has said where the beds were placed, but since the auditorium seats were bolted to the floor, we have to assume the press's and lawyers' tables were moved aside to make room in the shadow of the judge's bench.

A strange way to do things. Presumably, the men had an opportunity to shower and shave. And sooner or later, they slept.

Sunday, they were off. But they weren't allowed to leave the courthouse grounds, and so, being as how no Jew, Muslim, or Hindu had been selected to deliberate Ruth's fate, Christian church service came to them.

After breakfast, the men were shepherded to the courthouse lawn to await the transformation of their living quarters into a place of worship. A pulpit flanked by gold-leafed chairs with plush red seats and backs was placed in front of the judge's bench. One chair was meant for the Trinity Methodist minister Garland Holloman, one for, perhaps, a member of his choir. Or even the choir director.

The jurors filed back in to listen to a sermon on Christian justice. After the final "Amen," church was dismantled, Sunday dinner was provided, and, sometime that afternoon, the jurors returned to the quarters set up for them, to wait for Monday.

. . . .

Meanwhile, beyond courthouse business, Delta life rolled right along. Sharing the front-page banner headline of Sunday's *Delta Democrat-Times*, "PROSECUTION RESTS CASE," was a story about the construction of a new and up-to-date Greenville country club, including ballroom, kitchen, caddy shack, pro shop, and eighteen-hole golf course, out on Highway 1.

Further back in the paper, on the society page, Mrs. Judge Rabun Jones announced the names of the girls to be presented to society on December 23 in the Gold Room of the Hotel Greenville. Beside the story was a full-length portrait of Mrs. Jones, dressed regal as a queen in a frothy white-beaded gown and pearl-encrusted tiara.

For that day's *Delta Democrat-Times* editorial, Hodding Carter had penned an opinion piece called "And They Denounce Movies" in which he gently slapped the wrists of parents who decried the influence of "motion pictures which contain unchildlike scenes" yet took their children to the Dickins trial, where they listened to gory descriptions hardly designed for young ears. Finding it "rather out of keeping that youngsters denied lurid picture shows should be on the front row of this trial," he also took a swipe at the many spectators who showed up every day only because they found a graphic murder trial entertaining. Hearing their "low-voiced comments" about the defendant, he wondered "how far from the Roman games we really are."

"Perhaps," the editorial concluded, "the children at least could be left at home."

. . . .

Once the trial has concluded, the Jackson paper will run the first news photograph of Ruth's jurors. Seated in the jury box, the twelve men are all looking to their left, past the defense table, on which John Dickins has, as usual, placed his hat. Most of them have tilted their chairs back. Eleven are in shirtsleeves. The lone man in light-colored sport coat and striped tie is one of two wearing eyeglasses. Two seem to be dressed in knit golfing shirts, one of them in a more casual collarless T-shirt. The mahogany bar separating them from the lawyers and spectators comes up to their waists, obscuring all but two of the men's lower bodies. Those men are in very light-colored khakis.

The picture is blurry, but all twelve men seem to be deeply engaged, and maybe it's the casualness of their attire that makes them look more like farmers than businessmen.

. . . .

Once again, the Dickinses shuttered themselves in their home. Dell was away at summer camp, but Dorothy Jane was in Leland, having been cared for all week by friends and members of the family. Relatives came and went. Staying for a while and then quickly making their way to their cars, heads ducked in case somebody from one of the newspapers was out there or somebody sneaking around hoping to steal a quick look at them.

Ben and B. B. Wilkes studied their witness list and put finishing touches on their case while Sanders and McIlwain prepared to challenge whatever they came up with.

. . . .

As for us, my girlfriends and me, along with doting mothers, aunts, and girl cousins, we consumed every written word, studied every picture, speculated endlessly, imagining, envisioning, casting back to remember where we were when we heard the news, who told us, exaggerating what we knew and how it affected us, to create the story we passionately wanted, needed, to believe.

The end of which never changed. It was, for us, a foregone conclusion. She did it. Of course she did.

FROM THE DEFENSE

Monday. The Dickinses arrived at nine sharp. Wearing the tan-and-white cord dress from the week before, Ruth seems to have recovered her previously dependable calm facade and even managed a slight show of optimism, perhaps because her side was taking charge. She sat facing forward. Toying with an unlit cigar, John was the one who looked strained today, maybe because he was in line to testify.

The courtroom hummed like a stretched wire. When on his way into the courthouse, Wilkes was asked again about Ruth taking the stand, he said only, "Probably." Accompanied by his nephew, he entered the courtroom and took his seat near Ruth and John.

But a good part of today's crowd seemed to have little interest in the defense attorneys or even Ruth herself. Their gaze remained fixed on the courtroom door. And when Stanny Sanders appeared there, he made Washington County history. Never before in courtroom memory had the very sight of a lawyer caused an audience to burst into spontaneous applause.

Sanders, surprised and either embarrassed or secretly pleased, kept walking, followed closely by Willard McIlwain.

Sheriff Foote, standing in the hall with the judge, hustled in and rapped for silence.

"The judge," he warned, "says you'll have to refrain from hand-patting or any other display or there'll be some hereafter."

"Hand patting" is a pretty nutty way to say it, but "some hereafter" hits the jackpot.

McIlwain and Sanders sat. Stanny opened his accordion file.

Once the room had settled down, Judge Jordan took the bench, and within minutes the defense called its first witness, the photographer Bern Keating.

. . . .

Keating and his wife, Franke (pronounced "Frankie"), came to Greenville in 1946, a move some people credit as an instant upgrading of the town's quotient of worldly awareness and cosmopolitan style. The Canadian-born Bern grew up in Chicago and had lived all over the country, while Franke hailed from McGehee, Arkansas, a farm-rich if desultory little town across the river. By the time they decided to move to Greenville, having heard it was an up-and-coming arty kind of town, Bern had decided to make a career of taking pictures, with Franke by his side.

Within the next couple of years they'd opened a studio downtown and had quickly established themselves as skilled, in-demand photographers. As a couple they contributed to a 1961 Pulitzer Prize–winning volume of photographs of Civil War battlefields. They traveled together, wrote and illustrated books, gave lectures, were invited to contribute to various magazines, and eventually cut a wide swath in Greenville and beyond.

But in 1949 they hadn't been in the Delta long enough for their star to climb that high—the studio was still advertising free baby pictures—and so when Ben Wilkes hired Keating to shoot pictures of Idella Thompson's house and its surroundings, he wasn't thinking of name recognition. He just wanted to confirm Ruth's story.

The most noteworthy shot Keating took was from the back steps looking into the house, through the porch door toward the back hall and the bathroom door. Wilkes was inside, pressed flat against the wall next to the commode, where Ruth said the killer had hidden when she came in. Indeed, the photograph corroborated a significant detail of Ruth's account. Although Wilkes was a much larger man than the one Ruth described, no part of him could be seen. Other photographs—long shots of the area behind the house—illustrated a possible escape route from the Deer Creek house to the compress and the neighborhood beyond.

After Sanders's rather too long and inconsequential cross-examination, Keating stepped down.

. . . .

The case offered by the defense team depended on convincing the jury of a few basic premises:

1. That there wasn't much blood on the bathroom floor. Just "spots here and there," smears and droplets, despite the estimated 150 wounds on Mrs. Thompson's body. This, they assumed, would constitute proof that the person who hacked Mrs. Thompson to death could have fled across the back porch, down the steps, through the yard, and over the wall without leaving behind a telltale footprint or drop of blood.

2. That, further concerning the blood mass, it was the sheriff himself who ordered the bathroom floor mopped and that, contrary to Hughey's statement, Mildred Thompson Hood and Demetra Lee Thompson were merely following his instructions when they rang Jimmy Banks and had him come inside and carry them out. The idea, then, was Hughey's, not theirs.

3. That if the sheriff had done what he said he did and made sure people stayed out of the backyard, maybe the dogs would have found a trail. In contrast to other witnesses, Ruth's family remembered sightseers, policemen, and assorted neighbors roaming at will back there, destroying or corrupting any evidence that otherwise might have been detected, whether by Nick and Red or by careful evidence collection by police officers.

4. That Ruth had bruises on the back of her neck, which both Mildred and Demetra thought might have come from a man's hand as he grabbed and held her.

5. That Idella Thompson had no problem with John Dickins's ownership of the land that had been in her family since before her birth.

6. That Ruth was a perfect daughter, devoted to her mother, in fact if anything overly patient with her, having never lost her temper with the woman they characterized as "difficult" and "hotheaded." And that although Jimmy was her favorite, Idella returned Ruth's devotion in kind.

7. Bottom line? The Lizzie Borden hypothesis, based on inductive reasoning. If the good-natured Sunday school teacher Ruth Dickins *could not* have done anything as heinous as killing her own mother, that proved she *did not*. And if the death of Idella Thompson left only a smattering of blood on the bathroom floor, the man Ruth described *could have* run out the back without leaving blood drops behind; therefore why not accept what the family considered odds-on probability, if not sheer certainty: that he *did*.

As for the crucial question of whether Attorney Ben Wilkes would put his client on the stand, conventional wisdom stood firmly against it. Wilkes wouldn't say definitely yes or no, but if he decided to defy convention and put her on, courthouse regulars thought hers would be the lengthiest testimony of the trial.

A Stovall relative told me she didn't know why Wilkes didn't put Ruth on the stand and that they'd all wondered. Because wasn't it human nature to think an innocent person would insist on clearing her name? People took *not* testifying as an obvious sign of guilt.

But, she shrugged, Ben Wilkes was supposed to be the best lawyer in the state, and maybe he thought Ruth's appearance might work against her, the haircut, her clothes and plainspokenness. That voice. Deep and gravelly, like a man's. Maybe he thought . . . ?

Thought what?

She shook her head.

My guess is that Wilkes never had any intention of allowing Ruth to testify. What today would be called her "relatability quotient" was close to zero. And Stanny Sanders had proved to be a far worthier opponent than anybody had anticipated. If he was able to wring from her the same kind of convoluted and wavery testimony as the one she made from her bed—and there was no reason to think he couldn't—his cross-examination might well sink her.

. . . .

After spending several minutes eliciting further scene-setting testimony from an aerial photographer, Wilkes called Ruth's big brother, James

Wynn Thompson, the first of twenty defense witnesses to take the stand, fully half of whom were related to his client either by ancestry or by marriage.

Dressed in a light-colored boxy short-sleeved shirt, loose khaki pants, and dark leather shoes, Jimmy entered the courtroom looking worried and hopeless, like always, eyebrows and mouth punched down at the outside edge. At forty-four, he had a receding hairline, with winged points of skin on either side of his dark, slicked-back hair.

Sworn in, he took the stand.

Once he'd established Jimmy's name, age, and connection to the defendant, Wilkes moved to the rent checks.

Had Jimmy seen this one? He offered Collier's check for $1,852.50, made out to James W. Thompson.

He had.

And when did he receive it?

Tuesday, November 16, 1948.

As if wondering if perhaps he hadn't heard correctly, Wilkes asked for a do-over. Did he mean the day *before* his mother died?

That was correct.

From whom did he receive it?

From his sister. Ruth.

Had he spoken to Hampton Collier about picking up the check?

He had. On the sixteenth. And Collier said he would leave it with L. E. Ware. And his sister picked it up that same day. And yes, he had it in his possession the night *before* his mother was killed. The sixteenth.

. . . .

The main reason to call Jim Thompson as his first eyewitness was to establish Ruth's whereabouts on the day of the murder. *If* he was up to it. To sell the jury on a hypothesis of innocence, he had to repudiate the testimony of L. E. Ware and Hampton Collier, both of whom had sworn that Jimmy called Collier about the checks on the morning of the seventeenth, the day Idella Thompson was murdered. They further testified that his sister Ruth had come by the gin three times on that same day to pick up the checks. None of which Ruth included in her official statement.

. . . .

Jimmy Thompson's radically altered timeline was a shocker. If what he said proved out, that meant Collier and Ware had not only perjured themselves but had done so in brilliant, corroborative detail. And if Ruth *didn't* spend a good part of the morning of November 17 driving from her mother's house to the cotton gin and back, she and Jimmy could well have left for Greenville shortly after noon as she'd said in her statement, once she'd given Dorothy Jane her pill, talked to Beatrice Smith about that night's meal, delivered her mother's midday repast, and waited until she'd eaten it and Jimmy was ready to go.

The morning would have proceeded, for them, in a far more easygoing fashion, knowing that the checks were in hand and that Jimmy would be able to cash his and get it in the mail that same day and thereby preserve his hold on his land.

But the bigger question remained: What would persuade Collier and Ware to put their hands on the Bible and swear to tell the truth, then step up on the stand and tell one lie after another? If it was to settle a beef with Ruth, Jimmy, or even John Dickins, what could it have been? And why didn't Wilkes pursue this particular line of questioning when he cross-examined the two men instead of asking only about Ruth's loving care of her mother?

Urged by Wilkes to move from the checks to the next item of business, Jimmy began to re-create the hours he spent with his sister Ruth on the day of their mother's murder. When he finished shaving, he pulled himself together to go to Greenville. His big sister, Mildred, was still there, sitting with their mother, settling her down for a nap before going home to eat her own lunch.

He and Ruth left. Ruth drove. Jimmy had only one job all day: to endorse Hampton Collier's check. Ruth would take care of everything else. The Greenville Bank & Trust Company—housed in a narrow and unusually graceful white marble building with columns reaching from the sidewalk to the roof and a wall of solid windows along one side—was located downtown on Washington Avenue between the main post office and a high-end ladies' dress shop featuring designer clothing. Called Nelms and Blum, the store was half a block from the town's favorite coffee shop and diner, Jim's Café, the only one of those establishments still in operation today.

Ruth parked across the street from the bank and took one of Hampton Collier's checks inside. Although the check had been made out to and endorsed by him, Jimmy didn't go in with her but instead walked down the block to the café.

. . . .

John Dickins had gone into the cotton-buying business on his own some years earlier. His was one of the offices lined up along what was known as Cotton Row, a block of Poplar Street, which ran perpendicular to Washington and was less than a block away from the bank. But Ruth made no effort to stop in to say hello to her husband. She was busy, he was busy, there was no need. He was planning to come home early anyway. And she had to get back home to see about Idella. And Dorothy Jane. On the other hand—remembering her "Don't tell John" proviso—perhaps this was another need-to-know situation.

Ruth deposited Jimmy's $1,852.50 check and then purchased a "Memphis exchange"—the equivalent of a cashier's check—for $1,724 of the money, payable to the John Hancock Company, which presumably held her brother's land as collateral on a loan. She kept the remaining $128.50 in cash for her brother's everyday use. Ordinarily, the bank would have charged a fee for the exchange service, but because she and John had an account there, the purchase was granted without charge.

As one of the bank's directors, the Thompson lawyer Billy Wynn had offices in the building. When he saw Ruth in the bank, he went over to her. They spoke briefly before she left, heading for Jim's Café to fetch Jimmy.

Hector Townsend, who worked at the Palace Barber Shop next door to Jim's, happened to be in the café as well, waiting for his wife to join him for lunch. He remembered seeing Ruth come in at 12:45. She went over to her brother. A few minutes later, the two left together.

After Ruth gave Jimmy his cash, they retraced their steps back down Washington Avenue to the post office. Jimmy waited outside while Ruth went in and, fully aware that his payment needed to get to Memphis right away, sent it registered mail.

. . . .

And, Wilkes asked, his sister Ruth did all of this for him, why?

Because, Jimmy said, "she has always attended to my business since my father died in 1939." The death of J. W. Thompson was not, at this point, germane to the defense's strategy, and so, to emphasize Jimmy's reliability as a witness, Wilkes reminded him of the other, more practical reason. Wasn't it also because if *he* deposited the check and asked for a Memphis exchange, he had to pay for it and Ruth didn't?

Yes, Jim said. But that wasn't the main thing. The main reason was she "had always attended to my business."

Wilkes moved on.

Once Ruth sent the check and exited the post office, they walked across the street to her car. Jimmy had decided to stay in Greenville and get a haircut, but Ruth left right away. It was a little past one, he remembered. He didn't see his sister again until after he heard about his mother's murder. That was at four thirty or five. He was still in Greenville at the time and presumably found a ride to Leland, he didn't say who with.

He tried to get to Idella's house—*home,* he said—but the crowds were too big and he couldn't get through. He did somehow manage to meet up with Thompsie Hood, who, after confirming what Jimmy had heard about his mother, drove him to the Witte Clinic. Louise Azlin had taken Ruth there to have her injuries seen to. But by the time they got to the clinic, she'd already gone home, so they went there. They found her in bed, bruises on her arm, her forehead and elbow bandaged.

. . . .

Before passing his witness to the prosecution, Wilkes needed, once again, to establish Ruth's close relationship with her mother. In response, Jimmy set the tone and vocabulary for the rest of the family and every other defense witness. *Devoted,* they said. *A devoted daughter.* Her relationship with her mother? *Perfect.* She was a *perfect daughter.* They had a *perfect relationship.*

Jimmy had never seen such a devoted daughter; she was more devoted than any of the other children. His mother called on her for everything and more than once had told him she didn't know what she'd do if she didn't have Ruth to depend on.

And had he ever seen Ruth get out of patience with her mother?

Never. He couldn't imagine how Ruth could have such patience. He'd even told his mother so.

And—moving from family ties to the attack—had Ruth complained about injuries to her side and back when he saw her later that same day at her house? Yes, sir.

What about the backyard of the Thompson house? When Jimmy passed close to it, was it filled with people, all over the yard and in the house?

Yes, sir, it positively was. They were milling up and down the driveway and in the front and back yards and inside the front door.

Wilkes passed the witness.

. . . .

Stanny Sanders opened with inquiries into Jimmy's recent whereabouts. Was it true he'd left town with his brother and sister-in-law on the eve of the grand jury session in January?

It was.

And had he been gone until quite recently?

Yes.

Where exactly had he been?

Memphis, New Orleans, Texas, Mexico.

Sanders flew past the peculiarity of the trip's timing without further inquiry.

What about his relationship with the Collier brothers? Didn't they rent land from him? Yes. Still rented from him? Yes. And was their relationship good? Yes, perfectly fine, always had been, still was.

Could he think of any reason Collier and Ware would come to court and speak against his sister?

No, sir.

Nothing at all?

Not that he knew of.

The DA moved on to money: Ruth's reasons for making the deal with Nettles, her need for secrecy, why Jimmy had been in such urgent need to get his check off to the land bank when his records showed that he had more than $1,000, maybe closer to $2,000 in the bank, and why his mother didn't have the extra $3 or $4 to pay her way out of the hospital. What did he have to say about any of that?

When Jimmy didn't exactly answer any of those questions, Sanders didn't press him. Oh, he said, swerving into a new topic, by the way, was it true he was his mother's favorite?

Embarrassed, perhaps confused by the sudden switch, Jimmy skirted the question. That's what they say, he said. But after he looked in Ruth's direction, he came out with it. Yes, he said. He was his mother's favorite.

And was Jimmy positive he received his check on the sixteenth?

Yes, definitely.

And remind him again, what time was that?

In the afternoon.

And did Ruth have the other check from Hampton Collier, the one made out to their mother, with her when they went to Greenville?

No, sir, and he didn't know why she didn't, maybe because his mother didn't need the money and he did, he needed to send a payment to Memphis right away, otherwise he'd be in trouble and might not be able to hold on to his land. As for why, if Ruth had picked up both checks on the sixteenth, they didn't go ahead and cash Idella's to pay her way out of the hospital the next morning, instead of using the insurance check from her lockbox and having to borrow an extra $3 or $4 from Ruth, he didn't know.

Sanders didn't pursue the matter further but asked if for some reason perhaps Idella had *refused* to endorse the check. Not that he expected Jimmy to answer that one. The law didn't allow him to quote his mother on the subject or even to ruminate on her intentions or thoughts concerning it as "proof of the matter asserted." Throwing the question out was enough.

In addition to which, to avoid alienating the jury and risk a charge of badgering, he had to be particularly careful with this obviously fragile witness.

. . . .

Jimmy's reinvention of the timeline left at least two big gaps in the defense's case: an explanation for why Hampton Collier and L. E. Ware would lie about the day the Thompson checks were delivered to the gin office and the reason Idella didn't endorse her check before Ruth and Jimmy left for Greenville. And if they did leave at noon as he testified, of what benefit was that to Ruth's case when that gave her an hour longer to stab her mother to death and then, once she'd come to and realized what she'd done, clean up the scene—wipe her fingerprints off the pruning shears, throw her bloody handkerchief in the bathtub—and figure out what to do next?

Sanders turned to the Thompson property. What did Jimmy know about feelings Idella might have harbored toward John and Ruth once the land J. W. Thompson had worked so hard to acquire became, in essence, the Dickins plantation? Didn't his mother occasionally complain that "John Dickins got all the property that used to belong to us and Ruth is responsible for it"?

Not in his presence, no, sir. In his opinion the land had been wished off on John Dickins.

And after his father died, had his mother been involved in farming the land?

For one year, in partnership with Ruth and Wood.

And after that?

Only his brother, Wood, and his sister Ruth were interested in farming. He was not. His mother had been, but she dropped out. Wood and Ruth kept going as long as they could.

. . . .

Taking advantage of his right to examine his own witness after a cross-examination—called redirect—Ben Wilkes highlighted John Dickins's generosity, given the fact that when he bought the Thompson land it was heavily "involved"—in debt—and in a terrible state.

Jimmy agreed with Wilkes's assessment without actually forming an answer. It wasn't a real question anyway.

As for the matter of Ruth's having always attended to Jimmy's business. What, Wilkes wondered, was the current state of his health?

"I have been in bad health," Jim Thompson said for the third time, "since my father died." That's almost ten years of bad health. Including the months he served in the U.S. Army.

The prosecution had no further questions.

Jimmy stepped down.

· · · ·

Chronology had been reinvented; a death day's clock set to run. As a witness, Jimmy had done fairly well, but in the end his shaky emotional state and the chronological inconsistencies in his testimony surely countered the gains he otherwise might have contributed to his sister's cause.

After Billy Wynn placed Ruth in the bank between 12:30 and 1:00, Wilkes led him step by step through the legal afterlife of the J. W. Thompson estate, from the probate notice he and Mrs. Thompson ran in the paper through John Dickins's assumption of the family indebtedness, the accomplishment of which Wynn said depended on the willingness of the heirs to give him quitclaim deeds.

Once Wynn finished, a local banker made a short appearance to confirm Ruth's purchase of the Memphis exchange for Jim.

· · · ·

A lean young man with sharp features, Mildred Hood's son, Thompsie, had flashing dark eyes, black eyebrows, and a sleek short haircut that emphasized his large ears. At twenty-six, he dressed modern. For his appearance in court, he wore a loose-fitting white button-up shirt tucked neatly into dark flaring trousers topped by a thin white belt emphasizing his trim waistline. His shoes were white. Not a big man, he'd served in the U.S. Marines during the war and been awarded a Purple Heart for service in the Philippines. An only child, he seems to have had too much time on his hands in those years, always ready to hang out with Ruth at the drugstore or sit on the front porch with the dog doing nothing. Which in Ruth's eyes made him a perfect pal. She got a kick out of people ready to change plans on a dime, going this way instead of that, fulfilling her desire to stay on the move and have fun.

Thompsie knew what time he left home to go to Leland that day because *Queen for a Day* was on the car radio. It was a show he liked and he was listening to it as he drove the seven miles from Long Switch, where he lived with his parents, to the Drive. He'd come to town to collect one of "my tenant Negroes" from the Witte hospital, where he was recuperating from an appendectomy, but first he had to drop off a ham his mother had given him to take to his grandmother Idella Thompson.

He got there at one or so and had been there five or ten minutes when Ruth came in after stopping at her house to check on Dorothy Jane. They sat and talked and, as Ruth put it, "fooled around" a little, then, when he got up to go pick up his tenant, he told her he had a little time to spare and about six bits in his pocket, so why didn't she come with him to Azlin's for a cup of coffee?

As they headed out the front door, Ruth peeled off her pullover sweater. She would, she joked, burn up if she wore it, hot as Mrs. Azlin served her coffee. She left the sweater on her mother's dining room table.

They went in separate cars and had been at Azlin's no longer than fifteen minutes when Thompsie had to give up and go on over to the hospital. The coffee was too hot to drink, and he needed to get on with his task.

So he left Ruth talking to Mrs. Azlin and continued on his way to the hospital, then, once he picked up the tenant, drove east on the highway, back toward Long Switch. He took a gravel road off the highway and along it "unloaded the Negro into a wagon." And went home. This took, he said, something between half an hour and an hour.

To travel seven miles? Well, he guessed he must have been driving slow.

At any rate, he'd been sitting on his front steps for maybe ten or fifteen minutes picking cockleburs off his dog when his mother came tearing out of the house. Take her to town quick, she'd said, something had happened to Grandmother and she was too nervous to drive. So he drove as fast as he could. When he crossed the railroad tracks, he checked the station clock. It was 3:15.

A couple minutes later, they pulled in to Mrs. Thompson's drive and found Doc Witte and Chief Aldridge in her bedroom with Ruth.

They'd seen the body in the bathroom on their way in.

Thompsie's rundown of his day—what time it was when he first saw Ruth at his grandmother's house and persuaded her to go to Azlin's with him and how long it took to drive home—didn't perfectly match up with Ruth's or Jimmy's, and both he and Wilkes knew it. As did Stanny Sanders.

In his cross, the DA went hard at the young man about the half hour to an hour he said had passed between his parting with Ruth, the stop at the hospital, and his drive home. That Thompsie resented having to answer questions unfriendly to himself and his family came as no surprise to anyone who knew him. He was young and maybe more than a little arrogant and couldn't help balking at questions he didn't like. Sanders after all was trying to put his aunt—his pal—in prison maybe for the rest of her life. And besides, he came honestly by a thin-skinned nature he shared with his mother.

But when Sanders asked if Ruth was crying when he and his mother got to his grandmother's house, he answered honestly. No, he said. He didn't think she was.

. . . .

In 1949, Washington County trial transcripts identified witnesses only by their race. It comes as no surprise, then, that when "Beatrice Smith (COLORED)" testified, courtroom language shifted. The witness was addressed by her first name, without a courtesy title. Mrs. Dickins became Miss Ruth; Thompsie—who was years younger than Smith—Mr. Thompsie. Although every single person who took part in the trial in any capacity spoke with a deep southern accent, the transcript records their speeches in plain English. Smith's, on the other hand, was, from time to time, recorded phonetically in a caricature of dialect. When, for instance, she answered a question, "She sure did," the transcript has it as "She sho did."

Beatrice Smith had worked for the Dickinses for sixteen years. On the stand, she told of her employer's visit home to get the shavings for the kittens, which she insisted was the only time Ruth came home that day until after lunch, when Thompsie brought her there all bloody and Bea helped her change clothes in John's bedroom and cleaned her up so that Dorothy Jane wouldn't see her in that state. After Ruth told Bea, "For God's sake don't let the girls see these," she took the blood-drenched clothes to the laundry room and put them in a washtub to soak. Not that anybody told her to, but she didn't know what else to do with them. And yes, after they'd been soaking for a while, the water turned "real bloody."

When Ben Wilkes reminded Smith about the first trip Ruth said she made to her house, *before* she came for the shavings, when she got the pruning shears to cut back her mother's roses, Smith stood her ground.

Once, she said, to get the shavings. That was the only time she remembered.

On cross, Sanders tried to change Smith's mind by re-forming the question into a statement—"She didn't come by the house but once?"

But Beatrice Smith held fast. "Just one time," she said.

Wilkes refused to give up. "You didn't see her," he said, "when she got the shears?"

Smith didn't need to elaborate. She simply said, no, sir.

Asked about Ruth's relationship with her mother, Smith said it was "fine."

Asked how Mrs. Thompson treated colored people, she said the same thing. "Fine."

She turned out to be especially good at dodging the questions of both lawyers by saying she didn't remember whatever it was they were prodding her to come up with.

When it was clear to Wilkes and Sanders that they'd gotten everything she was going to give them, Beatrice Smith was excused from further questioning.

. . . .

Mildred Thompson Hood looked nothing like Ruth. A plain, fleshy woman, she parted her brown hair in the middle and finger waved it old-school style close to her wide face and over her ears. In court, she was prone to wearing loose dresses, printed in geometric or flowery patterns, belted across her large midsection. Staunchly proud, like her son, Thompsie, she did not tolerate contradiction, accusation, or bad talk about her family. Appointed Long Switch postmistress in 1939, she'd served the unincorporated town until 1947, when the local post office was closed and the government began sending mail directly to Leland.

She had, indeed, been there when her sister brought Idella home from the hospital and later had waited for Idella to finish eating her lunch so that Ruth and Jimmy could go ahead and drive to Greenville. After her mother had lain down to take a rest, Mildred headed home to eat her own noonday meal, promising to return soon afterward. But between 1:30 and 2:00, Idella phoned and said there was no need, she was feeling fine and would continue to rest as per Dr. Bunt's instructions, and anyway Ruth and Jimmy would be back soon. And so Mildred stayed home, leaving Idella alone in her house, waiting for Ruth to return.

Ruth called a little after three. Come quick, she said. Come see about Mother. Assuming Idella had had a stroke, Mildred rushed outside and told Thompsie he needed to drive her to Leland right away and they left. When he drove over the railroad tracks and onto Deer Creek Drive, she too checked the time. It was 3:15, she said. Just as Thompsie had said.

Which comes to about a ten-minute drive to downtown Leland and maybe two more to Mrs. Thompson's house.

Once she saw what was what and heard Ruth's story, Mildred started making phone calls. She called her husband, Shields, and her brother Wood's wife, Demetra, in Hollandale. She tried to get hold of Wood as well, but he was out and wouldn't hear the news until later when he stopped at George Lee's filling station for gas. She really wanted to call some of her friends after that, but Frank Aldridge said *he* needed to make some calls and she had to wait for him to finish. And even after she asked him if she might "interfere and call members of my family," he persisted. And she had to wait.

She described her mother's great love for her cats—"kitties," she called them—as a way of justifying Ruth's odd decision to see about them on her way to her car with Thompsie, despite her injuries and the slaughter of her mother.

But when asked about the blood on the bathroom floor, Mildred flared up. There wasn't "as much as what they said," and, no, she didn't make tracks after she went in there, and just to be clear, there was no blood on the rugs the way they said and since she was the one who cleaned up after the funeral she ought to know.

What about the front door? Was it closed to keep curious people out?

No, sir, it was wide open and in no time the house was full to overflowing, and it hurt her "to see such a crowd of curiosity seekers as Mother was such a person that she hated publicity, and they did that way for three days."

People in the backyard? Absolutely.

What Ben Wilkes didn't know was that Mildred was biding her time. She had something to say and by God she was going to say it. She saw her opportunity when Wilkes inquired about Idella's handedness. Was it true she was left-handed?

"Very left-handed," she said and then she went for it. *And,* she said, her mother had arthritis in that hand and couldn't hardly hold a fountain pen and "could not have held those shears and I am determined to say it. I am determined to get that in . . ."

The state was vociferously objecting, Judge Jordan was sustaining, and Wilkes was staying out of the fray when Mildred finally went quiet enough for Jordan to reprimand her. She apologized, pleading ignorance due to inexperience in courtroom procedure. But she'd done what she came to do: counter the theory that Mrs. Thompson had struck first, a possibility that, so far, had not been directly mentioned in court.

Wilkes returned to what he thought was safer ground, Ruth's devotion to her mother. Mildred said the usual: wonderful, patient, loved her to death, perfect. The perfect daughter. "She was just wonderful to our mother."

But she didn't stop there. "And that is the reason I know Ruth couldn't have done this."

Objection. Sustained. Apology.

When, for his final question, Wilkes asked if she saw Sheriff Foote with the shears, she said she did. She saw him out front with the shears with a lot of people gathered around looking at them.

. . . .

On cross, Sanders asked about the amount of blood on the bathroom floor, the decision to mop it, the timeline of Mildred's day. On redirect, she said yes to Wilkes's question about Ruth borrowing $750 from the Nettles loan brokerage outfit. Was that to send to her mother in Colorado? Yes. They often had to send her money "because she was sick so much." And they took Idella to Colorado every summer because "hot weather just killed her" and it was cheaper to send her out there. That August, when Ruth borrowed the $750 their mother had asked for, it was to pay for medical bills incurred when she stepped in a hole and broke a little bone in her ankle.

And did Ruth get it for her?

She certainly did.

The large woman stepped down.

. . . .

The testimonies of Wood and Demetra Thompson did little more than confirm what other members of the family had already asserted. Wood spoke of his and Ruth's failed attempt at farming as well as John Dickins's purchase and bailout. Demetra talked about Idella's health and their January trip to Texas with Jimmy. Both testified to Ruth's perfect relationship with her mother, the devotion she displayed, their unqualified opinion of her as the most loving, most perfect daughter they'd ever known.

. . . .

At that, Ben Wilkes called the day's final defense witness, John Dickins. Walking slightly bent at the waist the way big men often do, sometimes from old athletic injuries, he took his cigar with him.

After a quick trip through the basics, making clear that John was Ruth's husband, that they had been married for twenty years and had two daughters—Dell, fifteen, and Dorothy Jane, ten—Wilkes wondered if Ruth had been a good mother to her children.

John answered with enthusiasm. "Yes, siree."

Made a good home for him? Made him a good wife?

"Perfectly wonderful."

Would he please tell the court and the jury what kind of relationship existed between his wife and her mother, Idella Long Thompson?

"It was very close."

Had she looked after her mother and cared for her?

Dickins responded with a simple "Yes, sir." And then on his own, he went beyond the bounds of the lawyer's question. "And," he added, "she has taken care of them all."

Wilkes didn't pursue the matter of who exactly John might be talking about when he spoke of "them all." Or what he meant precisely by "taken care of." He simply allowed the statement to sink in with the jury and then moved on.

Did John know where he was the day Mrs. Thompson was killed?

. . . .

As if waiting to be asked, John plowed right in.

He left his office early that day, around three thirty, he guessed, and drove over to Leland. He had left some money at home he needed to get to his manager so that he could pay some cotton pickers for work they'd done the day before. He'd arrived in Leland at about four o'clock, but when he turned down Deer Creek Drive, he was forced to stop. The street, the yards, the creek bank, were jammed. Cars parked up and down the street. People standing around in groups. He rolled down his window and asked a neighbor what in the world the matter was and was told about the murder of Mrs. Thompson. Soon afterward he happened to see Thompsie Hood, who told him Ruth had been injured and Mrs. Azlin had taken her to the Witte Clinic, he should go over there and see about her.

By the time John got there, Dr. Bunt had finished tending to Ruth, so he took her home and put her in bed, but she was so sore she could only lie in a propped-up position with pillows behind her back. She had cut places across her head requiring, Ruth had told him, six to nine stitches, plus another place on her arm. There were deep prints on her forearm, two fingernails were torn off, and she had soreness about her legs. Later, he rubbed her down with a hot liniment his friend Charlie told him worked on his horses when they were stiff. Combined with heating pads and the medication Bunt had given her, Charlie's salve helped her sleep. John stayed home the rest of that week and into the next to tend to her and help with the children.

John Dickins never acknowledged a moment's doubt about his wife's innocence. Not that day or the next or any other during the rest of his life, which ended in 1977, nineteen years before Ruth's. On the stand he made no bones about this and, on cross, often became testy when Sanders asked questions he deemed inflammatory and prying, especially about money. A big, direct man, convinced of the incontestability of his reputation for honesty and fairness, he fiddled with his cigar and spoke in drawling, confident tones that were said to have "dominated" the courtroom.

When Wilkes referred to earlier testimony "insinuating to the effect that" he had taken over the Thompson property and that his mother-in-law had been indignant about that, John answered curtly.

Yes, he said, he'd heard it and he was happy for the opportunity to set things straight about the acreage.

There were, he said, 1,591 acres still out there in his name, and he owned another 1,200 of open land. The Bogue Phalia River took up some of what had been the Thompson land, and 200 acres had been worked under the government program. For three years, Ruth and her brother Wood had farmed 500 or 600 acres in cotton, some in alfalfa, and some in other crops. Those were bad years. Labor was hard to come by, and general storage was bad. The acreage had gradually been reduced. The property was all mortgaged. They rented mostly. But when the rent came in, it wasn't enough. And the "Negroes" who "owed them a lot of money" moved off without paying. Like everybody else, they were trying to get away from mule-and-plow farming and farm with all tractors, but "it had been handled slow and it looked like they could not last another year when they would have to hand the land back to the boll weevils."

By the time they came to him in late December 1945 and asked for his help, they were drowning in debt.

To the tune, Wilkes figured, of $143,000. Was that about right? John said yes.

And did Wood and Ruth ask him to take the property over?

Yes. They came to him and Wood said, "Dickins, how about giving me my equipment and I will rent Jim's land and take my equipment and my house and I will try fighting grass and rent Jim's land."

Not long after that, John said, "I took over."

Nobody he asked thought he should take on the property, but he did it anyway, for one reason only: Ruth didn't want to let it go. He paid off the loans and made the Thompson family a deal. And no, he didn't think Mrs. Thompson resented having to sign off on it. She seemed happy that the land was still in the family.

As to Ruth's questioning by Sheriff Foote and the others, John didn't know why they had to choose to put her through such an ordeal on the very day her mother was buried when she hadn't even had time to grieve. On the other hand, he'd done everything he could to set things up for them, chairs around the bed and all. But it was what happened the next week that riled him most. That was when Frank Aldridge made the call demanding that he bring Ruth to the courthouse. The day she took the lie detector test. The ordeal that day had a pretty bad effect on his wife. She was "plumb worn out from their talking to her and she had nobody with her and nothing to eat." And now, more than six months later, she was still having trouble sleeping.

Unmentioned in John's testimony was the reason Ruth had nobody with her when she took the lie detector test or, for that matter, when she made her bedside statement: his and the Thompson family's refusal to hire a defense lawyer for her.

. . . .

When Sanders took up cross for the prosecution, he wanted to question John right away about the clothes Ruth wore the day her mother was killed, but because of his earlier ruling the judge sustained Wilkes's motion to disallow Sanders's right to ask questions about them. But he okayed asking the jury to leave so that Sanders could pose his questions, at which point Dickins further confused the issue by saying *he* was the one who put the bloody clothes in the washtub. And that when Hollingsworth came to get them, they were not on the clothesline but still soaking. And that he, Dickins himself, lifted them out of the water. This contradicted the testimonies of both Beatrice Smith and Hollingsworth, but the jurors weren't allowed to hear it and so Sanders let that be.

The jury returned. Wilkes's objection stood. Evidence lurking within the bloody threads of Ruth's jacket, skirt, blouse, girdle, and stockings remains unknown.

Dickins's answers to the question about a reward were particularly significant, not just within the context of the trial, but as a reminder of race relations at that time and in that place. When asked if he'd offered a reward for the "apprehension of a Negro," Dickins said yes, he'd offered a $1,000 reward and that his brother-in-law Shields Hood had added another $500. He then supplied a list of the people he'd told about it, all of them "trustworthy Negroes." There was Red and Ruby, Smoky, also Bea Smith's husband, James Smith, and a few others.

He didn't have it published in the newspaper, because, in his opinion, "it takes a Negro to catch a Negro." And he didn't tell the sheriff about it, because "it wasn't the sheriff's business." Or Frank Aldridge for the same reason. He did tell G. B. Swafford, the only policeman who'd agreed with the Thompsons about the backyard being full of people. But in general he thought if you caught a Black man where he was gambling or with a woman or if you knew somebody who was mad at him, other Black men were more likely to say so than if you published it all over the country in a newspaper read by white people.

When asked about the wall at the back of Mrs. Thompson's property, Dickins had gone back there and climbed over it but assured Wilkes that "a Negro could jump over it." And when he went down to the compress beyond Second Street and asked the manager about the space underneath the compress, he assured him that a "Negro could crawl under it."

After being excused, Dickins walked back to Ruth's side and, before sitting, leaned down to finger her hair and speak quietly to her. The moment had arrived for Wilkes to call Ruth to the stand; instead, he announced that the defense would close the following day.

At that, Judge Jordan called for a recess until nine the next morning.

. . . .

A final note about John Dickins's quadruple role as husband of the defendant, outspoken champion of her innocence, steady presence in the courtroom during her trial, and defense witness. Mississippi didn't adopt federal guidelines regarding the exclusion of witnesses from the courtroom during other testimony—generally known as the Rule—until 1975. Prior to that, according to a Leland lawyer, Mississippi trials were like the Old West. Decisions were based on English common law: derived from custom and precedent rather than statutes. Based ideally on the "sound discretion of the court," rulings were made on the spot. It was up to the judge to hash things out. Realistically speaking, this meant it was within the scope of his discretion to assess the trustworthiness of a witness and to give latitude where, according to the judge's opinion, based to some extent on community standards, it was deserved.

Today, before a trial opens, the judge will ask if both sides agree to "invoke the Rule," which in Mississippi comes in specifically as number 615 of the state's extensive Rules of Evidence. Lawyers routinely agree that in order to discourage and expose falsification, inaccuracy, and collusion, nonexpert witnesses should be excluded from attending the deposition of other witnesses.

In Ruth's trial, John Dickins never left his wife's side. When he took the stand and said he was happy to have the opportunity to clear up the acreage question, he was referring to testimony he'd sat there and listened to. When asked if he'd heard it said in court that Mrs. Thompson resented his takeover of her land, he said simply, "I heard."

In 1949 Mississippi, nothing on the books ruled against this. The prosecution didn't object. If it had, Wilkes could have countered by characterizing Dickins as a character witness whose testimony referred only to sideline issues, not germane to the case itself, the murder charge. Either way, John would have managed to keep his seat beside his wife, the defendant.

. . . .

When the Dickinses exited the courtroom and the lawyers were packing up, a reporter asked Wilkes if Ruth would take the stand the next day. Once again, he waffled.

Depends, he said.

DEFENSE RESTS

For the final day of her trial, Ruth wore a brown broadcloth golf dress with split sleeves, which one writer thought "made her dark-hued skin seem even darker." She seemed, he thought, "weary of the trial." Preceding her, a small girl of about ten entered, holding the hand of B. B. Wilkes. Wearing a "cotton frock of pink marked off into squares," eyeglasses, and a pink ribbon binding her dark blond hair—cut in bangs over her forehead and falling to her neck pageboy style—Dorothy Jane Dickins, "pale but calm," chatted smiling at other members of the family as she was led past them to the door of the witness room.

. . . .

The first witness Ben Wilkes called was Idella Thompson's second cousin John A. Stovall. A licensed mortician, embalmer, and graduate of the Gupton-Jones College of Mortuary Science, he estimated that in thirteen years of experience he'd embalmed a thousand, maybe twelve hundred, bodies. Including his cousin the late Idella Thompson. A man of forthright confidence, when he assertively testified that upon his arrival at around four o'clock on the afternoon of the murder Mrs. Thompson had lost perhaps a quart of blood but certainly no more than that, and, yes, there were spots of blood on the bathroom floor, the tub, and the walls but not a river of it and it had not yet coagulated, he certainly seemed to assume that the jury and everybody else in the courtroom would accept his as the final word.

Yes, the temple bone was broken, the skull crushed by a terrific blow into the cranial cavity resulting in a wound that must have been an inch and a half deep—you could actually look down into the skull—and her arm was broken, fingers were broken, there were bruises and abrasions, but not that much blood. Even though, yes, there was a flap of bone with a hairnet on it and you could lift the whole thing up because it was all stuck together and came away in one piece.

When Stanny Sanders's turn came to question Stovall, he lit straight into him. Implying he was helping the defense hide the truth, he first reminded the jury of the funeral director's blood kinship, not just to the victim in this case, but to the defendant as well.

"I believe you said Mrs. Dickins is your second cousin?"

Yes, sir.

After subsequently establishing Stovall's absence of medical training, he moved on to the burning of Idella Thompson's clothes.

Surely, he said, as a former sheriff he must have realized that the clothes of a victim were important in solving a crime; didn't Mr. Foote, the sheriff, tell you to *hold* Idella Thompson's clothes? Without acknowledging Hughey, Stovall said he did hold the clothes for a few days at his funeral establishment but nobody came for them.

"Isn't it a fact," Sanders snapped, "that Mr. Foote worked for your administration when you were sheriff . . . and you fired him?"

Yes, sir.

And does he have animosity toward Mr. Foote?

No, sir.

The next exchange put the lie to his denial: "You knew that burning the clothes would hamper him in his investigation?"

"Mr. Foote knew that I was busy."

Sanders: "Mr. Foote was busy too?"

Stovall, in a snit: "Well, I was busy too."

This cat-and-mouse skirmish did neither man credit. It ended when in response to Sanders's question as to why he burned the clothes, Stovall sat tight: "I didn't. They were burned by my men." Because they were obnoxious and smelly? That's what they said.

And no, he and his two helpers didn't track blood into the house when they lifted Mrs. Thompson's body and took it to the other bathroom to disrobe and wash. There wasn't that much blood. And her wounds weren't as horrific as others have said.

Even though, yes, you could pick up that flap of her skull and put it down. And it was mangled? Yes. Badly mangled? Yes. Gruesome? Yes.

Yet he can tell the jury she could have sustained all of those blows and still lived? Yes. If she'd been a younger woman.

. . . .

Wilkes's next-to-last witness was Dr. E. T. White, a pathologist called to offset the testimony of Doc Witte about the state of Mrs. Thompson's body when he arrived, specifically that rigor mortis had already set in, which he knew by the state of her wrist when he picked it up to check for a pulse and found it already turning cold. Then, when he let it drop and it hit the floor with a kind of thud, his conclusion was that she'd been dead for longer than Ruth claimed. Making it possible that Ruth's phone call to him had been delayed while she cleaned up after herself after murdering her mother.

The pathologist did a good job of casting doubt on a medical doctor's ability to assess the state of postmortem rigor. Doctors, he said, usually pronounced a person dead, then went out and spoke with the family. And that was the end of their responsibility. They didn't deal with the process of death as he, as a pathologist, did.

He was convincing. Lawyers in the courtroom thought perhaps the hit to the prosecution's case was fatal.

. . . .

If science is the crescendo, the testimony of a little girl in a pink dress might be thought of as its coda. Dorothy Jane Dickins was there ostensibly to confirm Ruth's story that, yes, she was sick on the morning of November 17 and, yes, her mother was there to administer her pills that morning and, yes, she went regularly to school and Sunday school and, yes, she knew what telling the truth meant.

But mostly she was there to be her ten-year-old self and to highlight Ruth's role as a loving mother. Stepping down from the witness box, Dorothy Jane smiled at Ruth. After B. B. Wilkes escorted her from the courtroom, Ruth lowered her head to the table and wept.

But by 11:15, when Ben Wilkes rested his case without calling his client to the stand, she'd recovered somewhat. John and the Thompsons had also relaxed. Everyone had performed well. Nobody flubbed or caused too much commotion (except maybe Mildred, but not seriously enough to make a difference). The defense case seemed strong especially compared with what the state was able to come up with, even without Ruth's testimony.

. . . .

When the judge called for a recess until 1:30, Ruth and John gathered up their daughter and drove home for lunch.

The four lawyers meanwhile went into deep seclusion to prepare their closing statements.

CLOSINGS

We long for answers. When a crime is committed, we comb relevant stories for details: the what-happened? Once we've digested that, we set off across a broad field of helter-skelter speculation. Who could do such a thing? Who might have? And why? A process that takes us from probability/likelihood to solution and motive. A trial should fill in the gaps. We keep hoping, once the verdict comes in, we'll know. We want "Guilty as charged" to translate as "It was her." She did it. Acquittal as "Not her. Somebody else." Certainty helps make us feel safer. We rest easier once a wrongdoer has been identified and punished, relieved that violence isn't random or on the loose and truth is both knowable and precise.

Lawyers know better. For them a trial is a blood-sport negotiation, fungible and pragmatic, a profession akin to horse trading. They are adversaries, not truth seekers. We know this. We've heard TV lawyers say it time and again, innocent until proven guilty, beyond a reasonable doubt, and so on. In Britain there's a third possibility: unproven. A convenient if frustrating option, leaving observers to think, so yes, she probably did it but the prosecution couldn't or didn't prove it. So she flies free. Even if she's guilty as sin.

We know all of this but cannot quiet the desire to believe. To know. Listen to interviews with the parents of a victim. To them, "Proven guilty" equates with "He/she did it. Killed our loved one." Open the door to the cell, the execution chamber. In *State of Mississippi v. Ruth Thompson Dickins*, neither side seems to have presented a strong enough case to unequivocally nail down a verdict. Lawyers attending the trial or making a point of keeping up with it thought absolutely the state had failed to prove guilt beyond a reasonable doubt. But the courtroom crowd and a great many people in the region stood with the DA, firmly against her.

. . . .

Judge Jordan had given the lawyers an hour-and-a-half recess in which to perfect their closing statements. In the meantime, he retained his seat on the bench for another of his jobs: to sentence ten recently convicted felons, one of whom was the young man known as the Sweet Potato Slayer.

Because the Chinese grocer Jeu Sing didn't die immediately after Alex Clark Jr. hit him with the potato, the case wasn't open-and-shut. In Clark's defense, his pro bono lawyer—a flamboyant litigator known around town as the attorney you wanted to hire if you were guilty— argued that the real cause of death was not the hurled vegetable but age and frailty. But after deliberating for four hours, the jury found eighteen-year-old Clark guilty of manslaughter, and on June 28, 1949, between noon and one o'clock, while Ruth and John Dickins were at home trying to calm themselves and feel optimistic, Judge Jordan sentenced him to two years in the Mississippi State Penitentiary. Clark and the other nine inmates he sent there would be held in county jail for three to five more days, after which they'd be shackled together by the state's official "traveling sergeant," known throughout the state as the Long Chain Man, and loaded into a special van to make the trip to their new home.

Confinement in Mississippi's state prison would forever change the life of a man as young as Alex Clark. One of only four U.S. state prisons to still make use of the lash—a five-foot-long, thick leather strap known as Black Annie—as a means of discipline and control, the sixteen-thousand-acre Mississippi State Penitentiary was not a conventional prison. There were no perimeter walls and no barred cells or guard towers. No razor wire. It was designed as, and continued to be, a working farm. And like other farms, it existed primarily to make a profit.

As a result, Parchman Penal Farm, as the penitentiary was known, offered no education or rehabilitation programs, nothing that might give a released convict a shot at starting a new, perhaps more fulfilling life. And because inmates were segregated only by race and gender, Alex Clark would be housed in a bullpen-type camp with anywhere from 75 to 180 other Black men, including murderers, rapists, and the many so-called feeblemindeds who roamed the premises.

Once the ten sentenced men had been escorted from the courtroom, Judge Jordan could leave as well.

· · · ·

At that, many members of the audience took the opportunity to stand, stretch their limbs, and cool their backsides. Until the last minute, people were still batting opinions across rows and seats: which side presented the best case, what the jury might be thinking especially concerning Ruth taking the stand or not, who would make the strongest closing argument and what he would say. Strangers had become known to one another during the week. They asked after each other's family and health. They weren't friends; once this was over, they'd go their separate ways and likely never meet again. But a trial like this—a local spectacle—can create a temporary bond among the attendees. By now everybody knew who was who on which side of the guilt-or-innocent fence, the great majority of whom were against Ruth and for her conviction. Opinionated tropes had become like a song you can't get out of your head. An earworm, thrumming in the background. *She did it, I know she did, look at her. Expressionless as a poker shark. Scary. A born killer.*

· · · ·

At 1:30, once Ruth and John and the lawyers were present, the judge entered the courtroom and from the bench asked for the jury to be brought in.

The temperature outside still hovered in the middle nineties. Inside felt, if anything, even hotter, more oppressive. People with paper fans waved them in front of their faces. For today only, the judge allowed a certain number of attendees to stand in the rear of the courtroom just inside the wide double doors. A few people mimicked the kids and brought wooden soft drink crates to stand on. Those too late to squeeze in ambled around the lawn.

Because burden of proof is on the state, the prosecution had one last chance to challenge arguments brought by the defense. For his first rebuttal witness, Sanders recalled Sheriff Foote, who insisted that, contrary to some witnesses' testimony, Mrs. Dickins had been well treated by himself and his officers. Anytime he wanted to talk to her, he always consulted her husband first. Made the appointment with *him.* Got his approval. And she never seemed to mind answering questions but conducted herself in a calm and collected manner no matter what he asked her. Furthermore, he didn't *make* her go to the Greenville doctor's office the day of the lie detector test; he *asked* her would she go and she said she would and John agreed to take her and no officers went along. As for the blood on the bathroom floor, Demetra Thompson was the one who *asked* him if they could have the floors mopped. Trying to do right by the family: *that* was the reason he agreed to let her and Mildred Hood call the handyman, Jimmy Banks, to come inside and take care of the job. The shears? He certainly did *not* take them out into the yard for the crowd out there to look at; in fact he was "so particular with the shears that I tied a string to them so that nothing could touch them."

When Ben Wilkes took over and asked the sheriff why he didn't say anything before now about those ladies asking if they could mop the floor, Foote said he figured he had.

Undaunted, Wilkes reframed the question and asked it again.

This time Foote turned sullen. "You didn't ask me," he said.

Wilkes responded in kind. That was because, he said, "I didn't know whether you would tell me or not."

Foote: "Then why didn't you ask me and find out?"

Things were getting out of hand. Both sides turning fractious. Exhaustion and dread taking their toll.

Two other men took the stand to contradict defense testimony claiming the Thompson yard had been overrun with sightseers and cops the day of the murder. Frank Aldridge adamantly denied having told John Dickins to bring Ruth down to the courthouse the way John said he did or that he was rude enough to ask, "What the hell's the matter with *her?*" He had always been as courteous to Mrs. Dickins as courteous could be.

The final rebuttal witness was Dr. Bunt Witte, who stood behind his father's explanation of rigor mortis and subsequent estimation of the time of the victim's death. Once he was excused, both sides rested.

. . . .

The judge turned toward the jury.

The charge by the state against Ruth Thompson Dickins, he said, was murder in the first degree, the definition of which assumed malice aforethought. In response to which they could return one of five verdicts:

1. Guilty as charged, which carried with it a death sentence in the electric chair.
2. Guilty as charged with sentence set by the jury at life imprisonment.
3. Guilty as charged but unable to agree on punishment, in which case the judge would have no other option than to issue a sentence of life in prison.
4. Guilty of manslaughter, the killing of a human being without malice, in the heat of passion, and not in necessary self-defense. Which carried a maximum sentence of twenty years.
5. Acquittal.

Additional instructions requested by either the state or the defense and approved by the judge would also apply. The judge read these aloud.

One from the state defined "malice" as implied by law from the nature and character of the weapon used. Another, that malice aforethought did not have to exist in the mind of the slayer for any given length of time, but might set in at the very moment the fatal blows were being delivered, *if* they were being inflicted with the deliberate design to take the life of the victim. Yet another of the prosecution's instructions charged that the jury did not have to know beyond the shadow of a doubt that the defendant was guilty before convicting her; they had only to believe that, *from the evidence beyond a reasonable doubt and to the exclusion of every reasonable hypothesis other than guilt, she is guilty. And if they so believe, it is their sworn duty to so find.*

In its instructions, the defense urged the jury to proceed with utmost caution and vigilance when considering circumstantial evidence and to consider that, *if there remains within the evidence or want of it some other reasonable hypothesis consistent with innocence, they should so find.* In other words, "circumstances proved may produce a strong suspicion of guilt but that is insufficient to justify a verdict of guilty." And if there were two theories growing out of the evidence or lack thereof, both reasonable, one pointing to the defendant's guilt, the other to her innocence, and they are unable to say which was true, it was their duty to accept the theory pointing to her innocence, even though the theory pointing to her guilt may be stronger and supported by better evidence.

. . . .

There would be, the judge said, four closing statements, each with a one-hour limit. The prosecution would take the first slot, after which the defense would have two opportunities to speak. Because it brought the case to court and had the burden of proof, the state would speak last.

At 2:40, Jordan called for the state to begin.

By then, an unlucky pigeon had found its way into the courtroom. Searching for a way out, the desperate bird flew round and around, high above the proceedings, just beneath the ceiling fans. As Willard McIlwain rose and moved toward the jury box, the bird flapped its wings and kept going, flying from one side of the room to the other.

People looked up. There was nothing to do.

At McIlwain's first utterance, Ruth bent her head and hid her face in her arms. When strands of her hair fell over her forehead, John Dickins motioned to Demetra to come sit beside her on her other side. After reviewing the defendant's statement to the police, McIlwain began pointing out its inconsistencies and implausible reasoning. After which he moved on to a number of race-baiting hypotheticals, including one declaring that "if she'd been fighting a Negro she would have been panting over the telephone when she called the Witte Clinic."

He also revisited the four possible verdicts for conviction. Given the state's attitude throughout the trial, the general expectation was that, if the prosecutors didn't request the death penalty, they'd certainly go for life imprisonment. But after pointing out that, as defined by law, malice concerned the kind of weapon and the type of death, he went in the other direction and reminded the jury of its fifth, alternative option: if it found that Mrs. Thompson's death came about without malice aforethought but in the heat of passion, it could return a verdict of manslaughter.

McIlwain returned to his seat.

The very mention of manslaughter indicated the prosecution's willingness to accept the lesser charge, perhaps because even they knew their case was a web of circumstance and possibility. Punishment for manslaughter ranged from a fine and no jail time to twenty years. Were Sanders and McIlwain announcing their willingness to accept even the lightest sentence on offer in order to save the win?

. . . .

The defense attorney B. B. Wilkes's blast at the prosecution employed a closing lawyer's favorite mode of attack: sarcasm. They have, he said, "established no motive whatsoever. It looks like the state is trying to convict Mrs. Dickins by the process of elimination," a last-man-standing strategy based on no evidence at all.

. . . .

In his turn, Ben Wilkes took a more deliberate tone, focusing on the state's burden of proof, once again pointing out that unless contradicted by facts that prove guilt beyond doubt, the story Ruth Dickins told—the intruder, the shears, the scuffle, his escape—should be accepted: that was their sworn duty, that was the law. As for manslaughter, the defense rejected the option. His client was innocent. The state had not proven otherwise. Wilkes asked for nothing less than acquittal.

He was all in, and certainly the family had approved the gamble. And in the end, you have to wonder how much any jury is swayed by a lawyer's last-ditch bombast. After a week, wouldn't those twelve men be ready to do their job and decide how this thing will end?

Wilkes edged toward his conclusion by gesturing toward John Dickins, who draped a comforting arm across his wife's shoulders.

"If John Dickins," he said, "had even the remotest suspicion his wife committed this crime, do you think he would let her go on raising his children?"

He was here, he said, in this courtroom, standing before this jury "to defend this woman who raised children." He lifted his voice to an evangelical pitch.

"I am here," he declared, "to defend one of those whom we men of the South place on a pedestal next to God!"

A maniac, Wilkes concluded, killed Mrs. Thompson. Only a maniac was capable of committing such a crime.

Having once again extolled the virtues of the man who stood behind the defendant, followed by a reprise of the question of *who could or could not have* committed this murder, Ben Wilkes returned to his seat.

. . . .

Prosecutor Sanders rose. It was 5:30. With an hour to go, the speechifying had grown tedious, the day having already extended beyond the five o'clock adjournment the audience had grown accustomed to, beyond the time for babysitter pickup, dinner prep, and—especially important in the Delta—cocktail hour. But no one budged. Sanders's performance was what they'd been waiting for. But for the steady flapping of the pigeon's wings, the courtroom was silent.

He approached the jury box, taking his usual spot, close enough to the railing to pound it if he so desired.

"There has been," he began, "a horrible murder committed. The people have a right to demand that the murderer be punished. The reason Mrs. Dickins is on trial here is that her mother was brutally murdered and"—hitting his fist on the rail, he reminded jurors of the one inescapable element of what B. B. Wilkes labeled the state's process of elimination—"she was the only one there."

There were, he went on, only two reasonable possibilities to consider: either "a Negro" committed the crime, or Mrs. Dickins did. And because "there was not a trace of evidence that a Negro was in that house . . . the guilt falls squarely on the shoulders of Mrs. Dickins."

He revisited every grotesque detail of the murder and the defendant's unseemly scramble for secrecy and money. And ended by playing on the jurors' inborn racial prejudice, urging them to ask themselves if they seriously believed a "Negro walked into Mrs. Thompson's house at four o'clock on a bright sunny day in that exclusive neighborhood and with only a pair of garden shears as a possible weapon" proceeded to murder that frail lady.

Garden shears? Wouldn't he at least have had a knife? Did they really think "a Negro" would have left Mrs. Dickins, a living witness, sprawled on the bathroom floor "within four jumps of the telephone"? Did that make sense?

He pounded his fist to the beat of his assertions.

"Somebody washed those shears. A wet and bloody handkerchief was found in the bathtub by the body."

In the time-honored ploy known as waving the bloody flag, he grabbed the lady's brown linen handkerchief and held it aloft.

"That handkerchief," he shouted, "was used to wipe those shears."

After a pause he asked the twelve Mississippi Delta white men a rhetorical, if culturally empowered, question.

"Does a Negro man," he quietly wondered, "carry this kind of handkerchief with him?"

He paused. Let the question linger before quietly mounting his final appeal. He was certain now that when the jury considered the evidence, they would vote . . . He went on with the usual boilerplate prosecutorial windup, citing justice for the victim, the people's right to seek it, and so on.

At 6:30 p.m., after officially handing over the case to the jurors, Judge Jordan assured them he'd be on call whenever they were ready, no matter what time, and the men filed past him, into a stuffy anteroom guarded by a bailiff, to begin deliberations.

The judge left, followed by the defense attorneys, the defendant, and the prosecutors. Once the Thompson relatives had disappeared through the door, the courtroom quietly emptied. Most spectators got in their cars and drove away. But some stuck around outside on the lawn with news reporters, hoping to be the first to hear what came next.

At 8:30, when Judge Jordan felt sure there would be no verdict that night, he released the jurors for their dinner break and asked the courthouse staff to clean the courtroom and prepare it for an overnight stay.

Hearing the news, some of those waiting outside went home, while others—the die-hard *I was there first-ers*—lingered until the early morning hours when the court clerk told them a verdict had been reached but court wouldn't convene until after ten. At which point they went home or to Jim's Café for breakfast, vowing to be back in time to get the news first.

VERDICT

It happened fast. Less than sixteen hours after they began deliberating, the jury foreman, Wilson Webb, advised the judge they were ready to report. Jordan called the Dickinses' residence at 10:05. John notified everybody else. Accompanied by her husband, her brothers, and Demetra, Ruth—dressed in the blue chambray dress she wore the previous Friday—arrived from Leland at 10:30 to find her sister, Mildred, already there, accompanied by her son, Thompsie, and her husband, Shields Hood. Oddly enough, the courtroom audience had thinned out considerably, leaving many seats unoccupied, perhaps revealing a greater interest in the chase than the finish, but in the end who knows. Some people chose rather to find a spot outside, close to the back door. If the verdict went against Ruth, she'd come that way, down the steps toward the women's quarters of the jail. They wanted to be there for that.

Jordan summoned the jury. At 10:36, the twelve men entered. According to one onlooker, Ruth focused on the foreman's face, as if searching for a sign of what was ahead. The men stood in a semicircle in front of the judge, facing the defendant, as instructed by the court clerk. Thin and pale, when asked to stand in place, Ruth clasped her hands at her waist and leaned into her husband, who, aided by Demetra Thompson, all but held her upright.

"Have you gentlemen agreed on a verdict?" the judge asked.

The foreman, Webb, said they had and handed the penciled verdict to the court clerk, who read it aloud: "We, the jury, find the defendant guilty as charged but disagree as to punishment."

When "guilty as charged" rolled through the courtroom, John Dickins bowed his head and put his arms around his wife. Ruth's face didn't change. She stared as if into space. After the judge praised the jury for its work and dismissed the men from further duty, they filed out and he summoned Ruth to the bench. Looking dazed, John remained on her right side, while Ben Wilkes took Demetra's place on her left.

"You understand, Mrs. Dickins," the judge said quietly, "I have no discretion in this case. The jury found you guilty but disagreed as to the punishment. It is therefore mandatory for me to send you to the penitentiary for the rest of your natural life."

Grasping the mahogany railing before her for support, Ruth nodded, then returned to the defense table and dropped heavily into her chair. John and the family gathered behind her, leaning down to cradle her upper body, saying nothing, muted by disbelief.

Sheriff Foote approached, carrying an order from the judge to take the defendant into custody. Her life sentence would begin immediately. With Wilkes's and Dickins's help, Ruth followed Foote and his deputy out of the courtroom, trailed by family members. The courtroom audience waited. No one moved or spoke until Ruth and her family had cleared the room, when they slipped quietly into the corridor, in single file, as if organized.

Foote and Deputy Sheriff Murray Etheridge led their prisoner down the back steps and across Courthouse Alley to the small, squat building—square, like a box—with barred windows, which sat next to the men's far larger, two-story jail. Built in 1872, both buildings were made of crumbling, concrete-coated brick painted white.

While Ruth waited with her family in the jailer's office, Wilkes rushed back into the courthouse to file a motion for a new trial, based on objections he'd raised during the trial and rebuttal. When Judge Jordan overruled the motion, Wilkes immediately requested the reinstatement of the $10,000 bail she'd posted in January, pending the outcome of her appeal to the state supreme court.

Remarking that he would "assume from the verdict that the woman is guilty," the judge said that while it was within the discretion of the court to grant bond following a conviction, an "atrocious crime" had been committed and caution should be taken. With that in mind, he "wouldn't be in a frame of mind to admit bail this afternoon," but would take the request under advisement. Reminding Wilkes that court would adjourn the next day until mid-July, he asked him to pick a future time and place for further discussion. With that, he left. Wilkes returned to the jail to give Ruth the news.

Her old friend Hughey Foote escorted her to her eight-by-ten-foot private cell. Known as the "white woman's room," it had a steel door with a small triangular window at about eye level, clear enough to see through. The windows were barred, the floor concrete, the corrugated steel ceiling ten feet high. Furnishings had been set up in advance: two electric fans, two armchairs (one a rocker), a double-decker bunk with linens, a small table, a lamp, and a private bathroom with shower, sink, and toilet.

She'd have privacy, reading space, her own bathroom. Entering alone, she made only one comment. "It's awful," she said. "Awful."

And that was that. Imagining what Dorothy Jane must have felt when her father came home alone is not an easy or pleasant thing to do. Nor is wondering what it might be like to be Dell, off at camp, waiting for a telephone call.

· · · ·

The news spread fast, coast to coast. Front page. Prominent sportswoman. Socialite. Guilty of Hacking Mother to Death. Rose Shears. Hedge Shears. Pruning Shears. An editorial posted in a Shreveport, Louisiana, paper waxed sentimental: "No one could have other than a sinking feeling over the conviction of a woman of breeding, education and earned prominence for murder of her own mother, brutally through hacking with a pair of rose shears."

The *McComb Enterprise-Journal* declined to indulge in such sympathetic imagining. A page 1 story referred to Ruth as "just another prisoner in old Washington County Jail today."

Ruth's brother Wood and his wife, Demetra, visited her that afternoon, bringing sandwiches and a pitcher of iced water.

APPEAL

According to the sheriff, after a night in her cell Ruth was already viewing her conviction more stoically. She even ate her breakfast before receiving her first visit from her husband, who came by before work to assure her that a mistake had been made. Some members of the jury didn't realize that once they voted her guilty of first-degree murder, the judge had no choice but to sentence her to life. The mistake would be corrected. When asked by a reporter if he'd continue to fight for his wife's release, Ruth's "wealthy cotton broker husband, broad-shouldered John Dickins," roared back, "You're damn right we will."

But the Mississippi statute concerning bail for persons convicted of murder was strict. "Only on the condition of medical testimony to the effect that confinement in prison could seriously impair the health or endanger the life of a defendant can bond be granted those convicted of murder." But what exactly constituted impairment, and at what point had it become serious? Compared with what and according to whom?

When Judge Jordan next held court in July, two weeks after the sentencing, both Wilkeses were present to speak for Ruth. As were the prosecutors Sanders and McIlwain. John Dickins and Shields Hood waited in the visitors' gallery. To support his petition, Ben Wilkes presented affidavits from two doctors who, after separately examining Ruth in the county jail, had issued similar findings. Ruth's heart, they reported, was at "low voltage," her blood pressure below normal, her blood count verging on "an anemic condition." These reports, Wilkes argued, indicated a fragile state of health, which a period of confinement could only serve to aggravate.

Sanders objected. The state hadn't been given a chance to cross-examine the doctors, and if he and McIlwain had known she was receiving a physical examination, they'd have sent their own doctors to do the same thing. When Sheriff Foote was called, he noted an improvement in "the prisoner's" outward appearance since her imprisonment. She'd made only one complaint. After her first night in jail, she said her cot was uncomfortable and she hadn't been able to sleep. Hughey ordered up a sturdier, more comfortable bed that very morning. Next day, she said she slept better.

Georgia McIver, identified as the "Negro woman who waits on Mrs. Dickins in jail," reported that Ruth "took" three meals a day and even ate between meals. And when, each morning, McIver asked how she felt, Mrs. Dickins always said fine. The jailer J. W. McElwee thought Mrs. Dickins looked better than when she came in, more than likely because she'd taken a good rest and was in a nicely fixed-up private cell with her own private bath. As for a doctor or medicine, she hadn't requested either one. Not once.

Citing the lack of evidence indicating a decline in Mrs. Dickins's health, Judge Jordan denied bail. When Wilkes then motioned for a new trial based on the assertion that three jurors misunderstood the sentencing law, the judge denied that as well.

Wilkes had failed again.

Nine days later he had a heart attack. He seemed to recover well enough. But two days after that, he had another. The summer term of the circuit court had ended by then, and so he and his wife took off on a short vacation in the Poconos, where he planned to take some much-needed time off as well as work on his appeal.

But on the morning of August 1, two days before his fifty-ninth birthday, after waking up in good spirits, he collapsed in his motel room and fell immediately into a coma. He died shortly afterward.

To this day, most people believe that given the shock of how it all came out, especially with the odds so firmly fixed in his favor and he being so highly thought of, the Dickins trial killed Ben Wilkes.

. . . .

Ten days after his uncle's death, B. B. Wilkes filed an appeal bond with the Washington County Circuit Court clerk, who certified it. A few days later, he sent the 444-page trial record, including testimony, motions, orders, and instructions as well as all of the exhibits—fingernails, hair, the handkerchief, the shears—to the state supreme court in Jackson. By that time, John Dickins had replaced B. B. Wilkes with an experienced appellate attorney, the former assistant attorney general W. D. "Buck" Conn Jr.

The supreme court would hear verbal arguments before December 1. Conn was expected to be eloquent and aggressive in his attempt to schedule a new trial for his client.

. . . .

Middle of November, around the one-year anniversary of Idella's murder, a thirteen-by-ten tabloid called *Tragedy-of-the-Month* hit newsstands all over the country. It sold for twenty-five cents a copy.

Published by the Philadelphia-based Triangle Publications and Walter Annenberg—best known for his ownership of *The Philadelphia Inquirer* and the *Daily Racing Form*—the magazine devoted each issue to one approximately forty-page crime story. On the cover of only the second issue in the magazine's history, beneath the masthead, was the title of that month's feature: "Baring the Monstrous Murder of Ma'am Idella."

A lot of Greenville and Leland people sneered at that. Southern men often respond in passing to women with a tip of the hat and a murmured "ma'am." They may answer a question with "Yes, ma'am" or "No, ma'am." But I have never heard anybody use "ma'am" as a form of address. In the Delta as in most of the South, we—both men and women—pay our respects to a woman of some years by using the courtesy title "Miss." *Miss* Idella. Perhaps the Philadelphians thought the use of "Miss" denoted young and unmarried, the same as "Mademoiselle" in customary French, while "Madam" referred to a married, widowed, or older woman.

The cover art featured a nine-by-nine close-up of Ruth at the defense table. Her small hands clasped in a loose basket, she'd turned her head to the left, where Ben Wilkes usually sat, and was concentrating hard, mouth slightly open, eyes fixed. At her elbow, John's summer hat lay angled and almost upside down to protect the brim. Next to it were

Ruth's zippered white plastic-tile clutch bag—1940s fashionable and a somewhat surprising choice for her—and a book of some kind. Wavy and thick, so shiny black it looked almost lacquered, her famous bob swooped away from her forehead in a low pompadour to rest on the tip of her ear and end at the base of her skull. Perfectly contained. Every strand in place. She was wearing the zip-up springlike and rather girlish dress with the white collar and cuffs, and somehow the photographer caught her looking fresh, her cheeks not yet dragged down, eyes clear of dark pockets. She'd pushed her gold watch a full two inches above her wristbone. Her fingers stubby, rounded at the tip, nails unpolished and trimmed short, a gardener's hands. Strong, efficient, work hardy.

. . . .

By then I'd read every Nancy Drew and moved on to my mother's copy of Mickey Spillane's *I, the Jury* and anything written by Daphne du Maurier. Reading became my version of a sex education class, providing not how-to details but lessons in lust and the world of eros. Within a year, I'd managed to check out a copy of *Forever Amber* from the adults-only room of the downtown library by avoiding the librarian's eyes and trying to stand taller than I was. She asked no questions but simply stamped the circulation card and the book, reminding me of the due date.

My mother and I also shared a passion for true detective magazines. For us they were like Milk Duds at the movies: don't open the box if you're not ready to devour the entire contents. I vividly remember being in the new house one day when Mama handed me a magazine with Ruth on the cover. Inside were more pictures: shots of Ruth, John, Ruth's family, the courthouse, the courtroom jammed with spectators during recess, Mrs. Thompson's home, an aerial shot of the Deer Creek neighborhood, Ruth and John's home, the lawyers, and, of course, the pruning shears.

As a publication, *Tragedy-of-the-Month* itself seems to have quickly vanished from the tabloid world. But Joseph Fulling Fishman, the author of the "Ma'am Idella" story, was no ordinary hack. Educated as a penologist, hired by the FBI as one of its first agents, he was qualified to cover the story. By the time he came to Greenville, he'd been awarded a Guggenheim Fellowship and had published articles in several leading magazines.

But his take on the Idella Thompson murder and the Ruth Dickins trial leaned as heavily on standard romantic notions about ancestry and class in the Deep South as it did matricide.

Given this angle, the editors superimposed the cover photograph of Ruth on a long-range shot of the kind of allée popular during the days of the antebellum mansion: a tunnel of moss-draped cypress down which a horse-drawn carriage might rumble, carrying visiting ladies in hoopskirts and gentlemen in frock coats on their way to a Delta soiree.

Fishman perceived Ruth's family, the Longs, the Thompsons, and the Stovalls, as long-standing members of the Mississippi Delta "ladder of aristocracy," a societal structure that came into being before the Civil War and a hundred years later still existed. Because Ruth's family possessed "both wealth and influence as well as lineage," they dwelled at the very apex of that ladder. The vaunted "cream of the Old South," they embodied "the hope that their way of life would continue and never die out."

His language was full of clichés, but to be fair, a lot of the information he came up with—if certainly not all—is accurate, and the photographs are worth many, many times the two-bit price of the magazine. It is, beyond the nonsense, invaluable.

· · · ·

On November 28, Ruth's appellate attorney Buck Conn made his case before the Mississippi Supreme Court. First, he argued, the evidence presented in Mrs. Dickins's trial was insufficient to support the guilty verdict. Second, the court erred by allowing a "presumption of malice" charge to be read to the jury. And further, no evidence had been submitted to show that Mrs. Dickins actually struck the blows. These errors, he argued, qualified her for a reversal of the original trial and the scheduling of another.

Speaking for the State of Mississippi, the attorney general disputed Conn's contentions one by one and ended his verbal arguments with "According to the facts in the record, the court was justified in its action. The jury was fully instructed in every phase of the law pertaining to the case. The instructions issued at the defendant's request were elaborate and gave her every benefit of the doubt."

The justices went into session. Two weeks later, on December 12, in an opinion that painstakingly covered every point raised in Buck Conn's appeals brief, the supreme court unanimously and lengthily upheld the trial court's decision.

Its pages included a blunt and quite testy response to Ruth's story of the murderous intruder: the evidence, it said, did not disclose one thing, "a button, a hair, a hat, or anything whatsoever to indicate that a third person had taken part in the affray." And while the jury might reasonably have presumed that Mrs. Dickins and her mother had participated in a struggle, "the physical facts pointing to the presence of a Negro are entirely and significantly absent, except for Mrs. Dickins' statement."

By employing the conditional tense of its verbs, the court also went to great lengths to conjure up the jury's possible thought processes as it made its way toward its verdict: "The jury *could well have been* of the opinion that Mrs. Dickins *could not have taken* the shears from any Negro man in the fashion set out in her statement. They *could have further believed* it unreasonable to suppose that a Negro who had killed Mrs. Thompson *would have fled* leaving Mrs. Dickins, a witness, prostrate on the floor and just a few feet from a telephone . . . and that this Negro *would have killed* Mrs. Dickins as well." In discussing the struggle that cost Mrs. Thompson her life, the opinion said the jury *could have also decided* that the nature of the multitudinous wounds incurred in the prolonged fight indicated the act of a woman, considering the comparatively brief time and many fewer lacerations it would have taken a man to kill the frail and aged victim.

As for the "malice" argument, the court "presumes malice from the killing of another with a deadly weapon *unless* facts in evidence change the character of the killing by showing some justification or necessity." Because Ruth made no explanation of the facts in evidence but denied the killing, there was no evidence that might have justified the deliberate use of a deadly weapon. Therefore the "presumption of the law characterizes the act as murder."

The lengthy opinion fairly steamed with righteous certainty.

"Mrs. Dickins Must Serve Term," *The Delta Democrat-Times* declared.

Prison officials, it went on, expected "Mississippi Delta socialite Ruth Dickins" to join six other white women inmates right away. Because she was convicted of a capital crime and given a life sentence, she wouldn't be eligible for parole for ten years. When the attorney Buck Conn was asked if he planned to appeal to the U.S. Supreme Court, he said that in his opinion there was no federal issue in the case strong enough to warrant a hearing.

Ruth had spent the previous Christmas—1948—at home with her family. This year she'd be alone, locked up in county, awaiting transfer.

LATE 1949, EARLY 1950

By this time, the Fey family was living large. We'd been to the Edge-water Beach Hotel that summer for a vacation. My mother had a section of the concrete-floored patio of our new house enclosed and made into a nice sunporch. She bought wicker and bamboo furniture and put down a sisal rug that scratched the bottom of your feet when you walked barefoot across it. And she'd come through in response to my relentless requests for a baby sister. She was pregnant. The baby was due in May. She and I planned to name her Judith Marie. I was proud of her for being the youngest mother among my friends, still able and willing to have another baby.

One of the wicker chairs was like a king's throne. When my father sat in it, which was often, he looked like Sydney Greenstreet in *The Maltese Falcon*. He was still traveling and putting in extra hours at a pharmacy near the hospital.

One day he arrived home from the road with a surprise: a newly issued RCA Victor 45 rpm record player, complete with an assortment of seven-inch multicolored vinyl records. In those days, everybody was listening to Columbia 78s or the new 33⅓ LPs, but RCA was after a younger market, teenagers and college kids who liked quicker hits, three minutes of music a side. In many ways, my father fit right into that market. And he liked to be in on new things.

The four of us gathered while he unboxed the small machine and plugged it in. My brother, David, and I were skeptical. We couldn't believe something so small would produce the kind of sound we were used to. Daddy set the company's demo record on the changer and pressed "Play." The record dropped instantly, the player arm swung quickly into place, and once the needle dropped, a man's voice filled the room, explaining the setup and giving us samples of the kind of music we'd be listening to. Country, semiclassical, R&B, popular—each genre represented by its own color vinyl.

We put on Vaughn Monroe doing "Riders in the Sky," a semiclassical instrumental called, I think, "A Night in the Forest." Mama loved José Iturbi's "Clair de Lune" and anything by Perry Como. None of us went for country music, but we liked to hear Bob Nolan and the Sons of the Pioneers doing "Cool Water," mainly because they starred in Roy Rogers movies. Daddy liked the jump and swing tunes. Mainly Count Basie.

We kept the bright-colored records separated and in place for a little while, but Mama was the only orderly one among us, and in no time we were leaving them scattered all over the place. They easily scratched and warped. We lost interest.

But the player itself was to take on a new importance when Daddy entered us in the annual citywide outdoor Christmas decoration contest sponsored by the Green Thumb Garden Club, first prize, a check for $25. The No. 1 pop-music single that year was "Rudolph the Red-Nosed Reindeer," sung by Gene Autry. The Rudolph cartoon short had come out the year before, but what caught the country's attention was the song, which sold 2.5 million copies. As a result, Rudolph decorations were showing up all over town.

Not at our house. My father decided to go all out for the prize by bucking the trend. He took a picture of the Nativity scene, complete with Mary, Joseph, and the baby Jesus, the manger, halos, shepherds, wise men, and the rest, to a sign shop and had a life-size plywood cutout built, painted, delivered, and set up. We did nothing. Just looked out and there it was: haloed Mary cradling the swaddled baby, one hand curled around his head, the other cradling his bottom. Joseph, the wise men, and the shepherds huddled around looking bedazzled. A floodlight representing the Star of Bethlehem. The manger filled with hay. He set up the 45 rpm player, covered it with a tarp, and plugged it in to a speaker. Put a record on the spindle, clicked "Play" and "Repeat."

Twenty-four hours a day, the world's fastest record changer dropped Perry Como singing "Ave Maria" in Latin to the turntable. Up and down Washington Avenue, his languid voice drifted, swooned, lifted, paused, and, after the click of the player arm as it swung to one side, then set its needle back on the vinyl, began again. After a few nights, a neighbor from across the street called and, when Daddy answered, sang a phrase of the song he'd heard so many times he'd memorized it.

In Latin. From then on, Daddy switched off the music at ten.

. . . .

For its Christmas celebration, Leland staged a repeat of the year before with a couple of added attractions. There would be a fourth light-swathed tree afloat on Deer Creek—two between the bridges, two on the other side of each—and on opening night the (white) high school band would march from the schoolyard to the Drive playing Christmas carols.

The plan, Mayor Caraway announced, was to add a tree every year.

Ruth's family visited her in jail, bringing food and gifts. Thompsie often showed up with lunch and sat with her in her cell. John Dickins consulted with Buck Conn, who had one more trick up his sleeve before giving up on appeals.

. . . .

There were complaints when our Nativity scene won the grand prize for outdoor decoration. Mary's robe was not *pink*, a woman wrote in a letter to the newspaper. It was *blue*. Others thought the idea was for families to create something together. Not go out and order it.

Ever the salesman, my father figured winning the contest was a fine way to announce our presence on one of the best streets in town. He was also making plans to go into business and thought the attention would serve him well.

On December 28, "social activities in the Mississippi Delta were climaxed" when sixty-two girls in white ball gowns, carrying bouquets of lavender orchids, made their debut in the Gold Room of the Hotel Greenville. For its decorative theme, a "Greek pavilion effect" had been created.

On New Year's Day, the Sunday edition of the New York *Daily News* devoted two full pages to the murder of Idella Thompson and the trial and conviction of her daughter. Called "Did Justice Prevail?," the article used the Lizzie Borden story to fuel Ruth's. It opened, "Mrs. Ruth

Thompson Dickins, bright-eyed and thin-lipped, may follow Lizzie Borden into macabre immortality," and ended with a predictable reflection: "Doubt hung like a cloud over Lizzie Borden, who went free. And doubt may linger about Ruth Dickins, who went to prison."

The close-up headshot of Ruth accompanying the story may well be a mug shot taken at the Washington County Jail. She's wearing an open-collared black-striped white blouse or dress and has the look of somebody told to look straight at the camera. Her eyes are ringed in darkness, eyebrows pressed down at the outside edges, lips pursed tightly together.

There's a picture of Idella's house one column over. In the fourteen months since her murder, it had deteriorated. The paint looked worn and patchy. The trees needed trimming. Two cheap lawn chairs sat on the front porch, and a long hose snaked down the front sidewalk, as if casually dropped and forgotten.

The article contained many errors. But it told an irresistible story of murder, matricide, savagery, and greed among the upper class. A Deep South redo of its New England precedent, it was undoubtedly read widely and hotly commented upon.

The Sugar Bowl went badly for Louisianians who attended when the LSU Tigers were trounced by the Oklahoma Sooners, 35–0.

. . . .

On January 9, Buck Conn filed a do-or-die motion with the state supreme court, pointing out two instances of error in the opinion the court had released in December, one having to do with the insufficiency of the facts of evidence submitted in the trial court; the other, instructions regarding the definition of malice.

To nobody's surprise, on the twenty-third the court rejected Conn's suggestion of error. Sheriff Foote said he would transfer Ruth to Parchman once he received the official order to deliver her, probably in about five days.

But a week later, Ruth remained in county. When Parchman superintendent Marvin Wiggins was asked about the situation, he said that before he could send over there to get her, he had to have a mandate from the state court. On the other hand, if the sheriff wanted to transfer her himself, he'd go along.

On February 1, Foote had a heart attack. Recovering at home, he said he was feeling fine but made no statement regarding Ruth.

Curiosity among townspeople grew. Her jurors began to wonder. Shouldn't she be serving the sentence the judge handed down? Didn't Judge Jordan say the Long Chain Man usually gathered up convicted felons within three to five days of their sentencing?

. . . .

Finally, just after lunch on February 2, 1950, Ruth Dickins quietly exited the Washington County Jail, escorted by Deputy Sheriff W. A. Clark and accompanied by her husband, who had been given permission to take the trip with her. No Long Chain Man, no chains or cuffs. Just husband, wife, and a driver.

No one appears to have questioned this extraordinarily special treatment. Nothing in the paper, no rumors anybody remembers. But then, she was no ordinary convict.

III

———

PRISON

Women in their "up-and-downs," lined up for mail call at the Parchman Post Office. This photo is part of the Mississippi Department of Archives and History Photograph Collection and was probably taken in the 1920s. It provides a visual sense of the dresses the incarcerated women were given and what the women did to vary and improve them. The number of women lined up to get mail is impressive and may well have been staged as a way to indicate to a curious public how well inmates were treated and how happy they were to get letters. I have found no pictures of white female inmates at Parchman, and research proves that few photographs were taken of imprisoned women at all.

1950: A NEW LIFE

The straightest shot from Courthouse Alley to the gates of the prison would put Ruth and the two men on South Washington Avenue for eight blocks before taking a left on Highway 82, a familiar route to all three, especially John, who drove it on his way to and from work every day of the week. After passing the drive-in movie theater and Mink's Dine and Dance, they came to the Leland city limits and, in short order, on their left, the road to Deer Creek Drive. Unless the deputy gave Ruth a last-chance cruise past her house, they'd stay on 82 past Lillo's Supper Club and the land she and her brother tried to farm. Not long after that they'd take State Highway 49 West into Sunflower County, its flat black cotton fields at rest at this time of year, waiting to be turned and planted.

Indianola, the county seat, has been home to a few famous people, Minnie Cox for one. A graduate of Fisk University and a teacher at the local "colored" school, she was appointed postmistress of Holmes County by President Benjamin Harrison in 1891, the first Black woman in Mississippi to hold that position. She even managed to hang on to the post through the dark days of what the South called Redemption until 1902, when the white supremacist spokesman and future Mississippi governor James "White Chief" Vardaman berated the county for tolerating "a negro wench as postmaster" and demanded her resignation. The new U.S. president, Theodore Roosevelt, refused to bend to Vardaman's demands or accept Cox's resignation. Instead, he closed the post office entirely but kept Cox on the federal payroll for the remainder of her term of office.

The bluesmen Albert King and Little Arthur Duncan also hailed from there. B. B. King wasn't born there, but as a teenager he worked in nearby cotton fields and at a local cotton gin, and when asked, he always named

Indianola as his hometown. But King was long gone by the time Ruth traveled through town on her way to prison, having established himself in Memphis as a radio and live performer, often singing with Bobby "Blue" Bland and Johnny Ace in a group called the Beale Streeters. In 2008, the B. B. King Museum and Delta Interpretive Center opened in what remained of the Indianola cotton gin where he worked, its stated goal "to honor the life and music of one of the most accomplished musicians of our time" and "to share the rich cultural heritage of the Mississippi Delta."

In all likelihood, nobody in the car headed for Parchman Farm had heard of him.

. . . .

On June 29, 1949, in his annual report, the Mississippi State Senate Prison Committee chairman, Senator Fred Jones from Sunflower County, called Parchman's continued use of the lash a "relic of barbarism [that] has no place in an institution provided by the organized society of an enlightened and Christian people for the detention of the delinquent members."

The story ran on page 1 of the Greenville paper, side by side with news of Ruth's conviction and sentence.

But Marvin Wiggins, the prison's superintendent, didn't take kindly to criticism. He issued a statement the next day, denying that acts of brutality occurred at the penitentiary. In addition to which, he added, the responsibility for practices inside the prison was "that of prison officials, not the people of the state or the legislature." In short, nobody's business but his.

Inmates called Wiggins "Mr. Marvin." What they knew was that Mr. Marvin was boss. *His* farm. *His* rules. *His* convicts.

He might have been expected to have the same influence over Ruth's life in the coming years.

. . . .

From two-lane 49W, a dusty road led to a gatehouse manned by a couple of guards, its entranceway protected by a barrier arm that would swing open upon official approval of a would-be visitor. Like a storefront sign, a corrugated aluminum canopy, painted yellow, sat atop the gatehouse.

Imprinted across it, silvery block letters announced the official title of the institution within: MISSISSIPPI STATE PENITENTIARY.

Deputy Clark turned in.

There were no walls. No barbed wire. No guard towers. Nothing inherently forbidding in sight. Cheap building materials and a Dollar General aesthetic lent the entranceway a benign appearance. Nearby, in the grass, a worn billboard, something like an old-time football scoreboard, welcomed visitors while promoting Coca-Cola, the only soft drink the prison offered.

The deputy sheriff drove to the gatehouse and presented the orders Foote had received from Jackson, authorizing him to deliver Ruth Thompson Dickins to the prison.

The barrier arm lifted. Inside the gates, Clark pulled in to a parking place at the administration building.

. . . .

The original state penitentiary was built in 1830 in the heart of downtown Jackson. Called "a source of civic pride . . . rising with feudal majesty," occupying six blocks of the central capital city, it was razed by the Union general William T. Sherman in 1863. Late in the century, the state began a program of renovation, but soon abandoned it in favor of a convict leasing system, leaving the once grand penitentiary to further deteriorate. In 1900, the legislature sanctioned the building of a new state prison, not a replica of the original, but a for-profit penal farm.

After a search for available property, they settled on a sixteen-thousand-acre tract of rich Delta bottomland in north Sunflower County, more than half of which had once been owned by a locally prominent family named Parchman. Intentionally modeled on an antebellum plantation—complete with a superintendent to act as master, prisoners as slaves, sergeants as overseers, assistant sergeants as drivers, and trusties as shooters—the prison and the town that arose around it soon became exclusively known by the name of the family who once lived and farmed there. Its patriarch, J. M. Parchman, rode in on the deal. Appointed the prison's first superintendent because of his experience as a Delta cotton farmer, he moved into the lavishly ornate, Queen Anne–style Big House built especially for him and his family.

By the time the prison opened its gates in 1906, the White Chief—Vardaman—had been elected governor. Reflecting his vision, the Mississippi Code of 1906 defined the state penal system as a "plantation known as Parchman . . . operated by the state in the enforcement of penal servitude."

At the time of his 1944 appointment, Superintendent Marvin Wiggins had been a Sunflower County planter for some thirty-five years. Commenting on his selection, Governor Thomas Bailey praised Wiggins for his thorough familiarity with "Delta agricultural conditions." This made sense. A Parchman superintendent's primary responsibility was to manage crop production at a profit. Inmates, usually close to 90 percent Black men, worked the fields, brought in the crops, and operated the cotton gin, the slaughterhouse, and the brickworks. White drivers rode horseback among them, giving orders, while trusty-shooters, many of them Black, patrolled the grounds on foot, each cradling a .30-.30 Winchester rifle, barrel pointed toward the sky. The superintendent's annual report to the legislature was basically a profit-and-loss statement focusing on the number of cotton bales produced and the prices paid.

Wiggins was a hatchet-faced man, dark hair pasted flat to his high pale forehead, eyes in a perpetual scowl behind rimless glasses, mouth a grim slot. A Mississippi historian described him as a man with "the temperament of a rattlesnake and the eye of a gunfighter." Before moving in, Wiggins had the original superintendent's house torn down and replaced with a ranch-style one-story. More modern, more practical. Fewer geegaws. More to his liking.

To his credit, Wiggins did institute some forward-looking policies. Soon after his appointment, he set up a Christmas furlough system—the first in the nation—based on an inmate's good behavior and a minimum of five years of prior imprisonment. In his six-year tenure, more than fourteen hundred inmates had been awarded ten-day suspensions of their sentences, with—according to his reports—only six cases of late arrival or escape attempts. The approximately three hundred men and women chosen each year were divided randomly into groups of thirty-five to fifty, the furloughs staggered in ten-day intervals between December and the end of March.

Mr. Marvin praised this program as an incentive for good behavior and morale building. He felt similarly about the Sunday "conjugal" visits he allowed male inmates to enjoy without offering legal proof of marriage.

When he was asked if he'd be the one to process Ruth, the superintendent's answer was brisk. "Mrs. Dickins," Wiggins snapped, "will be treated exactly like any other prisoner."

. . . .

Ruth and John said their goodbyes, and he and Deputy Clark drove off. In Greenville, Sheriff Foote—still recuperating at home from his heart attack—phoned *The Delta Democrat-Times* to report Ruth's arrival at Parchman. Asked if John Dickins rode with her, he said he had granted John permission to accompany his wife to prison and "supposed" that Deputy Clark had allowed him to ride with her in the same car.

Inside the building at the front desk, Ruth was assigned an MSP number—19813—and photographed. After which, the registrar entered a summary of her physical characteristics in the official description book. Color of eyes, hair, complexion. Height. Weight.

Once registered, Ruth was taken to the prison hospital, where she was given a full physical examination as well as a psychological screening. She spent her first night there.

. . . .

Parchman Farm housed felons only. Men incarcerated there lived in one of the fifteen "field camps," spread out over the prison's forty-six square miles. Generally, thirteen of the camps were reserved for Black inmates; two for white. Surrounded by a wall and barbed wire, each camp housed as many as 180 inmates along with guards, trusties, and a resident sergeant responsible for every minute of the prisoners' lives, including work and sleep schedules, meals, recreation, discipline, punishment, and furlough recommendation. There was, within each of the fences, a large garden where vegetables served to both prisoners and officers were grown. Inside the dormitories, called "cages," the men slept in bunk beds—"racks"—jammed along the walls, less than three feet apart.

The main job of male inmates, whatever their skin color, was field work, sunup to sundown, six days a week. This might be thought of as a living example of racial equality, but it was bitterly resented by a good many white men, who considered labor in the fields strictly "nigger work."

Black women worked long hours as well. Some canned vegetables, cooked, and, during picking time, worked in the fields. But most of them spent their days hunched over Singer sewing machines making and repairing prison garments and bedclothes. Though their numbers were far lower—maybe ninety to a hundred Black women at any one time, no more than eight whites, usually far fewer—the racial percentages matched the men's.

The women's dresses, made of stiff white duck fabric with broad black stripes running vertically from neckline to hem, were known as "up-and-downs." Full skirted and baggy, the dresses narrowed slightly at the waist, a feature some women sought to improve by applying careful stitches here and there or putting on a white waist-length shirt or cardigan sweater as a kind of spiffy cover-up. Men wore "ring-arounds," loose shirts and pajama-like pants made of the same stiff fabric but with stripes running horizontally. The only men given up-and-downs were the armed trusties, as a distinguishing sign of their highly desirable position as snitches, free to gun down an inmate who ran for home.

The trusty-shooter position was highly prized.

"Only idiots risked their up-and-downs," one inmate cracked.

. . . .

The next morning, Ruth was given her prison dress. Escorted by a guard, she walked the short distance from the administration building to nearby Camp 9. There were fences, a guardhouse, and two buildings: a white brick cottage with benches and a flower garden out front, and—separated from the cottage by only a driveway and a fence—a long metal shedlike structure. The smaller of the two living quarters was Ruth's new home. The large metal building was reserved for incarcerated Black women, who slept the way the men did, in bunk beds lined up close together, military-barracks style.

The cottage, however, was divided into two separate living quarters, called apartments. Ruth was assigned a bunk in one. She would share the space with three other women. There was a bathroom with toilet stalls and showers; a radio; a library; daily newspapers. An additional three women shared the other apartment. Meals were brought to the cottage. The women had two hours off for lunch and worked only until about five. Before supper, they were free to work in the flower garden or read books from the prison library. Afterward, they could sit outside. Not that there was much to see beyond the guardhouse, where a female trusty sat with a rifle across her lap. But relaxing outside in the open air provided the women with a feeling of margins. A break. Breathing room. No men lived anywhere near Camp 9. The nearest building was half a mile away.

Some questionable stories about Ruth's Parchman life still make the rounds. One alleges she was allowed to wear her own clothes; another, that she was given permission to bring her own china and silver from home. There's no proof that either of these privileges was granted, and in all likelihood they weren't. One thing any incarcerated person will tell you is, the first thing a new arrival has to figure out is how to operate within two systems: one defined by the authorities, the other by the inmates themselves.

"I spent the first twenty-four hours I was locked up holding up the walls," a female inmate from Texas told me. By the next night she'd figured out what she had to do. She studied the routines, made her peace with the rules, learned to adjust. And when the rules changed or the makeup of her particular community shifted—new people in, friends transferred out—she found a way to readjust.

Ruth was different enough from the others already, without further emphasizing the gap between them. She was older than the other women, had been to college, read books and the newspaper. Her family came to see her every week. Her husband and daughters believed in her, wanted her home, worked to win her release, looked down on her housemates. And she was a quick study: this cottage, that sewing room, her housemates and workmates, and the guards constituted her world, at least until John found a way to get her out. And if he didn't, he didn't. She had to set long-term expectations and assumptions aside and find a way to work within the hour-by-hour givens.

Had to and did. It seems to me the last thing Ruth Dickins, Latin scholar, college graduate, would want was to stand apart as somehow better than, more entitled than, her new sisters. Her daughters and husband could afford to discriminate against the other women in her behalf, but she could not.

But people love to tell Ruth stories. Once when I was in Greenville, a young man called me aside to relate a story his grandmother had told him. She said she actually met Ruth at Parchman when she toured the prison with a college sociology class. It's not clear how much of the prison the students visited, but she was walking through the white women's cottage when a woman with a low, gravelly voice spoke to her.

She turned. And there stood the infamous Ruth Dickins, easily recognizable to any Mississippian who read the newspaper. She was, according to the grandmother, behind bars. (Not so, a former prison employee told me. There were no bars inside the women's quarters. Or the men's.) Looking quite friendly, if still scary to one predisposed to see her that way.

"I see," Ruth said, pointing to the sorority pin the visiting coed wore on her sweater, "you're a Tri-Delt." And when the surprised student affirmed this, Ruth said, "I'm a Tri-Delt too."

A good story, except for the simple fact that Ruth was a member of Chi Omega sorority, not Delta Delta Delta. Did the grandmother misremember? Make the whole thing up and in time come to believe it really happened? Or was Ruth using her considerable wit to connect with a young visitor if only for the briefest sliver of time, as a way of reaching out to somebody new or perhaps simply to amuse herself on a boring day?

. . . .

I belong to a Facebook page called "You from the Delta Ain'tchu?" From the profile photos people post, a great majority of the members appear to be white and most have, like me, moved away. They write in from afar, sharing photos of themselves taken back in the day or to say how shocked they were when they went back to their hometowns. Those from Clarksdale were dismayed to learn that the last big grocery store, a Kroger, had closed, leaving only Double Quicks and other fast-food marts for local food shopping. In Greenville, the grand old Elks Club had been reduced to a pile of pale green rubble, and even the Salvation Army had packed up and moved to Cleveland, the only town in the

Delta that didn't look if not dead, then dying. Cleveland had attracted a high-tech industry as well as the only Grammy Museum outside Los Angeles. The library of a local college, Delta State University, had just opened a special archives collection.

If any town could call itself Queen City of the Delta these days, it's Cleveland, not Greenville.

I'm not a frequent visitor to Facebook, but one day recently a Rosedale friend said there was a post on the "Ain'tchu" page I needed to see. Willard McIlwain Jr., the son of Ruth's prosecutor, had written in wondering if anybody knew about a Leland woman who'd slashed her aunt to death with hedge clippers. Somebody answered him right away. It wasn't her aunt, they said. It was her *mother*. Other people then contributed anecdotes and witty comments. One woman said the thing she remembered about Ruth Dickins was how she honked her car horn whenever she got behind a slow driver and wanted him to either pull over or speed up. Another person remembered how she used to drive up to the gate of the garden nursery and just sit there honking her horn until somebody came over to take her order. There were also admonitions from relatives, shaming the "Ain'tchu" contributors for making light of a sensitive subject.

After reading the comments, I wrote to Willard McIlwain Jr. privately and said that while I realized he was only two years old when the murder came down, did he remember his father mentioning the trial or saying anything about Ruth?

He remembered only two comments. His father said he received death threats for trying to put Ruth Dickins in prison. And once, when he was working a defense case, he went to Parchman to visit his client and, while he was there, made a side trip to the women's quarters to see Ruth.

When he asked how she was doing, she was ready with a snappy rejoinder.

"Oh," she said with a sigh, "I'm just convicting around."

The prosecutor's anecdote enriched my notion of what Ruth was like and is the one prison story, of all I've heard, that smacks of authenticity.

. . . .

Ruth's new life took on a dependable rhythm. She did her work, kept her religion and her sense of humor, got through weekdays and Saturday knowing Sunday was ahead, when her husband and daughters visited, bringing food, stories, love, and reading materials. They never missed.

. . . .

Ruth was the only Mississippi white woman convicted of first-degree murder in 1949. But in December of that year, one day after the state supreme court ruled against her appeal, an Amite County white woman named Irene Locke Hughes was charged with and held without bail for the first-degree murder of her husband, Talmadge Hughes, a tenant farmer. Known as the Coffee Cup Slayer, Hughes, the mother of two young boys, had confessed to lacing the dead man's morning coffee with strychnine. When she implicated her lover and neighbor, Allie Duck, he too was jailed and charged.

By April 1950, Irene and Ruth were housemates. Though convicted of the same crime and given identical sentences, the two women were unlikely to have heard of each other beforehand. Amite County was located far south of Leland, just north of the instep of the Louisiana boot, culturally a world away from the Delta. Down there, farmers were called farmers, not planters. The two women had only the one unusual circumstance in common.

Irene was assigned to a bunk in the other apartment.

Two months later, a convicted embezzler from Jackson named Janie Brister, once the highest-paid woman in the state tax office, moved in to Ruth's quarters.

. . . .

In no time, Irene Locke Hughes began to chat with her bunkmate Virginia Countryman, a twenty-eight-year-old red-haired escape artist who'd been convicted of grand larceny and sentenced to five years. When Myrtis Blackwell, a short-termer caught forging checks, arrived later that fall, she joined the conversation. The fourth inmate sharing their quarters listened.

Incarceration makes for unusual attachments as well as unspoken, even unforeseen, avoidances. Ruth and Irene might well have turned instantly away from each other. Although each had been convicted of the horrific murder of a family member, an act that landed them where they now lived, one of them was a confessed participant while the other swore it was somebody else.

While Ruth was born into automatic prominence, Irene's biological parents placed her, along with her sister, in an orphanage when she was a tiny baby. When she was two, she was taken to be raised by an older farming couple with no children. By the time she was twelve, her so-called foster father was molesting her. By the time she was sixteen, she'd been married off to a neighbor, also a tenant farmer. At twenty-one, she had two sons and a lover, the neighboring farmer Allie Duck. Needing to get on with her life and be with Duck, she poured a dose of strychnine—locals called it crow poison—into her husband's coffee. He died a horrible death. Quickly arrested, she freely confessed and posed for pictures, lying in her cell in a fluffy bathrobe, combing her long dark hair. When she was sent to prison, history repeated itself when her two small sons were placed in an orphanage.

Other than being convicted of first-degree murder for the brutal slaying of a close family member, the two women had little in common except whatever memories they retained of that event. A circumstance that more than likely sealed the chances of their estrangement.

Obviously, I don't know that. But from what I know from other imprisoned people, it seems likely. On her part, Ruth took up instead with the churchgoing Janie Brister, a professional woman who'd been convicted of a white-collar crime executed in order to support and care for her dying mother.

. . . .

Back in Greenville, my family life continued on the upswing, socially, personally, and, as far as I knew, financially. My father was still traveling, but he'd also introduced a new kind of service to the town, something like the Instacart of today. Called City Delivery Service, it offered residents a way to get anything from prescriptions to a piano delivered to their door. Within a few months, he expanded. At City Delivery Service Rent-a-Car, customers could rent cars by the hour, the day, or the week. He'd also managed to become the local agent for Inter-city Trucking, a southern-based moving and storage company. He was gathering ground, ginning up speed, taking out jazzy, high-pitched advertisements in the paper. On the move. Establishing a larger presence.

Because in the Delta dancing was everything, three of my friends and I marked the occasion of our elementary school graduation with a dance at the community center, hosted by our parents. I was two months shy of twelve and wore a pale green evening dress, taffeta with a layer of net on top. My date sent a yellow carnation corsage. In a photograph taken that night, I look breathlessly happy and so does he. Our faces shine with youthful, unimpeded delight, mine in particular: the night before, my mother had given birth to a baby boy. Not Judith Marie. Edward Lawson. We adored him totally.

In Leland, John Dickins added a wing off the kitchen of his house for his cousin Allee Brown, who moved in as a kind of nanny for his daughters. Dell's name appeared regularly in the newspaper. She attended parties, competed in oratory contests, did theater work, and played tennis in statewide doubles matches. She and Dorothy Jane both went to camp, though not together and not to the same camp. Dell stayed within state bounds, while Dorothy Jane and one of her friends traveled to North Carolina. Dorothy Jane played in a group piano recital. Knowing his daughters were cared for and were living a fairly normal life in spite of everything gave John the freedom to pursue the goal that soon consumed his life: getting his wife out of prison. He had allies, including the powerful chairman of the Mississippi house Ways and Means Committee, Representative Hilton Waits from Leland.

Waits's support gained public notice when, shortly after Ruth's arrival at Parchman, a bill came before the house reducing family visits to the prison from two hours every Sunday to one visit a month. Specifically citing Ruth as a mother of children who wished to see their confined parent as often as possible, he vowed never to stand by and see that privilege reduced or taken away.

The legislators who sponsored the bill quickly backed down.

What John knew was that springing Ruth depended on steering a path directly to the governor's office. To accomplish which, he needed Waits's help.

. . . .

That same year, 1950, Leland became one of only a few districts in the
state to organize a "colored" consolidated school district. The city subsequently approved a $75,000 bond issue to pay for construction of a new
high school—which was, the mayor bragged, fully accredited—that, once
completed, was considered one of the finest "Negro" schools in the state.

Unspoken was the ulterior motive of white voters: to safeguard the
unimpeded racial segregation of schoolchildren and confirm the "separate but equal" stance that states' righters like the current governor
worked to perpetuate. Also kept hush-hush was the indisputable fact
that despite claims of an ongoing process of racial "equalization," the
state was spending three times more of its educational budget on white
schools than Black.

To residents of both races, this was business as usual in the state of
Mississippi.

. . . .

Ruth's forty-fourth birthday came and went.

In August, Sheriff Hughey Foote suffered his final heart attack at
home. Although his widow declined to run for the remainder of his
term, she did ask the city for some "small benefit" that would have
accrued to him, especially—she didn't say this—if he'd lived to continue
collecting tax money from bootleggers.

The second anniversary of Idella Thompson's murder, November 17,
passed without notice.

Christmas Eve fell on a Sunday, which gave Dell and Dorothy Jane
Dickins an opportunity to celebrate the afternoon with their mother.
The day was warm and muggy. No rain. They could sit outside.

David Fey appeared as Santa Claus at a party given for a dozen or so
children attending the Junior Auxiliary Nursery School. His snow-white
beard was glued to his face with spirit gum so that children could tug
it with all their might without loosening a hair. His bright red velvet
suit, trimmed in pure white bunny fur, was impeccable. The children
surrounding him look starry-eyed and happy, and so does he.

SUSPECTS, ESCAPES, CAPTURES, AND RUTH

JANUARY 1951

Ruth's appellate attorney, W. D. "Buck" Conn, had been writing to Governor Fielding Wright for months, asking him to grant permission for his client to visit Whitfield, the state mental institution. Charlie Ferguson, a Whitfield escapee one newspaper referred to as a "Negro homicidal maniac," had recently been recaptured after spending almost three years on the lam. Authorities found him working in a cotton field near Leland.

Ferguson had confessed in 1947 to a double murder, and he'd been in the Delta when Idella Thompson was killed. He was also tall and muscular, in no way matching Ruth's description, but Buck Conn thought Ruth had the right to view a lineup of Black men, to see if she could identify him as her mother's murderer.

Conn didn't come up with this notion on his own. Though no longer on the Thompson payroll, the Jackson private investigator A. E. Crawford had never stopped searching for a suspect who even slightly fit Ruth's description. And so, hearing of the fugitive's capture, he took it upon himself to look into the escapee's whereabouts during his years at large. He had even visited a few of the young man's relatives.

Conn was not filing a formal appeal, nor was he requesting a hearing. He was asking the governor for special treatment. When Stanny Sanders heard about the request, he protested. In his opinion and in the minds of other state officials, Mrs. Dickins had been given a fair trial before an impartial jury that unanimously voted her guilty of murder, and five and a half months later the Mississippi Supreme Court unanimously confirmed the verdict, having declared her guilt "conclusively determined."What gave her the right to challenge lawfully determined, unambiguous decisions?

Greenville police officers and investigators made no comment. Hughey Foote was dead. The lawyer and former state legislator Scott Thompson (no relation to Idella) had been elected to serve the last two years of his term. But Sheriff Thompson had no personal stake in Ruth's fate. And no call to step into a situation that might well resolve itself without his participation.

When Governor Wright granted Conn's request, Marvin Wiggins— who served as Parchman superintendent at the governor's pleasure—had no choice but to comply. And so it happened that on January 5, 1951, less than a year after Ruth arrived at Parchman, two armed guards loaded her into a state vehicle and headed toward Whitfield, Mississippi.

Parchman to Jackson's about 135 miles, a nice drive straight through the Delta—Drew, then Ruleville, Indianola, Belzoni. Just past Yazoo City, the highway crosses the river the town was named for, then comes to the trip's first ridges and hills. There the Delta ends.

Ruth, of course, loved road trips, and this one must have particularly pleased her: two or so hours to Jackson, the same coming back, no Singer machine whirls and clackings, no guards watching over her every move, nothing to do but feel the motion of the car and watch out the window as the dirt changed from black to rust and, as if on command, the generous shade trees of the Delta—the tap-rooted oaks and pecans, the sycamores and sweet gum—vanished, replaced by the cool distance of tall, stalwart pines.

For most of us, the sudden change never fails to remind us where we came from. The shift in the landscape is startling. To me, the pines seem unfriendly, somehow threatening. I'm always relieved when, traveling into the Delta, the big climbables of my past show up.

. . . .

Reaching Jackson, the trio veered into Rankin County with only ten miles to go. Although it was originally named the Mississippi State Lunatic Asylum, and later refashioned as the Mississippi State Insane Hospital and then the Mississippi State Hospital, everybody I knew called it Whitfield, which historians dismissed as its "colloquial" title.

None of us knew it as anything else or that Whitfield was actually a town named for a governor. Everything we knew about mental institutions came from the 1948 movie *The Snake Pit*. For us, Whitfield and snake pits were synonymous.

As with all Mississippi institutions, race determined the asylum's map, its architecture, and the rhythms and routines of its everyday life. There were two campuses, one for Black inmates, one for white, widely separated by acreage and an imposing administration building.

Presumably, Ruth was taken to the white people's building and escorted by Parchman guards to a seat between the director of the asylum and a staff physician. A couple of newspapers claimed that Buck Conn was also there, but he said he was in Jackson at the time and had nothing to do with the lineup; matter of fact he didn't know Ruth had been to Whitfield until somebody told him.

And by the way, he added, he'd hoped to get the viewing done without "all this publicity." Unfortunately, however, it "got out of hand."

. . . .

The "hopelessly insane" Charlie Ferguson had been sent to the state mental hospital after confessing to the murder of the elderly Black shopkeepers Charlie and Mabel Baskin, following an argument over the purchase of a five-cent candy bar. The store where the dispute took place was a small, isolated establishment located on the Claude Romine plantation, about fifteen miles from Leland, just off the Tribbett Road, in Tralake, in Washington County, not far from where Ruth's sister, Mildred, lived with her family. Having lost the argument, Ferguson stormed out. The store stayed open late. In winter, the sky out where it was, in the middle of nowhere, turned black early. Once it was dark, Charlie left home armed with a loaded shotgun and a blackjack. Arriving at the store, he burst in and without a word shot Mabel Baskins in the face, blasting her head from her body. Before the old man could move or speak, Charlie beat him to death with the blackjack. And went back home.

Quickly caught, he freely admitted the killings.

He was not yet twelve years old.

Too young to be tried, he was sent to Whitfield and locked up in the disturbed ward. Seven months later, he escaped, reportedly by bending the bars of his cell. Although he spent the whole time he was out with various family members, he remained at large until July 1950.

Once A. E. Crawford heard where he'd been found and what he'd done to get himself locked up, he notified Buck Conn, who wrote to the governor.

. . . .

The lineup was extensive. Fourteen young Black men, some of them inmates, some attendants. Ruth made her choice. That one, she said, pointing at Charlie Ferguson. When, later that day, she was presented with a photographic lineup, she chose Ferguson again. In a face-to-face meeting with Ruth, the young man said he'd never seen her in his life.

He was sixteen when Ruth fingered him. That would put him at thirteen or fourteen when Idella was killed. A boy. A very big boy, strong enough to bend iron and beat a man to death with a blackjack, therefore, surely capable of killing a small, elderly woman in many fewer strokes than Idella suffered, as well as easily preventing a woman of Ruth's size from wresting a pair of pruning shears from his grasp.

Here are a few of the headlines the next day: "Mrs. Dickins Claims Insane Negro Murdered Her Mother," the *Hattiesburg American;* "Mrs. Dickins Fingers Negro from Whitfield as Mother's Attacker," Jackson *Clarion-Ledger;* "Ruth Dickins Points Finger at Negro Homicidal Maniac," the *Greenwood Commonwealth*. Other stories appeared in newspapers in Lubbock, Texas; Montgomery, Alabama; and all over the South.

. . . .

Ruth was returned to Parchman that same afternoon. In a fairly inscrutable postscript, Buck Conn assured the public that even though his client had identified the slayer, he was not personally, under the present conditions, "asking anyone as of now to believe it."

Four days later, Charlie Ferguson's aunt and grandmother emerged to declare that Charlie was with them from October 1948 until close to Christmas, when he left to look for his mother. They lived three hours south of Leland, in McComb. Investigators searched school records to find out if he registered for classes there, but nothing turned up.

Charlie's mother confirmed the information. Her son, she said, had spent Christmas 1948 with her, in the Delta, near Leland, in Bourbon, Mississippi. Before that, he was in McComb.

. . . .

Some people considered the women's statements suspect, but the aunt was a respected schoolteacher, and her testimony must have seemed too solid to contradict; otherwise, Buck Conn, A. E. Crawford, and John Dickins would have jumped on it. Instead, they all seemed to put Ruth's identification of Charlie Ferguson behind them as a worthwhile possibility going nowhere.

But Ruth's name was never out of the news for long, whether for reasons directly related to her case and her family or, as sometimes happened, because of events she was only tangentially connected to.

Two weeks after she returned from Whitfield, late on the night of Saturday, January 20, three of her housemates—the chatty women in the other apartment, namely Irene Locke Hughes, Myrtis Blackwell, and Virginia Countryman—set off a sizable storm when they got together and, on a sudden whim, decided to abscond.

According to Irene Hughes, the women didn't spend a lot of time making plans.

"We just decided to do it," she said. "And we did it."

It was past 11:00 p.m. by the time the women had, in time-honored Hollywood fashion, rolled clothes and towels into a lengthwise bundle and put them under their blankets to look like sleeping bodies. The house was quiet. The resident sergeant had conducted bed check and gone home. If Ruth or any of the other women heard anything, they didn't say so.

When the caper was discovered at 8:30 the next morning, the inmates' means of escape became obvious: they had piled a table and some chairs underneath a ceiling ventilator to create what a guard described as a "precarious pyramid"; then one by one climbed up it, careful not to dislodge the furniture. The first to make it to the top removed the ventilator cover and set it aside, then "wiggled" into the attic. The others followed.

All three women were small—between five three and five five, 105 to 117 pounds—and could easily fit. Once they'd made it into the attic, they replaced the covering, crawled across the floor to another ventilator shaft, removed its cover, let themselves down into a different room, and made it "through a front window and across a field to Highway 61" without a hitch.

By 11:30, the three women were on their way.

I nominate red-haired Virginia Countryman as instigator of the decampment. Sentenced to five years by circuit court judge Arthur Jordan for drugging and robbing a plumber, she'd staged a breakout from the Washington County jail when, while waiting to receive her sentence, she and a male inmate managed to make a run for it. They were quickly spotted and returned to their cells. Nonetheless, Countryman had clearly demonstrated a yen to flee and the ability to persuade others to join in. Otherwise, why would Myrtis Blackwell, an accountant who'd been sent up for two years for forging checks, make the inexplicable choice to take part when she'd already served half her term?

The third runner was twenty-two-year-old Irene Locke Hughes, the Coffee Cup Slayer. The fourth roommate knew about the plan, but didn't take part.

A Saturday night escape made sense. Sundays, Parchman life slowed. Prisoners got the day off to relax, attend religious services, play softball, listen to the radio, write letters. Men visited the "red room," where they engaged in quick sex with women they swore were their wives. Lucky inmates like Ruth awaited the arrival of family.

By the time the precarious pyramid was discovered, the three absconders had caught a ride to Clarksdale, twenty-five miles away, and were soon on their way north through the state, into Tennessee, heading for Missouri.

Irene Hughes told a reporter she was forced to participate. "They made me go along," she explained. "For fear I'd talk." But Irene was known for blaming other people for her actions, a habit that brought her few friends and made for a lot of resentment. In addition to which, she'd already tried to escape prison life when, after only a month inside, she cut her wrists. Her intent might have been serious, but either she made the cut wrong or whoever found her got there fast enough to save her life. Because of the nature of the crime she'd confessed to, her unapologetic abandonment of her children, and her willingness to talk about the murder of her husband, she'd already been taken to Whitfield for one psychological exam. After the suicide attempt, she was sent back for another but once again was pronounced sane.

Unlike Ruth, Irene craved attention, whatever its origin and aim. When the other two women kept going north, she turned back, made it to Arkansas, where she visited her "foster" parents, who'd moved there, and then flagged a ride to Blytheville, where she turned herself in to the local police and happily agreed to an interview with the local press.

Once again, Irene made the news. Her crow poison story was lapped up by an audience within and beyond the state lines of Mississippi and Arkansas. Prettily photogenic, when pictures were snapped, she widened her eyes and looked straight into the camera lens. And she revealed the strategy of their breakout and described its progress, through two states and into a third and fourth . . . a first, not just for Mr. Marvin, but for Parchman Farm itself.

Her fame was short-lived. Three days after turning herself in, she'd been returned to the white stone cottage inside Camp 9. Her fellow fugitives, Countryman and Blackwell, were picked up in St. Louis a month and a half later. The three women were labeled troublemakers and put under twenty-four-hour lockdown. They worked and ate where they lived, isolated from Ruth and the other inmates.

Irene's twenty-third birthday came and went.

People end their own lives for various reasons, but mostly it comes from the inability to see a bearable way forward. Having never spent time making a plan in her life, in all likelihood Irene didn't make one on this occasion either. On July 23, 1951—one day short of six months after she was returned to Parchman from Blytheville, Arkansas—she stripped an electric wire from a lamp, took it into the bathroom, and hanged herself. This time she made it out. Her body was discovered at midnight.

Next of kin were informed, but nobody showed up to claim her remains. She was buried in the Parchman Farm Cemetery. Her story ends there.

. . . .

Or does it? Ruth was there. She knew Irene. Heard the commotion surrounding the breakout, the dismantling of their escape route, the return of Irene and later the other two. And could not have escaped the ruckus when Irene's body was discovered or the sight of it, bagged and being removed. A young woman, half Ruth's age.

One of the few public comments she made about her years in Parchman was "I think I did some good there."

Ruth never mentioned Irene. Or any of her other housemates. But Ruth was Ruth. She liked to be in on things. Wanted to help, liked taking charge, was especially drawn to young women. She had daughters, taught Sunday school to girls.

Certainly she would have been affected by, would have mourned, the young woman's lonely death. And, as the good Baptist she was, she would have doubtless prayed for her soul.

. . . .

Six months after Charlie Ferguson's aunt and grandmother provided testimony clearing him from the Idella Thompson murder charge, he again escaped from Whitfield, by slipping out the back porch door with the garbage detail.

Familiar with Ferguson's slipperiness, the state police wasted no time sending flyers to police departments and newspapers all over the state.

A week later, he was nabbed in another cotton field near Greenville. The Washington County sheriff, Scott Thompson, had gone to Rolling Fork with a deputy to arrest an unrelated suspect and there was Charlie, in a line of cotton pickers, calmly filling his burlap sack. Thompson recognized him right off. When he drew on him and told him to put his hands up, Charlie refused. He wasn't, he said, the right man. But he quickly gave that up, and Thompson took him to the county jail to wait for somebody from Whitfield to come get him.

Ferguson didn't want to go back. He wasn't insane, he said. He wanted to stand trial. In Greenville.

For murder?

Yes.

Sheriff Thompson listened to his plea but said nothing when the Whitfield detail arrived and transported him back to the asylum, where Charlie Ferguson was once again put behind lock and key in the disturbed ward.

LETTERS FROM LELAND

Toward the end of 1951, while John Dickins was gathering support for a petition he planned to send to the parole board, three letters arrived in Governor Wright's office: two supporting clemency for Ruth in the form of either parole, pardon, or the suspension of her sentence, the other one taking an adamant stand against her discharge.

The first voluntary pro-Ruth appeal came from Emmett Harty, a Greenville lawyer and municipal judge who was, he wrote, "interested in and troubled about Ruth Thompson Dickins to the extent that she has rarely been out of my thoughts since her incarceration." He had known her since she was a child, playing around on his office floor with another child, and he knew her to be "kind, generous to a fault, a good wife and mother." Considering all of that, it was inconceivable to him that she could be guilty of the heinous crime of which she was convicted.

But Ruth's innocence was not the basis of Harty's plea for clemency. She had been, he argued, deprived of her constitutional right to a fair and impartial jury and had, in addition, paid her debt to society for "whatever crime she may have committed."

Including, presumably, murder.

To support his argument, Harty sneered sarcastically at the "godly, Christian people of Leland" who not only had convinced themselves of her guilt within twenty-four hours of the murder but also had set about with the zeal of witch-hunters "by hue and cry to bring everyone else in the county to their point of view." Newspapers, he added, "rendered invaluable assistance"; dime detective magazines attempted to prove "by innuendo and the attendant circumstances" that Ruth alone could have committed the crime. The presumption of innocence that rightfully was hers was lost. And "Ruth stood guilty by public opinion long before she was ever brought before the bar of justice."

He went on at some length, describing the raucous behavior of the curiosity seekers who attended the trial and the circus-like atmosphere in the courtroom, and ended by describing Ruth as "a woman gently reared" who'd been torn from her husband and children, forced to spend two years in the "closest association with prostitutes, thieves and murderers, the *vilest of womankind*."

After wondering what more degrading and cruel punishment the rabble could possibly demand, he urged the governor to order executive clemency and grant "this unfortunate girl" a parole.

A month later, W. E. Bufkin, superintendent of the Leland Consolidated School system, also wrote in on Ruth's behalf, despite, he cautioned, certain unspecified "personal characteristics" she had exhibited, of which he disapproved. That aside, her husband and her fine young daughters needed her, and as far as Bufkin was concerned, her release on parole would harm no one. He too believed she'd been convicted on rumor as well as the physical inadequacy of her defense attorney, who, he reminded the governor, died soon after the verdict was rendered.

While the signers of the third letter realized that many people of "prominence and influence" had endorsed John Dickins's petition to the parole board, they on the other hand felt that Ruth had been afforded a fair and impartial trial. And that the evidence indicated her guilt. "If guilty when convicted less than three years ago of so heinous a crime," they reasoned, "surely she is yet guilty and her punishment in the sight of the law is not complete."

And while they were aware that the current request for parole had been subscribed to by many local people, they would not themselves endeavor to collect a large number of signatures. The governor should understand, however, that they were expressing the views and convictions of a "larger and equally interested number."

Some surprising names appeared at the bottom of this letter, including the new Delta Debutante Club leader, Mrs. Lawrence L. Paxton, and her husband, several members of the Dean, Aldridge, Branton, Hebron, and Allen families, as well as Ruth Mathis, whose daughter was married to a Stovall.

Letters to and from Mississippi governors are routinely archived. But if Governor Fielding Wright responded to these appeals, his letters did not make it into his files.

. . . .

In December, Hilton Waits and Buck Conn filed John Dickins's petition. Signed by some seven hundred supporters from all over Washington County, it asked the parole board to recommend "action favorable to" Ruth to the governor. Although a person serving a life sentence wasn't legally eligible for parole until after ten years, a Mississippi governor had the power to grant, at his pleasure, either a suspended sentence or a pardon.

Wright was on his way out. When the incoming governor, Hugh Lawson White, was inaugurated in early 1952, he would have the right either to approve or to countermand Wright's decision. But John Dickins didn't want to wait. He was hoping to get something done right away.

"I am convinced of my wife's innocence," he told *The Delta Democrat-Times,* "and I am not through investigating." What happened to Ruth was "a case of emotion sweeping the area" in which people grabbed on to circumstantial evidence and enlarged it, far out of proportion. They also said a lot of unproven things about her family. He'd known the Thompsons for more than twenty years and never found anything out of the ordinary about them.

"We are," he said, "people, just like anybody else." Solid Christians. At the time of her mother's murder, he reminded readers, Ruth was teaching thirteen-year-olds in Sunday school; they belonged to the Leland First Baptist Church, where he was the Sunday school superintendent.

"Those kinds of people," he blithely asserted, including himself and his wife as members of *those kinds,* "don't commit murder."

Among the signers of the petition were five members of Ruth's jury, twenty-three out of a total twenty-seven members of the Washington County Bar Association, the foreman of her grand jury, three members of the board of supervisors, and so on. John's likability and reputation having become an irresistible pull toward support for him and the "girls," people signed without thinking, often without considering Ruth's guilt or innocence or the murder of Mrs. Thompson at all.

The petition came around. A local resident told me her mother said. *The same names were on it every time. We all signed. When it came back around, we signed it again.*

I think once the jury said, "Guilty as charged," my friends and I forgot about Ruth Dickins, or if we didn't exactly forget, we didn't dwell on her anymore. The petitions were only paper. John said the same thing over and over again. And anyway, hadn't Ruth been sentenced to remain in prison for the rest of her natural-born life?

. . . .

To celebrate Christmas that year, the Dickinses went to great lengths to decorate their living room in cheerful Santa Claus array. Family gathered. Below their house, beyond the Drive, the creek was once again lit up, lights and floating Christmas trees attracting lines of pedestrians and cars that sometimes, at the end of the Drive, circled on a dirt U-turn road to the other bank, making the elongated circle again.

Parchman rules didn't allow for special holiday visits, but on Christmas Day the prison kitchen ramped up. Organized by the state dietitian, a sumptuous meal was served to the entire prison population, guards, trusties, office workers, convicted murderers, and petty thieves alike. Inmates got the day off. Carols were sung. Games played. Bibles read. Small gifts exchanged.

Ruth joined in while at the same time looking ahead, as she always did, toward the day her week aimed for: Sunday, when her family returned.

. . . .

One of the 1951 snapshots my mother held on to is of herself with her three children, sitting beneath the Christmas tree. She and I are wearing short satiny lounging jackets over our pajamas. David is sporting a stocking cap and holding a big teddy bear. The center of our attention, Eddy, is wearing a footed onesie, sitting in my mother's lap, and pointing at something in a picture book.

On the back, Mama wrote, "Eddy's first Xmas in G'ville. Bev is 12. D.Jr 9yrs old. Wonderful year. 1951." The underline is hers. A new baby, a magazine dream house reborn as home. Inspired by a magazine article, she'd spray-painted our Christmas tree a soft pink. She was happy.

A NEW YEAR

Cyndi Lauper says girls just want to have fun. Maybe she's onto something—about some girls at any rate. Others of us go for broke in another direction. Our quest, during our growing-up years within the nest of parents and siblings, is to be the girl of the girl of the collective American daddy's dream, unblemished, accomplished, in a word, perfect. The girl other daddies hope their daughter will exactly mirror.

Dell Dickins might have been one of those girls.

Nineteen fifty-two's a big year for her. Winner of oratorical contests, actress in plays, future class valedictorian, competitor in regional tennis tournaments, nonstop busy, she's a top all-around senior, graduation and college in sight. Early in the year, she's also entering her final days as a member of the Leland Junior Cotillion Club, known locally and throughout the Delta as a kind of rehearsal squad for those girls who hope or even expect to receive a late summer bid to membership from the mother of all invitation-only social clubs, the Delta Debutante Club.

By New Year's Day, she'll be ready for her presentation at the grand Junior Cotillion ball, held the first Friday night in January. Gown sewn up, white gloves purchased, hoopskirt bands inserted, she'll have chosen her escort. Attended rehearsals. Invited a girlfriend from Tunica to sleep over and enjoy the festivities. Included Dorothy Jane in the preparations. Depended on her aunt Mildred to take Ruth's place as substitute mother.

Historically, cotillions were organized to teach girls etiquette and manners: how to sit, stand, and curtsy, when to wear white gloves, how to perform certain dance steps. In the Delta, cotillions adhered to a stringent schedule. Sub-Deb Cotillion Club issued invitations to tenth-grade girls. Membership at this level came easy. But Junior Cotillion membership was harder to come by. Fewer invitations issued. More girls excluded.

During the week preceding the Leland ball, parties were nonstop. Thursday night, Dell hosted a buffet dinner in her home. For the occasion the family left the Christmas decorations up, including a mantelpiece Santa in a sleigh pulled by reindeer created from popcorn balls and cookies, its runners resting on waves of snow fashioned from hardened cake frosting. Cotillion members and their parents filled the small living and dining rooms of the Dickins house.

Some four hundred young people from all over the Delta were said to have attended the ball itself, which didn't begin until 10:00 p.m. and lasted until 2:00 in the morning with an intermission party at midnight. The Burt Taggart Orchestra, an all-white swing and 1930s-style band from Greenville, played. The high point of the evening, when outgoing members and their escorts were introduced, was emceed by John Aldridge, who—perhaps unknown to Dell and her father—had just signed a petition sent to the state parole board, protesting clemency of any kind for Ruth.

Dorothy Jane and I turned fourteen in 1952. At that age, we didn't yet matter much, socially speaking. We were still just *girls.* But our time approached. Sub-Deb membership was ahead. I would get into that one, but missed out on an invitation to the Junior Cotillion the next year. From what were then called the society pages of 1950s Delta newspapers, the importance of these girl-focused rituals becomes clear. Like lines drawn on a door frame marking the growth of children, by their membership in invitation-only clubs did select teenage girls contribute to the established social order, also known as *our way of life.* There were other, less fanciful forms of measurement. But none less enduring.

The long-established drill went girl by girl, exclusion by exclusion, year by year, providing assurance to those on top that life as they knew it would never change. Once a girl made it through the cotillions and had turned eighteen and made her debut, she was pretty much finished as society news until the day she announced her engagement to be married.

No more fervent wish filled the hearts of those who lived *almost* on the line of social acceptability during these years than to be included. To, by the social standards of our community, *matter.*

None of us considered the possibility that our desire to be invited to wear the hoop-skirted formal and elbow-length white gloves contributed to the continuance of something as darkly suggestive as white supremacy. If asked, we would have laughed. *Us?*

. . . .

Once the final Saturday morning breakfast had ended and Dell's guest had gone back to Tunica, the Dickinses switched gears. On Sunday, immediately following church services, they packed the car and headed for Parchman, arriving in time to be with Ruth by 1:30, when visiting hours began. Weather permitting, they ate and visited outside. On this particular Sunday, they had much to talk about. Ruth certainly would have wanted to hear about the buffet dinner. The ball. Dell's dress. Her escort. What part Dorothy Jane might have played. And there was the upcoming parole board hearing on Tuesday, only two days hence. The girls would make their plea and so would Ruth's sister, Mildred. Hundreds of petitions supporting Ruth's release had arrived on the board's desk. Word was, the opposition had enjoyed far less success, having persuaded only sixty people to sign on.

At 3:30, the girls and John headed back home. Ruth returned to her quarters.

. . . .

In Greenville the next day, John made a formal statement. Because of "a new and cruel rumor that they don't want their mother to come home," he had asked his daughters to go to Jackson with him, to appear before the parole board. It was hard to understand, he said, why a handful of people would resort to lies at the expense of children. The whole family knew Ruth was innocent. And the girls wanted their mother home, where she belonged.

Dell and Dorothy Jane's testimony, if recorded, was not archived, but when questioned afterward, Dell was poised and ready. "I've been without a mother all through high school," she told the army of reporters before her. "And now I'm graduating in June." She stopped. Her sister joined her. Standing side by side, the two girls refuted the rumors. They said simply, "We want our mother home."

As for John, he repeated much of his Greenville statement, with a notable addition. "When this tragedy happened in 1948," he said, "people in Leland were in a frame of mind to believe anything because of short tempers about the heavy cotton crop and the scarcity of pickers"—an interesting cotton buyer's take on a community response to financial anxiety and the postwar draining of the labor force due to the migration north of Black families.

"Ruth," he continued, "was convicted on gossip, rumor, and circumstantial evidence," and if he'd thought for one minute she was guilty, he'd have had her plead self-defense or insanity. But she was innocent. The jury had made a mistake. As for Ruth, she was adamant about one thing. Whatever the parole board decided, she would never say she killed her mother, even if she had to stay in Parchman for the rest of her life.

"She said a Negro did it," John declared. "And I believe her."

There are those who wonder if he really did. Or if perhaps his determination to prove himself right and to get his wife out of prison and back home with her family didn't take precedence over his secret awareness of her guilt. Mrs. Thompson had been dead now for more than three years. John's declaration that "a Negro did it" served its purpose without unfairly singling out any particular person. In addition, by this time, he'd become a kind of celebrity in the press, interviewed, pressed for statements. To best serve his cause, he'd created a public self.

He then went on to make a curious case concerning his wife's mental state. To confirm her sanity, he declared, Ruth was willing to take any kind of psychological test the state wanted to throw at her. And he, in turn, was ready to accept whatever conditions they came up with. Or so he claimed before correcting himself by setting down stipulations. One, that the examination take place in a private institution. Another, that the family be allowed to hire its own physician to observe and make an independent diagnosis.

And there was a kicker: once Ruth was proven sane, she got her freedom.

Drawing a line in the sand, making demands as if he held all the cards, was, without doubt, a bold and fairly high-handed move on John's part. It's also hard to figure why he's proposing that a successful test of Ruth's sanity might serve as her ticket out when only people deemed sane qualified for imprisonment. But John Dickins was a cotton man, a trader who gambled in high-stakes odds and, when necessary, played a cutthroat game. He was used to all-out competition. And to winning.

Having made his offer, he returned to safer ground. There was, he said, a conspiratorial group of "five individuals who don't even live in Leland" who were "spreading vicious gossip and influencing Leland citizens to spread erroneous rumors," accusing him of making large payoffs to the Hugh White election campaign as a way to influence the new governor's decision regarding Ruth. Anyone who knew John Dickins knew that, as one of the good guys, he would not stoop to do anything underhanded to influence this or any other case. As for the campaign contribution rumor, he had never donated as much as a penny to a political campaign.

He finished up with a bit of good news. He'd just learned that some of the signers of the petition protesting Ruth's release had asked for their names to be withdrawn. On the downside, however, he had it from the head of the parole board that some of those same counter-petitioners— he referred to them as "that group"—had raised $50,000 to keep Ruth in prison. An allegation he never backed up or repeated.

. . . .

On his way out of office, Fielding Wright pardoned eight Parchman prisoners and indefinitely suspended the sentence of another. All nine were Black men serving sentences ranging from seven years to life, six for murder, three for manslaughter. And all were personally known to him, having worked in the executive mansion, serving his family, during his administration.

Asked about Ruth, he said, "I have not considered any action in the Dickins case. I do not intend to take any action in it." He didn't mention the parole board.

In his farewell address to the state legislature, Wright stood firmly behind "separate but equal" educational facilities, touting his sponsorship of new Negro schools and colleges and recommending racially equalized teacher pay while insisting on the retention of "our segregation program." When accused of having used the word "nigger" fifty-seven times in a radio speech, he denied the charge, insisting he'd been careful to enunciate "Negro" each time.

He also thought the state should do away with its practice of transporting its portable electric chair—there was only one—from one county to the next so that the condemned man could be publicly electrocuted in the place where the crime was committed. For those who supported capital punishment the reasoning behind this made some sense. But executions attracted such big crowds that smaller towns frequently had to cancel and quietly reschedule an electrocution. Wright's solution to the problem was to build a maximum-security cellblock unit at the state prison, with a specially isolated death row for condemned convicts and an execution chamber for the electric chair.

Superintendent Wiggins stood firmly against this idea. Parchman was a *farm,* its goals directed toward work and profit, not cells, solitary confinement, and electrocutions. He made no suggestion of an alternate plan.

. . . .

On Monday, January 14, the parole board announced its decision. It would neither recommend clemency for Ruth nor make any ruling on the case.

Two days later, John read a prepared statement. "When Ruth and I married on January 24, 1929," he said, "we married for keeps. We are determined not to let anything happen that will break up our home or wreck our lives." Ruth was, he said, in good spirits, and he would never give up trying to get her home again. Once again, he blamed her conviction on "small town rumors and amateur detective work."

Ruth dittoed that opinion in a letter written to her family and supporters. Her mind, she wrote, was made up; she'd climb any hills she was asked to climb; she owed that much to her "two angels." And even though it was all discouraging, whatever her family decided to do, they knew her well enough to know she'd say, "Come on, let's go." The letter, written on a lined prison form, had been checked by censors before it was mailed. Ruth ended with a confident "Our sails are open to the blast and I will take them all."

John took the parole board's refusal in stride. In a week, a new man would move into the governor's mansion. John would change nothing. He would simply keep at what he was already doing. For as long as it took to get what he wanted.

A NEW GOVERNOR, ANOTHER SUSPECT

On January 22, 1952, Hugh Lawson White stepped into the Mississippi governorship with the ease of a man slipping his arms into a favorite bathrobe. He'd been there before, having previously served from 1936 until 1940. A large, short man, when elected he was, at seventy, the oldest, the wealthiest, and, at 270 pounds, perhaps the *fattest* man ever to take up residency in the governor's mansion. As proud of his girth as if it were a puppy he'd raised and trained, he was known for bragging about his voracious appetite.

Unlike Fielding Wright—an acknowledged member of the planter aristocracy—he wasn't from the Delta. Born in Pike County, in the southern part of the state, he had previously drifted no farther from home than two counties to the east. In Marion County, he grew wealthy, but not from cotton. From industry. And lumber. That didn't mean he'd necessarily be downright unfair to John Dickins, his wife, or their supporters. He just wouldn't speak the same language and might not lean in the direction of Delta propensities.

. . . .

Less than a week later, on February 1, the murder of Idella Thompson and the trial and conviction of her daughter returned to public attention when a "short, dark 24-year old Negro who gave his name as Arthur Jones" was arrested in Clarksdale, Mississippi, on a charge of "malicious trespassing" after asking for food at a white home. When asked by Coahoma County authorities to list his previous arrests, Jones mentioned being hauled in for stealing a bicycle in Greenville "on the day that white lady was killed in Leland."

The sheriff perked up. The white lady killed in Leland? What else did Arthur Jones recall about that day?

Surprised by the acuity of Jones's memory regarding the murder, the sheriff decided to make a report. Normal protocol mandated a call to Washington County authorities, but he chose instead to inform the man who was still almost as doggedly invested in the case as John Dickins.

By the time A. E. Crawford showed up from Jackson the next day, Arthur Jones had confessed to the murder of Idella Thompson. When Crawford hooked him up to his trusty lie detector to get an official statement, Jones first confirmed the murder, then quickly did a one-eighty. Said he'd never killed anybody in his life.

Crawford told him the machine said he was lying.

When Jones refused to change his story, the PI made a more devastating threat.

He "talked about going to get the preacher," Jones said later. After that, he "told them what they wanted me to tell them."

The next morning, the Greenville police chief, Hollingsworth, headed to Clarksdale with a deputy and his captain, only to find an ambulance parked at the jail. It turned out, Jones had made a noose of his bedsheet and hanged himself in his cell during the night. But when medics applied artificial respiration, he revived. Once he was pronounced fit to travel, the Greenville officers took him in.

Elated, John Dickins called the arrest of Arthur Jones "our first break."

Washington County's sheriff, Scott Thompson, released a statement the next day saying that after Jones admitted and then denied killing Mrs. Thompson, he proceeded to own up to the murders of three other white women, two of them very much alive, including Mrs. Hugh White, the state's first lady. He also confessed to a number of other crimes, both real and imaginary, they knew he didn't commit.

Checking Jones's record, they found that while indeed he had been in Greenville the day of Idella Thompson's murder and was, as he claimed, arrested for stealing a bicycle, he'd been thoroughly interviewed and examined for traces of blood or a struggle. When the officers found nothing, they ceased questioning him.

Because of the conflicting nature of his confessions and his "agreeable reaction to any sort of suggestion," the Greenville sheriff sent Jones to Whitfield for observation. While there, somebody at the asylum decided to take photographs of the two Black men accused of the Thompson murder, standing side by side. The picture was widely published in Mississippi newspapers, presumably as a kind of jokey illustration of the suspects' stark physical dissimilarity. Jones was short, stocky, square shouldered; Ferguson, long-limbed, stoop shouldered, and a full head taller. They were strictly Mutt and Jeff. And because Mrs. Dickins had positively identified Charlie Ferguson as her mother's killer, there was no reason to pursue Arthur Jones further or for Ruth to go to Whitfield to check him out.

. . . .

The next day, February 2, Parchman Farm opened its gates to members of the Mississippi House Penitentiary Committee. Accompanied by selected members of the press, the legislators were there to make their annual inspection tour of the state penitentiary. Because approval of his budget depended on the general drift of the congressmen's report, Superintendent Wiggins made it his business to put on a big show for the occasion, scheduling various forms of entertainment, spiffing up the place, upgrading the meals, making sure inmates understood the importance of the visit.

The legislators' first stop was the women's camp, beginning with a peek inside the uniform plant, where they took in the rows of black Singer sewing machines with their foot-operated treadles and big silver handwheels, as well as the waist-high wooden tables used by inmates who pinned paper patterns to large swatches of fabric and scissored the cloth into uniform shapes. After a brief observation of the women's workroom, the visitors moved on to the small brick cottage nearby, where, according to the *McComb Enterprise-Journal* columnist Charles Hill, seven white women lived.

Five lived together in one large wing; the other two, in a separate, smaller space, to which they were confined, day and night. The latter were of course Virginia Countryman and Myrtis Blackwell, the "troublemakers," who, because of what Hill called their "escapade," had been restricted to quarters for more than a year. But Countryman and Blackwell were happy to talk to the visitors and didn't shy away from discussing their breakout, their subsequent recapture, and the sad fate of their fellow escapee, Irene Hughes.

The men then moved to the larger room, where they met Janie Brister and Ruth.

Brister said she was being well treated and the food was fine. "I never sewed," she cheerfully added. "But I'm doing it now." On the other hand, she did get tired of the restrictions and thought she'd been punished enough "for something I didn't do." When a member of the committee wondered, if she didn't take money from the state tax larder, who did, she crisply said she wasn't sure anybody did.

Ruth echoed Brister. She was, she said, being well treated. She and Brister walked from their quarters to the sewing room every day, to work alongside the Black women. Everything was fine. But when one of the visitors asked about the crime that landed her in prison, Ruth clammed up.

. . . .

The tourists were then led to the Black women's barracks, where, according to the McComb newspaper columnist, every inmate they interviewed was in for manslaughter. None was quoted or named.

In their comments on the men's camps, the legislators downplayed Black Annie. The lash was, they reported, simply a means of discipline, amounting to little more than a stinging spanking. Inmates said if they had to choose between the lash and solitary, they'd take Black Annie every time. Not that Parchman had solitary confinement cells, just making the comparison. To prove how infrequently the lash was used, Superintendent Wiggins showed the committee a record demonstrating that in one 180-man camp, only 57 inmates had been strapped in the past nine months. After checking out other camps and enjoying a sumptuous meal of prison-produced vegetables, fruits, and meat, the touring group left.

Wiggins was equally praised by reporters and committee members. The legislature approved his budget.

. . . .

The Fey and Dickins families puttered along for the next little piece of time.

New ads for City Delivery Service featured my father's photograph and an exhortation that read, "Don't Move Across the Street or Across the Nation Until You See David L. Fey, Agent for Allied Van Lines, Inc."

That last part was new.

. . . .

Dell and Dorothy Jane took a trip to Memphis to see the Ice Follies. I gave my friend Sang a surprise birthday party. David went to an all-boys' birthday party. My girlfriends and I relished any opportunity we could come by to take care of my baby brother and looked forward to the day when we had driver's licenses—at age fourteen and a half—and could take him with us when one of us could manage to get the family car and "ride around." Not just because we adored little Edward Lawson "Eddy" Fey—although we did—but also because he was our ticket into places where boys our age and older gathered.

So life seemed to progress in a steadily set groove for a while. It seemed normal. Until March of that year, when the city tax collector ran a notice in the classifieds announcing a property tax sale, as required by the Mississippi Code of 1942 when assessed taxes had not been paid. Commencing Monday, April 7, 1952, the listed properties would be offered "for sale and sell at public outcry to the highest bidder for cash at the south or front door of the Washington County courthouse . . . continuing from day to day until hereinafter described lands have been sold to the highest bidder for cash."

The notice ran all of March and into April. The only Park Addition property listed belonged to David Fey and wife: the north sixty-five feet of Lot 4, Block 4. That's us. The amount owed, $183.60.

What was up?

. . . .

That same month, when officials at Whitfield declared Arthur Jones sane and sent him back to the Washington County Jail, John Dickins again spoke out.

"Before the recent developments in the case which so vitally involve my wife and family become too beclouded and people go off on tangents in their thinking and talking," he wished to remind them of a few pertinent facts: Arthur Jones had been declared sane and had given his confession to the proper Coahoma County officials. He'd taken a lie detector test confirming his confession and was found hanging in his cell the next morning, a sure sign of guilt.

He asked "every citizen who is head of a family" to ask himself, "If I were John Dickins, and my wife and home were involved and the above facts true, what would I do?" He ended his statement with his usual "All I ask is fairness."

Greenville authorities sent Arthur Jones back to Clarksdale to face the malicious trespass charge. After a short stay, he was released.

. . . .

In Leland, a few days before her graduation, a determined Dell Dickins sat down and on personalized stationery composed a thirteen-page letter to the governor.

"Dear Governor White," she wrote. "I am a nobody and you are the most important man in our state."

As an opener? Brilliant. But then, Dell's a performer. In college, her major will be theater and journalism. She has a yen for drama and is practical-minded enough to know what plays, including a tone of girlish spontaneity. As if she were speaking to him personally, face-to-face.

"Although you don't know me," she admits, "please keep reading my letter—or should I say plea? Yes, this is a plea—a plea of a teenage girl for her mother."

Her handwriting is rounded and continuous, no hiccups, gaps, or decorations, no little bubbles to dot her i's in the popular style of the time. She writes with clarity and has her father's dogged, speechmaking persistence. The one surprise comes on the second page when she casts her mind back to 1949 when the grand jury "indicted Ruth." There might have been other Delta girls who called their mothers by their first names, but I didn't know any, and it certainly wasn't common practice. There's no reason to give particular significance to this, except perhaps to add it to the list of unusual characteristics displayed by the Dickins family. Once you read enough about them, you begin to appreciate their willingness to operate slightly outside the mores and manners of the very tightly wound society within which they lived. And in Ruth's case, with an added smack of upstart humor.

During the time between indictment and trial, Dell continued, when her mother was out on bail, Ruth assured her that no daughter could ever be cruel enough to kill her own mother and that no matter what happened or what anybody said, she was innocent. And Dell was glad she was at camp during the trial so that she didn't have to see the "jeering crowd," the "low-class jury with no respect for the rights of others," and the spectators in the courtroom unleashing "their barbarism" on an innocent woman. Ruth, she wrote, was accused not only of murder but "of insanity and several vices that can't even be put on paper."

Never losing track of her intended audience, Dell often addressed White directly: "Governor White, listen to this plea of a high school senior—a seventeen-year-old girl. I graduate Friday. Could you get Ruth home to see me graduate? Could you?"

She followed that up with a gutsy challenge: "You can, but will you?"

She was valedictorian of her class. In June, she would return to the same camp as before, this time as junior tennis counselor. In September she'd leave for Mississippi College, her father's alma mater. She needed her mother home. And, didn't he realize? The real killer had actually been caught! Arthur Jones, the "negro who killed grandmother . . . confessed to the murder. He's been declared sane." And yet her mother was still in prison with "women having absolutely no background and character."

Dell left few stones unturned. In a challenge to the governor's very manhood, she expressed her certainty that the governor had the "gumption" to make the decision on his own and give her "what rightfully belongs to me—a mother in her home."

She rounded out her plea with the specific request she made on page 1, asking White to "put Ruth in the audience on the night of May Thirtieth, my graduation."

If White responded, no copy of his letter was archived.

Dell graduated, returned to Gulf Park Summer Camp, taught tennis. Came home; got ready for dormitory life at Mississippi College; received an invitation to make her debut on December 30; accepted; celebrated with her little sister, Dorothy Jane, who would now be a shoo-in for her own debutante club invitation in 1956. John drove her to Clinton, helped her get settled in her dorm room. If her mother hadn't been in prison, Dell might well have attended a more exclusive school, somewhere farther away. Hollins perhaps, Ruth's alma mater. Or somewhere else up east. As it was, she'd be close enough to home to stay in touch, to travel to Parchman every Sunday and show up whenever her father or her sister needed her.

. . . .

By this time, Charlie Ferguson had made it out of Whitfield a third time by joining up with another inmate to lock a guard in a closet and steal his keys. After that, escape was a cinch. But the two men were quickly caught, sitting together on the side of a dusty highway in Washington County.

This time, the "eely" Ferguson was given his wish to go on trial rather than return to the insane asylum. Persuaded by his court-appointed lawyer to plead guilty to avoid the electric chair, now that he was old enough to be executed, he appeared before Ruth's judge, Arthur Jordan, who signed off on a mandatory life sentence.

On June 30, 1952, the Long Chain Man headed from Greenville to Parchman with ten prisoners. All were in for short stretches except nineteen-year-old Charlie Ferguson, who would spend at least ten years of his sentence locked up for a murder he committed when he was eleven years old.

His story ends there. Whether Ruth knew of his confinement in Parchman, somewhere beyond the fence surrounding her quarters, is unknown. There is no indication they ever ran across each other and no reason to think they did. But newspapers were delivered to Ruth's quarters every day. She was a reader. Ferguson's incarceration was front-page Greenville news. And he was the man she tagged as the intruder who slashed her mother to death. So maybe she knew. Probably, she did.

. . . .

Meanwhile, my father was running bigger ads, featuring the official Allied Van Lines' logo and illustrations. He'd had a professional photo made. Tan suit, Windsor-knotted tie, big smile.

He began calling himself the Big Mover. Like a lot of scam artists, he often had good instincts regarding odds and the nature of what lay ahead. This one was no exception.

Built in 1940, the Greenville Army Airfield, just north of town, operated during the war years as an airfield, a pilot training school, and an aircraft storage depot. It continued to operate under the auspices of the army until 1946, when it was deactivated, and soon became the home base of a commercial flying school out of Marianna, Florida. But in 1952, because of the Korean War, the company was told its term of operation would end January 1, 1953, when the U.S. military would take control. Which meant that some three hundred families would soon relocate from Greenville to Marianna.

The Big Mover was ready to accommodate them. There was, however, a problem. Allied didn't supply the vans, the warehouse, or the storage facilities. He had to find a way to come by the necessities on his own.

As for the rest of us? All good. Nice house. Big parties. Steaks, booze, stories, music.

By August, our house had been removed from the delinquent taxpayers' list, but a more ominous warning appeared in the *Delta Democrat-Times* Sunday classifieds.

"School Days Are Nearing," a half-page special section advised parents. The potential home buyer should, "for your own and your children's convenience, Buy a Home Near a School."

Below that were ads for houses located near white public schools, complete with photographs. Most were smallish bungalows, except for a handsome two-story "only two blocks from the new high school location and four from Carrie Stern [Elementary]," a "lovely home in a beautiful residential area" with three bedrooms, two and a half baths, hardwood floors, forced air and heat, a fully tiled kitchen. Available at a "most attractive price." The address was 830 South Washington. Our house.

Nothing happened. No sign in the front yard. No agent walking potential buyers through our bedrooms. Within weeks, I started the ninth grade. David entered sixth. Because neither of us saw the ad, we carried on believing we would live in our "lovely home" for as far into the future as we could think.

Maybe my father made a deal to put the house up as security on a loan and, once that was done, would take it off the market, I simply don't know. I figure he must have found a way to convince my mother that *of course* he wasn't going to sell her dream house, he was just working the situation. Everything would be fine.

. . . .

In statewide developments, Governor White began a conciliatory "charm" campaign with Black Mississippians, speaking with members of the newly established Regional Council of Negro Leadership and at Black colleges, promising to bring about a program of true "racial equalization" in public schools throughout Mississippi. In this way, by acknowledging the disparity between the two school systems, White hoped to stanch calls for desegregation. A young Medgar Evers was hired, along with his wife, Myrlie, to work at an insurance company in Jackson. He and other Black leaders joined together to advise members of the RCNL to boycott gas at stations that offered only "white toilets." The tactic worked. "Black toilets" began showing up in the Delta. When Evers also became a member of the National Association for the Advancement of Colored People, he made a move toward the federalization of his cause.

Most white Mississippians disregarded these and other suggestions of coming change.

1952: YEAR'S END

O nce he'd managed to take our house off the delinquent tax rolls
and the real estate market long enough to give him some breathing room, my father could set his next plan in motion. He lined up his
priorities. First he had to make a deal with Graham Aviation School
to move its employees from Greenville to Florida. Then he had to find
an Allied company to supply the vans and drivers he needed to fulfill
the terms of that agreement. And *then* he'd have to come up with the
money to pay his expenses.

In September, he was working nights as part-time pharmacist and
manager of a drugstore not far from our house, when a potential solution
to this particular problem walked in the door.

William C. "Billy" Keady and his family lived on Washington Avenue, not far from us. Born in 1913, the fifth and youngest child of an
Irish immigrant who'd settled in Greenville to work as a saloon keeper,
Keady was born with a deformed right arm, absent forearm and hand.
A determined boy, he played competitive tennis during his high school
years and in 1936 graduated from Washington University in St. Louis
with a law degree, having paid his way through college with scholarships
and part-time jobs. Married by then, he returned to Greenville, where
he practiced law and fathered two children. A model of rectitude, he
maintained a public persona of a man who was upright in the extreme.
Some years after this when he was appointed a federal judge, he became
known around town as simply—suitably—the Judge. Twenty years later,
he dictated a privately published memoir, *All Rise,* to his daughter. In its
pages, he devoted an entire chapter to my father, called "My Business
Ventures."

The Judge—who'd strolled to the drugstore after his dinner to purchase a cigar—was well acquainted with my father, having represented him in "several legal matters." Because the pharmacy was quiet and the two men were "no strangers," my father felt free to pull out a statement of his monthly business receipts and expenses and show them to the Judge, who was impressed enough with what he saw to express an interest in investing a limited amount of capital in the business on one condition: together, they had to persuade two other local citizens to do likewise. Which they did. Rhodes Wasson, an insurance agent, and J. Frank Norris Jr., the local Dodge-Plymouth dealer, soon matched the Judge's $3,000 investment in a limited partnership, naming my father as general operator and manager.

There was, however, a proviso: to check Daddy's numbers, the partners hired a local accountant to submit weekly accounts of the firm's gross profits and expenses. To write the annual report to submit to the state, they engaged the services of my parents' friend L. D. "Rob" Robertson, a licensed CPA.

In September, Mama and Daddy drove to Marianna, Florida, where he met with Graham Aviation executives to persuade them to lend their stamp of approval to his company as official transporters of their employees from Greenville to Marianna. When he left with a contract, Keady had to admit, this "proved that he was quite a salesman."

Within a month, the David L. Fey Storage and Transfer Company held a grand opening at its newly leased warehouse at 337 North Street, on the edge of "colored town." In that Sunday's paper, my father ran a much larger ad. "THE BIG MOVER . . . MOVES," it announced, below which was a more serious photo of him, surrounded by Allied's trademark illustrations: a mama cat carrying her baby in her mouth to illustrate "No. 1 specialist in local moving"; a duck migrating south symbolizing long-distance moving; a kangaroo with a baby in her pouch for packing; and a squirrel storing nuts, for storage. Among the features included at the new location were six cold storage units and one quick freeze; a sealed chamber for the storage of woolens and blankets; cedar-lined cabinets to protect upholstered furniture; racks for storing rugs without stretching or breaking fibers; ample storage space for merchandise, commodity items, and furniture. These were "just a few of the features that will enable the company to give the people of the Delta even more efficient service in storage as well as local and long-distance moving."

A week later, he ran a photograph of himself standing with three drivers beside two of the huge Allied moving vans that would soon begin transporting families from Greenville to Marianna.

He'd also scored another coup when he prevailed upon the Commodity Credit Corporation—a wing of the U.S. Agriculture Department, created to stabilize and support farm income and prices and to "maintain balanced and adequate supplies of agricultural commodities and to aid in their orderly distribution"—to store a large amount of government-owned cheese in the warehouse's cold storage lockers. The processed cheese had been developed during the war for use in military kitchens and in the early 1950s was being distributed to schools, especially those in poverty-stricken areas. It was all but inedible, and there was a big scandal when news came out that CCC was buying product from companies like Kraft and selling it to schools at a higher price. Whatever was going on with the government, the David L. Fey Storage and Transfer Company had happily stored the cheese in its temperature-controlled units, complete with a nationally known brand of automatic sprinklers in case of fire.

All good. The three partners, Keady reported, "were elated as we received weekly reports tending to reflect an excellent profit picture."

. . . .

In November, Governor White made an impromptu visit to Parchman. As farmers all over the state well knew, a prolonged "drouth" had devastated that year's cotton crop, including the nearly sixteen thousand acres grown in the fields of the state penal farm. In an all-day inspection tour, White found the prison's operations in "splendid condition," the prisoners well fed and clothed, all under control. On the other hand, the cotton crop was down almost 50 percent. Other crops—corn, beans, rice—were all but nonexistent. He was, as a result, asking the legislature to appropriate $100,000 in deficit spending to make up for the loss.

As a brief side note, he also reported having spoken to several prisoners, including Ruth. Nothing important, he said, brushing further questions aside. He made the visit "at the request of her husband."

The message back home was that John—and perhaps Dell—had made inroads. The new governor was listening. He was coming around.

. . . .

In early December, Ruth lost another roommate when, after serving the mandatory one-third of her prison sentence, Janie Brister was released. Called a model prisoner by the parole board, she moved back into the Jackson apartment she'd lived in when her mother's medical bills prompted her to embezzle a fair amount of money from the state coffers. A little more than two years after she got out, her suffrage rights were restored. By then, she'd also returned to a regular life of church, clubs, and office jobs. In the years to come, she'll contribute recipes to the women's page of the Jackson *Clarion-Ledger* and die in 1987, ninety-three years old, buried in a family plot beside her mother.

A new roommate joined Ruth and the other white women only months after Brister was released, a convicted young forger from Rankin County described by a newspaper as blond and pretty. The forged check that nailed Evelyn Stevens was for $10.

. . . .

Two days after White's conversation with Ruth, John wrote to thank him for his "gentlemanly manner" during their January meeting and for remembering his request when he extended Ruth a similar courtesy during his visit to Parchman. In the past four years, he added, he had learned that the "veneer of civilization is very thin and in times of trouble your fair weather friends always desert you." As if assuming the governor were his *real* friend.

. . . .

In Greenville, as military officers began making plans to rehabilitate the airbase in preparation for its conversion to a USAF jet training field, large orange moving vans rumbled daily through town, going from one household to another, giving the limited partners of the David L. Fey

Storage and Transfer Company reason to congratulate themselves on a wise and timely investment. For high school girls, however, the arrival of a new population at the air base came with parental warnings to stay away from "flyboys." They were older and more experienced. They wanted only one thing from a girl.

Most of us stuck to boys our own age. But within the next year, two of my friends were dating flyboys they eventually married.

. . . .

Christmas week, Daddy ran an ad featuring a new photo of himself, this time as Santa Claus, surrounded by a roomful of gobsmacked children. In full regalia—white beard and mustache, tasseled cap, red suit with white fur cuffs and lapels—he's looking up at the camera, smiling away, black eyes dancing. A happy, happy man. And why not? He's not just another performer in makeup. He is the show. The whole shebang.

"Merry Christmas to All," the ad proclaimed, "from the Big Mover. David L. Fey Storage and Transfer Co."

For a number of years, he'd been Greenville's number one Santa Claus, in demand all over town. Parents invited him to come by their houses on Christmas Eve to talk to their children; the price for his services, a fifth of Wild Turkey. Everything he did was designed to play out the fantasy that there was a real Santa Claus and here he was, fat, jolly, eyes dancing.

In the Christmas 1952 ad, he removed the mask. That wasn't Santa Claus in the room with those adoring children. It was the Big Mover.

Seeing that ad now, I think he knew. To survive as a respected, successful businessman, to fulfill the promises he'd made, he had to use whatever he could come up with, no matter the cost. Otherwise? He couldn't think about *otherwise.*

For once in his life he told the truth. Santa Claus—he as much as came out and said it—was a lie.

. . . .

Traditionally, girls make their debuts dressed in all white. But "Pink" was the theme of the 1952 Delta Debutante Ball. And so that year's debutantes were instructed to turn their backs on the past and have their gowns made in a soft blush color, pale as the throats of mimosa blossoms. In one of the many society-page photographs of the event, "Miss Dell Thompson Dickins" is featured receiving last-minute attention from her aunt Mildred, who seems to be smoothing the wide, billowing skirt of her satiny strapless gown. A slim, willowy girl, she's wearing her regular eyeglasses, and her short dark hair is cupped in soft curls around her face. She's very pretty—much more delicate-featured than either of her parents—and she looks exceedingly happy.

John Dickins walked his daughter through the "enchantingly beautiful, diamond-studded Tarleton arch" to a platform where, under a pink canopy festooned with bows, they paused for a well-rehearsed moment. The ballroom lay shiningly waxed before them, its walls and ceiling "transformed into an illusion of pink fairyland" with garlands of southern smilax hanging from the ceiling and chandelier lights covered with tiny pink shades. When her name was announced, Dell removed her hand from her father's arm, and as the Ole Miss Rebelaires played soft background music and a local businessman chronicled her ancestry and accomplishments, she moved toward two tuxedoed teenage boys, one of whom placed a lei of pink princess aloha orchids around her neck. At that moment, John stepped back and the three young people took charge, walking proudly through the long Greenville Country Club ballroom, toward the "society" of waiting adults.

Afterward, there was, of course, dancing. Boys formed stag lines, waiting for a turn. Girls and mothers counted to see which girl's line was longest.

There's a long-standing belief held by a good many Deltans that Ruth was there, having been given a holiday suspension that had been set especially during the week of the ball so that she could see Dell make her debut. This is an extremely popular notion, quoted by many, repeated in published magazine articles as established fact. I, for one, am pretty sure it never happened.

Letters from the governor approving the Christmas furloughs are collected in official files. By the week of the Pink Ball, Governor White's approval of Ruth's ten-day suspension had not yet been sent to the prison superintendent for one reason: Wiggins hadn't yet issued the request. This means that if Ruth *was* there, either the official record has been lost or destroyed, or she received a secret pass. Given Wiggins's disinclination to bend the rules and White's general position toward Ruth at this time, this seems unlikely. But odder things have happened. In any case, the Pink Ball rumor lives on.

. . . .

Whatever the rest of the world thinks about debutantism, John Dickins and Mildred Thompson Hood must have been over the moon that December night, watching Dell walk proudly between two tuxedoed young men down the shiny floor of the country-club ballroom, head high, keeping under wraps whatever sadness she might be experiencing, thinking about her mother's absence. For her father and her aunt, making the moment possible must have seemed the least—and most—they could do for such a fine, near-perfect girl whose year had begun and ended in an evening gown.

. . . .

Two front-page stories of racial note appeared in the Greenville paper that same day. One came from Alabama's Tuskegee Institute, which for seventy years had kept an annual record of U.S. violence against Negroes. Nineteen fifty-two, it reported, was the first year on record without a reported lynching. Another, "White Man Arrested Here on Charge of Raping Negro Girl," revealed that Ernest J. Singleton, twenty-eight, had been arrested for the statutory rape of an eleven-year-old girl at noon on the levee near the gravel company. Although he admitted having committed the act, Singleton denied using force, thus playing into the popular notion that Black girls matured sexually far faster than white ones and couldn't help preying on white men for favors and cash.

This story reflects a tiny measure of what might be called racial progress, if only in a compared-to-what? context. Nobody exactly *approved* of a white man forcing himself on a young girl, whatever her race, but generally the rapist's name was kept out of the newspaper, *if* he was arrested and *if* a story ran at all. But there it was, a white rapist called out by name, page 1. Victim, a Black child. Despite Singleton's protest, he was found guilty of molesting a minor and sentenced to the penitentiary for five years. Within six weeks of the crime, he was bundled up with five other white men and five Negroes and transported to Parchman. After his release, he either stayed clean for a good eleven years or managed to avoid arrest. But in 1968 he was back in court, once again on a molestation charge. That time he got off with a $300 fine and ninety days in county.

A closer reading of the Tuskegee report reveals some less hopeful trends across the South. A resurgence of the mob spirit "as expressed in beatings, floggings, incendiarism, bombings and the like" had occurred in many parts of the country, directed against synagogues and Catholic churches, as well as Black people attempting to move in to what were considered white neighborhoods and Black leaders who were believed by whites to be "too active in improving the status of their people."

FURLOUGH

New Year's Day 1953. Truman's finished, Eisenhower's in; second-ranked Georgia Tech is favored over seventh-ranked Ole Miss in the Sugar Bowl, especially considering the soggy field and prediction of more rain during the game. Many dogged Rebel fans planned to converge on New Orleans anyway. A lot of them, including Governor White, blamed the Rebels' 24–7 loss not on the weather but on the biased officiating. White even wrote to the Southeast Conference commissioner to complain. Not that anybody should have been shocked, he wrote, considering that three out of four of the referees lived in Georgia!

On January 17, 1953, eighteen days after Dell made her debut, Parchman's superintendent, Marvin Wiggins, sent a request to the governor's office, asking him to authorize a delayed ten-day Christmas furlough for Ruth Thompson Dickins, MSP 19813, who had received no punishments for violating prison rules and regulations and whose furlough had been recommended by the women's camp sergeant. White didn't reply until Monday, February 2, the third anniversary of Ruth's Parchman residency, when—after acknowledging the superintendent's need to stagger these holiday passes throughout the winter and early spring—he granted the suspension. The prison contacted John that day. Her holiday would begin a week later, on the ninth.

The call, John said, took him by surprise. He didn't even know she was eligible. Especially given the fact that she hadn't yet served the requisite five years of her term. But he and the girls were, of course, delighted.

"It's mighty fine," he said. "I don't know what she'll do, however." He was leaving that up to her.

On February 9, he drove to Parchman. Ruth was ready. When they got to Leland, reporters were waiting. Her black hair newly streaked with gray, she also looked thinner. Ruth confirmed this. As a matter of fact, she said, she'd lost 30 pounds during her forty-four months in prison, and had scaled down to what she considered a healthy 120. She was grateful for the ten days to get "reacquainted" with her family so that they could "have something like normal lives after more than four years of unreality." When asked about Idella's death, she responded briefly. She was sure, she said, the mystery of her mother's "horrible murder will eventually be solved." As for the furlough, it was given to her "automatically," as it was to all who complied with prison rules, not as any kind of special favor. She didn't ask for it and John didn't know anything about it until only a few days before she was allowed to come home.

Ruth and John threw an open house that Sunday afternoon. In addition to scores of friends and members of the family, Ruth's former cook, Beatrice Smith, and her husband drove down from Indianola to make an appearance. And for ten days the Dickinses seem to have fulfilled Ruth's wish to enjoy something close to a temporary normal life. When her holiday time was up, John drove her back to Parchman, and according to Wiggins, Ruth walked straight back into the women's camp without a problem, healthy and in good spirits. He was also pleased to report that all inmates given a furlough that year had returned on or before their deadline.

Seeing Ruth at home, looking thin and tired but mostly fine, mostly the same Ruth they all knew, made a huge difference to Lelanders. She was one of them, after all; *theirs*. A Deer Creek Drive homeowner, wife, mother, and Sunday school teacher. A member of their community. No matter what she might have done.

Clearly the open house served as an opportunity for John to rev up his letter-writing campaign and acquire more signatures. Ruth had hardly gotten back to Camp 9 and changed into her up-and-down when letters began tumbling into the governor's office. One arrived before she even made her way through the prison gates. After thanking White for his kindness in granting the furlough, this one went a step further: Couldn't he please see his way clear to pardon Mrs. Dickins entirely? Or failing that, to suspend her sentence?

Other letters described how happy the family had been, how satisfying it was to see them together, *as they were meant to be.* And how ridiculous it was to think that a person who'd led the kind of clean life Ruth had, as a young lady, a wife, and a mother, would do anything so terrible as kill her mother.

"You know these Delta negros were giving similar trouble all around here," one woman wrote, "committing brutal murders." And in truth, the only evidence against Ruth was "washed up by Doc Witte."

In his letter, the restaurateur and liquor dealer Tony Giardino introduced himself as "owner of Vince's Café here in town" and "that big fat boy 360 pounds you talked to at the Ole Miss–Maryland football game this last year." Vince's Café had been in Leland for thirty-two years, and Giardino wanted the governor to know he was a great Hugh White supporter, always had been, and he hated to bother him, but he wanted to ask a big favor. He'd visited with Mrs. Dickins when she was home on furlough and hoped the governor would believe him when he said she was definitely a *nice lady* and her husband was one of the nicest men he'd ever met. And by the way, he, Vince, was out in the public all the time, hearing what people said, and what he'd heard lately was, all of those people who once talked against her were now talking in favor of her. So *please help her.*

In reply, the governor issued boilerplate thanks and allowed as how he remembered Mr. Giardino "mighty well."

Mrs. W. E. Bufkin, however, perhaps influenced by her school superintendent husband, couldn't quite come up with that level of effusive praise. Although she and Mrs. Dickins had similar interests because of their children, Mrs. Bufkin wanted to make it clear they were not close friends and never had been. When she visited Ruth in the county jail, that was for her children's sake and so was the time she went to see her in Parchman. That said, having been in Ruth's home during her recent furlough, she thought things had changed. Whereas Mrs. Dickins had heretofore been a "somewhat arrogant person," she was now "humble and without malice toward anyone." There was also the matter of Dorothy Jane, who Mrs. Bufkin felt needed to be held to "a higher standard of scholastic achievement and personal conduct" than either John Dickins or his cousin Allee Brown could manage. Ruth could help out on that score. Last, she was now convinced that justice had been served and that if Ruth were to be returned home, she wouldn't "push herself on the community in any way that would be obnoxious to anyone."

Even Idella Thompson's little sister Addie Rogers wrote from Robstown, Texas, to ask the governor to pardon her niece, noting that Ruth's grief and suffering had been hard enough to bear already, "whether she killed her mother or not." She was certain that if her sister Idella could return to life and speak, she would ask Governor White to show mercy and grant her daughter a pardon. *Whether she killed her or not.*

As usual, most of the support went to John. A Mrs. Hill hoped it was God's will Ruth could soon be home with her little girls and husband, "who is one of the finest Christian men I have ever known." After chronicling his college friendship with John at Mississippi College, Howard Spell, now the school's dean, mentioned a conversation in which John told him his wife was experiencing "considerable trouble" with "the menopause period." This was admittedly a subject men hardly ever talked about, but one he felt compelled to mention, under the circumstances.

Many of the letter writers spoke of dropping by the Dickinses' home during Ruth's time off. Seeing how happy the family looked, how *right* it was for them to be together, moved them to write in support of her release.

. . . .

Governor White considered his options. Certainly a majority of the letters he received spoke in favor of clemency. In response, however, he unintentionally roused up the opposition when he told the Memphis *Commercial Appeal* that "a lot of pressure" was being brought on him regarding the Ruth Dickins case. Not—he quickly pointed out—that by saying that, he meant she'd be getting out anytime soon, only that there seemed to be a "change of sentiment of letting her out." In addition, he understood that "a lot of people who were against her during the trial are now on her side."

This statement inflamed a number of people, including one self-proclaimed "taxpayer, father and property owner" from Memphis who was convinced the people putting pressure on the governor were friends of *Mr.* Dickins, standing behind Ruth for the sake of the girls, whose parents, by the way, weren't as much interested in their daughters' welfare as in the "successful social marriages" they could make. Social prominence and wealth, the protesting letter writer reminded the governor, did not give a murderer the right to go free. For emphasis, he underlined his argument: <u>If a sharecropper committed the same crime, with no influential friends to bring pressure, he or she would remain there for life—at hard work.</u> He closed by begging White to keep Ruth where she belonged because "she is guilty and knows she is."

Stanny Sanders also wrote the governor to let him know that he and Willard McIlwain "have at no time recommended and do not recommend a parole, pardon, or suspension for Mrs. Dickins."

White wrote the prosecutors back to assure them that he would take no action in the case without giving them an opportunity to respond. And that he knows of "no such action at this time."

It's "pressure" that irked people. The very mention of it made them think White was preparing his constituents for a decision in that direction and was buttering them up to accept the idea in advance. Especially aggrieved by the term were residents of parts of the state other than the Delta, to whom even the slightest hint of pressure implied favoritism brought on by class, position, money, and—the descriptive term beloved by folks on both sides of the fence—prominence. Which entitled those who had it to lord it over plain folks like themselves.

In response, Governor White temporarily retreated from making comments about the Dickins case and would, going forward, refrain from making any statement suggesting that pressure of any kind was getting to him.

. . . .

In March, my father ran a quarter-page ad, saying, "READ THIS"—in bold uppercase lettering—"Unsolicited Testimony About THE BIG MOVER." Surrounded by Allied icons and slogans was a letter from a Mr. A. L. Taylor to a senior officer at the Greenville Air Force Base showering high praise on the David L. Fey Storage and Transfer Company, which recently transported his family's furniture, clothes, and equipment from Greenville to Marianna, Florida. Since 1946, Mr. Taylor had had to move six times because of his job, and as a result of the care and personal attention he and his family received this time around—including a visit from Mr. Fey himself on the morning of the move—this one was the most pleasant yet. Their belongings arrived on time. Not a scratch on anything. For once, the move, he said, "was a real pleasure."

Buoyed by a potentially deadly combination of inherent optimism and growing desperation, Daddy managed to add the Hertz "Driv-Ur-Self" rental car franchise to his list of available services. He'd been in the vehicle rental business for a while, but now he had the added bonus of the Hertz imprimatur and access to its "system."

We were living by the day without knowing it, assured by his ebullience and certainty that nothing would, or even could, go wrong. That we were *fine*. There were signs. His drinking increased. My mother's temper grew shorter, her migraines more frequent. I didn't notice any of this but with her encouragement kept my focus steadily set. I had my own life to think about. My future.

. . . .

A few days after the testimonial ran, my parents and the parents of five of my friends threw us a big, formal ninth-grade graduation dance, to be held in the country-club ballroom. To play for us, in great contrast to the fox-trot-leaning white bands who played for the cotillions and the debutante club, they hired the hottest band in the state, the all-Black Rebops, a band out of Vicksburg specializing in rhythm and blues, soul, and early rock. Unlike other Mississippi groups, they were known for performing for both Black audiences and white. They wore red cutaway jackets, soft black southern colonel ties, and shiny black pants, and they could rock like nobody else. This was a great thing, but we were barely into our teens, and while we listened raptly to R & B, most of us knew very little about what the "Sixty Minute Man" was talking about when he advertised fifteen minutes of teasing, fifteen minutes of pleasing, and fifteen minutes of blowin' his top, bopbopbop. Or what kind of thrill Fats Domino found on Blueberry Hill. But we loved the music and to boogie down as hard and dirty as we could manage or get away with.

If there's one commonality in Mississippi Delta homes, juke joints, country clubs, and formal ballrooms, it's music. Dance music. Music to move to. When the beat warms up, we rise out of our chairs and go to town.

That's everybody. Young, old, Black, white.

Not that we danced *together*. But we all did it.

MR. MARVIN, RUTH, AND THE PRESS

Other than the occasional complaint about the continued use of Black Annie, Marvin Wiggins had enjoyed a gold-star reputation as Parchman superintendent for almost nine years. But in the spring of 1953, he found himself involved in one ruckus after the other, not one of which he could ignore or explain away and for a simple reason: the rows and scrapes concerned white inmates. Whose parents assumed they had a right not only to ask questions but to expect answers to follow. They also felt certain that other white people would pay attention. As would the press. And the governor.

These racially based assumptions turned out to be correctly held. The advantage given to these particular parents—and the hot water in which Wiggins found himself unhappily thrashing—was due not to class, money, or prominence but whiteness.

. . . .

On April 14, 1953, James and Rena McGraw, residents of McComb, Mississippi, received a terse telegram from Parchman Farm informing them that their son, Edgar "Sonny" McGraw, had died. No other information was provided. Sonny was twenty-six years old. He had entered Parchman three days earlier. He and his parents were white.

The McGraws barely had time to digest the news when a van pulled up bearing their son's body. Again, there was no explanation for the young man's death. The attendants dropped off Sonny's casket and drove away. Only after several hours of inquiries made by the irate family and, subsequently, the *McComb Enterprise-Journal* were the McGraws able to learn what had happened.

. . . .

After Sonny was arrested in Natchez in February, charged with a string of small-time burglaries and robberies, one of them armed, he was taken to Jackson and locked up in the Hinds County Jail. There, he was offered a deal: plead guilty and turn state's evidence, and they'd forget about the armed robbery and get him a two-plus-two sentence, four years run in consecutive two-year terms. Good behavior would get him out in nine, ten months. He'd still be in his twenties, plenty of time to make a new start. Sonny took the deal. Well aware that revenge against squealers was commonplace at Parchman, the judge who heard Sonny's confession sent a notice to the county jail, warning officials to be careful where they housed him. When the accomplices he'd fingered were taken to the same jail Sonny was in, guards were instructed to make sure the new guys were placed in a different cellblock.

But secrets fly fast through a small jailhouse. While in the Hinds County lockup, one of the accomplices Sonny had ratted out confided in a very tough jail mate named William Wetzel, from New York State. Transferred to the penitentiary ahead of Sonny, Wetzel was assigned to Camp 5—known as the home of the most hardened white criminals in the pen. There, he quickly joined a "notorious Parchman gang" known for its violent opposition to informers.

Sonny got to the penitentiary on a Saturday. He spent the usual two days being photographed, weighed, measured, physically described, psychologically examined, and dressed in round-and-rounds. On Monday, he was also, despite the warnings, assigned to a cage in Camp 5. A sergeant and two guards escorted him to his barracks. He knew only one other man there, a friend from McComb. None of the revenge-minded gang members knew Sonny; they'd never laid eyes on him. But when one of the guards who brought him to their camp introduced him as the stool pigeon who squealed on "Muscles Crawford" (a pseudonym for one of the robbers), Wetzel and the others knew they had their man.

Sonny racked down in Camp 5 for one night. Tuesday morning, he went out with approximately a hundred other men to work the line, planting soybeans between stalks of corn. At 1:30, when he started toward the water wagon, four members of his work detail rushed him from behind. While inmates and trusties watched, one man grabbed Sonny by the hair and threw back his head, one steadied his head in position, one stood in front of him chest to chest in case he tried to run, while the fourth, Wetzel, rushed up and, holding a switchblade pocket knife known as a crab-apple switch, kneed him in the back and slit his throat from his windpipe to the left side of his neck. Bleeding all over himself and the other prisoners, McGraw grabbed his neck, stumbled a few steps, then fell down between the corn rows. Within minutes, he was dead. The knife was found buried in soft earth nearby, wrapped in a bandanna, the blade protruding from a hole punched in the fabric. There were no fingerprints. Mr. Marvin didn't expect to find any.

Inmate witnesses played dumb. They weren't sure who killed Sonny, it happened so fast. One man thought he might have committed suicide. But trusties talked and the guards knew about the gang. Sonny's killers were quickly rounded up.

Prison officials dodged phone calls. But after Sonny's body was delivered to his parents, word got out, the press made a stink, and the district attorney from Brookhaven, E. C. Barlow, was sent to investigate. Unfortunately for the prison staff, Barlow took his job seriously. He stayed at Parchman several days, digging up clues and conducting interviews. By the time he left, he had uncovered every detail surrounding the death of Sonny McGraw and shared the information with the press, including the names of the killers and how, when, and why the whole thing had come down.

Once Oliver Emmerich's *McComb Enterprise-Journal* got hold of the story, Governor White weighed in. He was outraged; the murder of Edgar "Sonny" McGraw was "premeditated, planned and executed by gangland action." This would not be tolerated. "Gangland action" resonated with the citizenry. Something had to be done. In a relatively lame response, Wiggins came up with a new order: from that moment on, the "bunching" of inmates working the line was prohibited. No gathering together, no confabs or huddles. Straight lines only. An order to be strictly enforced by armed trusties.

A member of the legislative committee appointed to investigate the matter gave the prison and its superintendent a clean bill of health.

Twelve days later, *The Delta Democrat-Times* ramped up the discussion when the managing editor, Tom Karsell, ran a page 1 story about the "execution" of Sonny McGraw, noting that no one had seen fit to "comment upon the secrecy at the time of the murder or the subsequent cloaking of information concerning what took place in a public institution."

Thus did the Greenville paper fire the first shot in a battle with Wiggins that didn't let up for months to come.

The governor stood behind the prison superintendent, praising him for his managerial skills, his ability to restore order, and his willingness to go along with the recent suggestion of a Bolivar County legislator to reduce the maximum number of stripes from the lash from fifteen to ten. From then on, the whacks would also be performed only by a camp sergeant and witnessed either by himself, the assistant superintendent, or a prison physician. An easy compromise, having nothing to do with the gang hit on Sonny McGraw.

By June, in an effort to counter the bad press, Governor White announced his plan to put together a press tour of the Parchman facilities, to which newsmen "from all over the state" would be invited.

But before the governor could issue invitations, six white inmates working the fields were riddled with buckshot by a trusty who claimed the men had defied Wiggins's new rule outlawing "bunching." None of the men was seriously wounded, but all were hit with buckshot. One of the injured inmates reported the attack to his mother, who began making noise. Before the incident, her boy had been a Sunday school teacher at the prison. Afterwards, Wiggins took away his Bible and his teaching privileges. Also, her son had been put back on the line the day after he was hit, even though his arm contained a good bit of buckshot.

The Delta Democrat-Times took on the story. It quoted Wiggins, who said the shooting had been caused by a "convict uprising," a minor case of insubordination. A "routine" matter. In context, it wasn't clear whether by "routine" Mr. Marvin meant the "uprising" or the shooting of the prisoners, but the managing editor, Karsell, chose the latter interpretation. The newspaper ran daily stories raking Wiggins over the coals, dragging his sidekick, the governor, along with him. The editor Hodding Carter's Sunday editorial supported Karsell, castigating Wiggins for his lack of education and his outdated, inhumane practices.

Wiggins retaliated. Having agreed to go along with the superintendent's request, the governor sent invitations to reporters from newspapers in Jackson, Indianola, McComb, Greenwood, Drew, Ruleville, and even New Orleans and Memphis, but not Greenville. This in spite of the town's status as second-most-populous city in the state and Hodding Carter's Pulitzer Prize.

Carter and Karsell could not have been happier. War with the farmer-superintendent would provide front-page stories for weeks to come.

Further trouble arrived for Wiggins when the body of a seventeen-year-old white male prisoner was sent home to Vicksburg for burial. No date of death was supplied. But when the local funeral director opened the casket, he found a decomposed body. The boy had been dead for at least a year. The parents had not been told.

The Delta Democrat-Times ran a big story; other papers followed suit.

Another flap ensued when the governor announced the date of his public relations tour and Karsell called it "the first trip a governor has made [to Parchman] in several years."

White blew up. Karsell was, he said, a "dirty liar." To even the score, he wrote to *The Delta Democrat-Times*'s editor, reminding him of the several visits he'd made to the pen since taking office.

Carter printed a retraction, but Karsell infuriated Wiggins all over again when he criticized his continued use of the lash and his resistance to recommended rehabilitation programs and the hiring of a psychiatrist or a Black chaplain.

Wiggins had had enough: he closed the prison gates to *Delta Democrat-Times* reporters, including the staff photographer. Only representatives of what were deemed *fair* and *reputable* newspapers would be allowed on the penal farm grounds.

Carter countered with a scathing editorial taking the superintendent to task on many fronts: the arrogance of his assertion that he was qualified to pass judgment on the professional reputation of a newspaperman; his use of an antiquated system that included the lash; the alleged cover-up of the killing of an inmate; his dismissal of the recent multiple shootings by an armed trusty as routine. The editorial was accompanied by a cartoon depicting a beefy trusty in striped pants standing before two bodies on the ground while aiming his shotgun at another group of unsuspecting prisoners. In the foreground, a long-faced, square-jawed white man in suit coat, tie, and fedora has turned his head toward us, his sly, conspiratorial smile indicating a private joke between him and his audience.

In a wickedly sarcastic riposte, Carter challenged Wiggins to a kind of moral arm wrestle refereed by national representatives of professional organizations who would rate his performance as editor, Wiggins's as prison warden. The loser, Carter suggested, would surrender his bare bottom to ten Black Annie stripes. No response from Mr. Marvin.

· · · ·

Two weeks before the press tour was set to begin, John Dickins wrote to the governor. His letter began, "Since all the furor has been raised about Parchman, and since I have been asked by individuals and the press for any statement I felt like making, I thought it best to get in touch with those in authority and let them know personally what I feel."

He'd been to Parchman the day before—a Tuesday, only two days after a visit to see Ruth—and after "a long talk with Mr. Wiggins" wished to offer an opinion.

That he might have consulted with Ruth, Wiggins, Waits, or all three about writing to Governor White seems likely. After all, the "furor," as he called it, between the Greenville newspaper—its printing press located only half a block from his office—and the administrator of the prison where his wife had been incarcerated for more than three years provided a convenient opportunity for him to make a statement in support of the governor, Mr. Marvin, and Ruth.

His letter began with a rehash of his wife's experience behind bars, both in county and at the state penitentiary, for "a crime she did not commit." He praised the system at Parchman, where "she was thoroughly examined and given a number, and a record sheet with her name and number on it was sent to the front." After that, a prisoner was on his own, responsible for his own behavior. Any false statements, jealousies, or hatreds were recorded. And only that record was taken into account, nothing else. If his wife had "received that same unbiased treatment prior to her trial, in the 'Free World'... she would never have been made the victim of a lawful lynching." As it was, she was indicted, tried, convicted, and lynched before the grand jury even went into session.

Having given the governor permission to use his statement in any way he desired, Dickins ended with "This is all that I have to say at this time."

Hugh White didn't refer to John's comments but responded, as always, with a formal thank-you.

And so on July 11, 1953, when Superintendent Wiggins threw open the prison gates to "refute some of the charges of recent days," no representative of *The Delta Democrat-Times* was among the reporters who entered.

. . . .

The Jackson *Clarion-Ledger* ran reporter Gene Roper's lengthy, entirely favorable account of the visit and the state of the prison, on page 1. The governor himself led the caravan of reporters on a six-hour tour of the camps and cages, the canning plant, the laundry, and the sewing room, expounding on his theories about penal obligations and philosophy as he went. Against Wiggins's often-stated wishes, the governor touted his idea about the building of a maximum-security unit with solitary confinement cells for up to fifty convicts. This would, White repeatedly stated, separate the incorrigibles from the rest of the inmates and take the place of Black Annie. He was calling his new project "Little Alcatraz." But the citizens of Mississippi should rest assured: until its completion the legislature would have a hard time getting an act abolishing the strap by his desk.

As the July sun rose higher and the temperature began to rise, the reporters struggled to keep up with the indefatigable, if overweight, governor, who maintained his tour-guide enthusiasm and his pace as he showed off cotton, corn, and soybean fields, the peach orchards, the hospital, and the slaughterhouse, where the portly White was photographed with his entourage, looking down with obvious satisfaction at a row of sleeping hogs.

The early part of the tour ended in the kitchen, where lunch was being prepared. White went from one stove to the next, lifting lids from bubbling cauldrons of green beans and turnip greens grown on prison grounds, waving the aroma to his nostrils before lifting the cooking spoon to his lips to taste the vegetables, then cutting slices of fresh corn bread, topping them with pieces of fried trout, passing fresh peach cobbler made from the prison orchard to several of the newsmen.

Afterward, the visitors were divided into groups, one of which was escorted into the women's camp. Roper doesn't say much about the Negro women's quarters, but he does devote a fair number of column inches to interviews with Myrtis Blackwell, Evelyn Stevens, and Ruth Dickins. Before entering their freestanding building, he passed by a brick guardhouse some 150 feet from their dormitory. Inside, a white female trusty sat with a rifle over her arm, far enough from buildings and working individuals to cover any prisoner from any direction and to forestall any attempt to take her weapon. Roper found Blackwell and Stevens—both convicted of forgery—sitting on a bench outside the house.

When asked what kind of compensation she might have found in such a stigmatized and restrictive environment, Evelyn Stevens said that more than anything she looked forward to the two weekly letters she was allowed to write to her family. And actually, "this is really just like home. We all live in one dormitory and we do all the prison sewing, but we do have some time to ourselves when we're caught up with the work." There was, however, one thing she was concerned about. In only three months in prison, she'd already gained three and a half pounds.

Thoughts of impending freedom kept Myrtis Blackwell's spirits up. After serving almost all of her three-year stretch, she'd finally be out this coming October. She would have been freed months ago if she hadn't "taken a powder" with some other girls and lost most of her time off. But she'd dealt with that. And now she was going home.

Roper found Ruth inside, alone, reading. But when he walked in, she stood and greeted the reporter "graciously." Like the other women, she seemed to be in good spirits and—contradicting comments from her concerned neighbors and family—"the picture of health."

Under the circumstances, Ruth told the reporter, they were pretty well-off there. "Our dormitory is airy—you see today I've got the two windows next to my bed down because of the chill wind"—presumably at night when she was sleeping and the heat had dissipated. And they could do embroidery and knitting and read books when they had spare time from sewing. As for personal compensation, she "doted on the visits of her husband and two daughters every Sunday," when the family was allowed to have a "reception" on the lawn between their quarters and the guardhouse. Other family members and friends were allowed to visit every six months.

Ruth and the other women agreed that their dorm was well maintained. Floors swept and mopped. No vermin. The walls showed wear and tear but were clean. There were Bibles and pictures of loved ones on the beds and walls, as well as bits of knitting that seemed to have been recently laid aside.

As Ruth stood talking to Roper, the governor entered. Leading another party through her dormitory, he spoke to her by name. "Mrs. Dickins," he said, nodding. He didn't stop. But the momentary flash of recognition—*I know who you are and who your husband is*—was significant.

After a sumptuous meal hosted by Mr. Marvin and his wife, the journalists left to go back home and file their stories. Once they were gone, prisoners made their way to the fields. The women returned to the sewing room. All in all, the inmates took the news reporters' tour for what it was: another show.

. . . .

Summer brought another spate of letters to the governor's office. A notably articulate plea from the Leland entrepreneur and real estate magnate George Breisch began, "A matter about which I have done considerable thinking prompts me to write this letter and that is the case of Mrs. Ruth Dickins." He went on to say he'd known Ruth all her life and was friends with the family. Then this: "Since her father's death, Ruth took over the responsibilities of the entire family. I have never known a person who showed more devotion and patience than Ruth did toward her mother and I cannot make myself believe that she was in any way guilty of murdering her mother."

He went on to say that he believed poor investigation, rumors, and bad newspaper publicity played a major part in leading to her conviction. Because what he knew was, Ruth had a kind and happy disposition and was always thinking of others. He had even seen her "take old stray hungry dogs and feed and nurse them back to health." When she came home on furlough, she was welcomed by everyone, everywhere she went, and showed no bitterness toward anyone. When he asked about the crime, she said only that a great mistake had been made and that one of these days her innocence would be proved.

He ended with the usual plea for John and the girls, omitting any reference to the possibility of Ruth's innocence as the reason she should be allowed to go home.

"I cannot make myself believe" is intriguing. As if he'd tried to convince himself that Ruth had killed her mother and couldn't. Many of the people I talked to said something similar. They didn't think Ruth Dickins was capable of such a thing. She was too nice a person to have done such a thing. They couldn't *imagine* a woman like Ruth Dickins slashing her mother to death like that.

IV

CHANGES

The Feys, 1949. Biloxi, Mississippi. The Edgewater Beach Hotel. Glory days for my family, when the good times rolled and seemed to curl out before us as far as we could see or even imagine. This picture was taken by a professional photographer who worked the grounds of the hotel, snapping guests in their beach attire for a fee. I don't remember swimming in the Gulf of Mexico even though it was only steps from the hotel. My brother and I liked the pool. My mother liked the shade of an umbrella, with, for company, magazines and cigarettes. My father liked the golf course. And the bars. This photo is mine. It hangs on my bedroom wall.

THE FEYS, THE DICKINSES, THE SOUTH

Sometime around the middle years of my adult life, I came to the long-buried realization that the most dependable element of my family life was ongoing, uninterrupted uncertainty, artfully disguised as nonchalance. My friend Sang called it "flair." Whatever it looked like to others, however brilliant my father was at reaching beyond himself to create an alternate, more carefree, and cheerful reality, we were always floundering. Always waiting for the next uprooting and with it the chaos that inevitably bulldozed in and took charge.

On August 12, 1953, my parents signed a warranty deed transferring ownership of 830 South Washington Avenue to another family. August 12 was my brother David's birthday. He turned twelve that day. I'd turned fifteen two days earlier. Eddy was three.

I don't remember a buildup. Or mention of a foreclosure. I only remember going. We left together, my mother and brothers and me. In my memory, we're in the dining room, walking toward the bay windows overlooking the front garden, where the plywood Nativity scene once stood. The whole thing seemed unreal. I kept waiting for a turnaround, for the error to correct itself.

We moved in to a rental not far away. The house at 1276 South Main had been for sale for six months. The owner had already moved out. I don't know what kind of deal Daddy made to get us in. Maybe we were fill-in renters until somebody bought the house. Maybe Daddy made a cooked-up rent-to-own arrangement. I don't know. It was a nice house. Small, but okay. I think we lived in it for about a year.

Long after my parents' death I came across a statement that turned my head around. "Without stable shelter," Matthew Desmond, author of *Evicted: Poverty and Profit in the American City*, said in an interview, "everything else falls apart."

I didn't get it at the time or for years afterward, but our family life changed when we lost that house. We weren't without shelter. Whatever his faults, Daddy always managed to come up with a new job, a temporary dwelling, and some kind of transportation. But stability was nowhere in sight. We never knew how long we'd hold on to things or how many months we'd live in a place before word came down—from wherever and for whatever reason—telling us we had to move.

In a middle-class world, transience is unseemly. When called upon to face the truth, to own up to the shame we felt, we pretended. Brushed it off. Did what Daddy called "plike" and played like it didn't exist. While the ground beneath our feet quivered, quaked, and split.

I sometimes wonder why we stuck it out in Greenville for three more years. We had no roots there, no family in Mississippi. More than likely, it was because Daddy still figured he had a shot at getting things back on track. Maybe not the house, but the business, his reputation. Once that happened, he'd build Mama another house, a promise he made her many times during their fifty-three years together. If she had insisted on leaving Greenville, he might have gone along, but clearly she didn't. She was fierce. He was resilient. I was building a sterling résumé of accomplishments. Leaving is complicated. We stayed.

In the spring of 1982, when I was heading from Texas to Mississippi to participate in a Greenville literary festival, my mother confessed to a certain nervousness about my trip in her journal. She hoped, she wrote, I'd have a good time and be properly honored because she would "NEVER feel the same about Greenville" or forgive the people there and "how they treated us." Then, as if to tamp down her resentment, she reconsiders. Maybe, she writes, it was all "Big's" fault—Big being the name my father went by, at that time. He "never could make enough money" to pay the many people they owed and still have enough to live on. "I guess," she writes, "we always lived too high."

Reading this, I remember times when, at the breakfast table, my father often relayed dreams he'd had the night before. One he especially liked to describe was of flying. He'd flatten his hand and sail it like a paper airplane in front of his face to show how it felt to soar through the sky like a bird, looking down at places and people he recognized, above the fray of consequences, failures, and broken promises. Unreachable.

. . . .

By the end of that same summer, John Dickins was collaborating with Hilton Waits on a new one-two strategy. The setup was for John to write the governor a long personal letter laying out an argument for Ruth's release. After a couple of days, Waits would follow up with an official visit.

But Governor White's first eight months in office had been rough. He hadn't escaped criticism during Parchman's spring troubles, and with the trials of the four men charged with murdering Sonny McGraw coming up, newspapers would be all over the story once again. In addition, because McGraw was killed in Sunflower County, the trials would take place in Indianola, which was within the district assigned to Ruth's original judge, Arthur Jordan, and her chief prosecutor Stanny Sanders. Reminders of the Dickins case were, as always, everywhere.

Presumably, however, White read John's letter:

August 28, 1953

Dear Governor White,

I am writing you as a father and the head of a family, who is doing his best to see that some form of justice can come from a great miscarriage of justice that was dealt my wife over four years ago.

It was on Nov. 17, 1948 that the murder of Mrs. J. W. Thompson took place, and it was on Jan. 24th, 1949, over our 20th wedding anniversary that my wife was indicted for the murder of her mother. We have been a most bewildered family ever since.

I have done everything honorable and right that I know to do. I know that she is innocent and not once since this crime happened has anything ever transpired to cause me, in any way, to doubt the sincerity of my wife's claim of innocence.

The lie detector showed her innocent. She has co-operated with all officers, and all she knows she has told over and over and now, after practically five years, her story is the same, but the rumors that put her out of society have been proven false and for lack of foundation they have passed out of the picture.

There has never been a sadder Christmas in all our lives than the Christmas of 1948. There we were, trying as best we could to have a Happy Christmas for our daughters, age 10 and 14, our friends coming in with that look of sympathy and wishing you a Happy Christmas. We were most miserable, for we knew the rumors about my wife's connection with the crime were out and that nothing we could do would stop them. We became a "very peculiar family" all at once, and once the rumors started you could notice people driving by your house and looking in, people that never knew us but people with sadist[ic] tendencies. We couldn't think, we didn't know what to do. Not once during all of this time that my wife was under suspicion did the District Attorney or Prosecuting Attorney come by my house or make a statement to the press about letting the court handle the case instead of the press. There were newspaper articles that were written to be read between the lines and there were magazine stories. She was removed out of society before the grand jury ever went into session. We never hired an attorney until the indictment. All we knew was that she was innocent and we prayed that we would get justice. I have since learned that a Democracy is what they think most of the people want.

In my files with the Parole Board I have petitions signed by five of the jurors, also I have petitions signed by over seven hundred citizens of this section. These signatures include <u>24</u> of the 27 members of the Wash. Co. Bar Assn., foreman of the Grand Jury that indicted her, two other members of the Grand Jury, the County Judge Thomas, the City Judge, the mayors of Leland, Greenville, and Hollandale, all bank officials of the County banks, school superintendent, five ministers, nine doctors and countless housewives, laborers, and people from all walks of life. I might add that all of your colonels in this section are on that petition and it was made before you ran for Governor.

I am one of the few men who have had the privilege of fighting for his wife and family in a case that he knows is right. I will continue to do so. I need my wife home. My daughters need her, *especially the one that is just turning 15. Please don't break my kids hearts, they have gone through enough, and they want their mother.*

In all sincerity and humbleness, I ask that you study our files carefully, study the evidence and then, putting yourself in my place, make your own decision.

All we have ever asked for is fairness.

Sincerely,

This is certainly the most revealing of John's entreaties. While he repeated some of his usual appeals, he seems more spontaneous here, less prone to self-righteous speechifying, more willing to let stories speak for themselves.

Less than a week later, Hilton Waits appeared in Governor White's office bearing the same petitions and letters John had presented to Fielding Wright. He asked White to look them over and consider giving Mrs. Dickins early parole or some other form of clemency, perhaps an indefinite suspension of her sentence. What White knew was that Waits wasn't just another member of the house; he had clout. The governor could not afford to dismiss his solicitation out of hand. He promised to make time to read the letters. *And,* he warned, to ask Stanny Sanders for his opinion as well.

An additional stream of pro-Ruth letters soon followed, many of them taking on a slightly different slant, one that, in effect, both acknowledged and accepted her possible guilt without requesting a new trial. Guilty or innocent, a number of people opined, Ruth had been convicted on circumstantial evidence and unfairly sentenced. It was time to set her free. She'd been a model prisoner. Her continued confinement served no purpose. The girls needed her at home. She was convicted by the clamor of the mob and lurid stories in *The Delta Democrat-Times.* The orderly processes of the law had been abrogated. She was a Christian and therefore would never kill anyone, certainly not her mother. She wanted to take the stand in her own defense but wasn't allowed to. She was convicted on rumor. Convicted because of the atmosphere before and during the trial, which had been whipped up by ignorant outsiders.

One man wrote in to say that as one of only three members of her grand jury from Leland, he thought surely his word counted for something; after all, he and the other two Lelanders were the people who knew Ruth best, and wasn't it significant that none of them voted to indict her? As for how she would be received in Leland, the governor should know that the gossip and rumors had died down. The town was back to normal again. Calm.

Some gingerly castigated the victim as a way of justifying Ruth's actions. The mayor of Leland noted that "Mrs. Thompson . . . was an extremely difficult woman to get along with . . . known to have a very fiery disposition . . . [she was] entirely capable of striking the first blow" and that "the majority of people of Leland felt that if Ruth killed her mother it was during a fit of temporary insanity or unrational behavior caused by a lick on the head," presumably launched by her mother.

Governor White signed form letters of response to these pleas, but it seems unlikely he read them all. Other arguments included:

"Ruth will be accepted back in the community."

"John is a man of the highest character and Christian fortitude."

"She should not have been convicted of a crime higher than manslaughter."

"Those who object to clemency do so because of embarrassment over their part in spreading rumors . . . They seem to think the home life of the [Dickins] children won't be the same as their friends now . . . but Ruth I'm sure will never take or want her old place in the society of Leland again."

"An exemplary prisoner . . . needed at home."

The "negro she accused should be punished."

The private investigator A. E. Crawford wrote in to say that he considered Ruth's conviction "one of the most horrible miscarriages of justice ever in Mississippi." He knew the case backward and forward but hadn't been able to get the facts as he would have liked because people refused to tell him the truth. And he got "no cooperation from police officers."

In her letter, a kind of postscript to the one she wrote in 1952, Dell Dickins pointed out that now that she was a sophomore in college, she was a mature young lady who "could know Ruth as a personal friend." A group letter signed by some fifty "direct blood descendants of the late Mrs. Idella L. Thompson" and others "related to her by marriage" ran in the weekly *Leland Progress.* Piling on to the chorus of other proponents, it declared that while the undersigned believed in Ruth's innocence, they also thought that no matter what she'd done—including, presumably, the commission of murder—she'd been sufficiently punished for the "crime for which she was convicted."

. . . .

Though far fewer in number, letters opposing clemency of any kind were no less adamantly stated. Some raked Governor White over the coals for even *considering* making a change in Ruth's sentence.

For example:

"In my opinion and in everybody's opinion I have talked to relative to this case . . . it would be a travesty of justice to allow her to be freed."

And:

"Please bear this in mind . . . no person who is innocent of a crime will not take the witness stand in their behalf." Obviously, it was because Mrs. Dickins did not possess the earnestness of an innocent person that "her lawyers thought it best that she keep her seat on the sidelines where the less she said the better off she'd be."

A man from Vicksburg came up with a similar grievance: "Do not look upon the principal involved as a socially prominent woman from a wealthy Delta family, but just as a woman no different from the ones who [in]habit the streets of the small towns and hill counties of your state." And before deciding Ruth Dickins was eligible for a pardon, the governor should consider all the others in "our state prisons," many of whom were more entitled to a pardon than she. He also assailed Mrs. Dickins for failing to testify in her own behalf the way any innocent person would.

Dell Swett's family, also from Vicksburg, had lived in Mississippi, he assured the governor, for well over a hundred years, and up to now he and his wife had always felt their state was a safe place to raise their daughters. But now that the governor was considering letting a murderer out of prison without new and conclusive proof of her innocence, and even though her case had been duly considered by the courts and other elected officials, he was now ashamed to admit to his friends and children that he supported Hugh White for governor. You can feel Mr.

Swett's anger rise as he types his missive until, in closing, he poses a white-hot rhetorical question: "Just who do you think you are anyway, THE GREAT WHITE FATHER?"

From a former admirer of the governor: "Lighten her sentence and you might as well close your law courts in Mississippi." Another person thought if the governor saw fit to let Ruth go free, he should open the prison gates and let everybody go home. Yet another echoed remarks that the only reason people from the Delta signed the petition was to make sure the daughters made "socially prominent marriages."

A woman who was kin to Ruth by marriage: "If we respect law and order we must back decisions of our courts. If Mrs. Dickins be not guilty then a retrial rather than a pardon is in order. Those who say she's suffered enough should remember she's not an embezzler or a thief, not accused of a minor crime but one of the most horrible crimes this section has ever known."

Another woman suggested that before suspending Mrs. Dickins's sentence, the governor get the pictures of Mrs. Thompson's body and see for himself the mercy and consideration she gave her mother.

A man named R. J. Landers considered petition signing the lowest form of political arm-twisting and anybody who signed one in support of Ruth or anybody else was dragging out a cheap strategy people resorted to only after every other tactic had failed. The Dickins petition had been circulated all over Washington County, often peddled by young boys who'd been paid for their services. Landers himself had been asked to sign not just once but any number of times, and while he personally always refused, he knew people who were afraid *not* to go along, having been made to think a refusal was tantamount to enmity toward John and the daughters. They feared being shamed by important people. People in a position to do so.

The well-placed Leland planter Leroy Allen wanted to let the governor know that unlike some others he and ten or fifteen of the "most prominent men of this community" were considerably concerned regarding the reopening of Ruth's case. They were hoping Governor White would agree to meet with them and allow them to present "certain information that we feel will be helpful to you in reaching a decision in the matter."

White had met with John Dickins and his daughters; he'd also spoken to Ruth at Parchman. And Hilton Waits. He could hardly refuse to hear what the other side had to say. And so he asked Leroy Allen to meet with him in his office on a certain morning in October. And would he please bring the other members of his group with him?

Their names were familiar. Homer Dean, John Aldridge, Dean Hebron, and Ruth's uncle K. L. "Doc" Witte. They had come to Jackson, their spokesman, Allen, told the governor, because they believed that if Ruth was released, it would "tear up our community," and because a lot of people who signed those other petitions in her favor "wished they had not been wheedled into it." According to Homer Dean, Ruth had been spoiled all her life with money, and it seemed obvious to him that Mrs. Thompson had refused to come up with whatever amount Ruth asked for that last time. Which sent Ruth into a rage.

And although he had no doubt but that Mrs. Thompson might well have struck the first blow, if evidence from the trial made one thing crystal clear, it was that Ruth did, in fact, kill her mother. Her release would not only frustrate the ends of justice; it would also cause people in Leland to live in "mortal fear of their lives."

J. E. Smith said he believed Ruth was guilty when he served on her jury and he still did, and while he'd been pressured into signing a petition on her behalf some years ago, he did so because it focused on respect for her husband and concern for her daughters, not Ruth. Plus, the petition didn't say she wasn't guilty, only that she'd been punished enough. And what right did he or anybody else have to make that call?

Once again, Ruth's nemesis, Doc Witte, spoke aggressively against his niece. He also brought word from his wife—Idella Thompson's sister Johnie—that she wished him to add her name to the protest. Whether it was premeditated murder, a slaying committed in a fit of passion, or Ruth's being crazy, Doc declared, she "should not be turned loose on society." He was after all the first man called to the house after the killing. And he made up his mind as soon as he "hit the house" that Ruth was the person who killed her mother.

When he examined her shoes, they'd been washed. Same thing with the shears: washed, little or no blood. No sign of the "Negro" she'd accused. Middle of the afternoon when "a Negro hanging about in a Deer

Creek backyard" would *not* go unnoticed? Not a chance. And there was Ruth, the only one in the house, the only one to tell, to virtually *create*, the story.

But he didn't need to get carried away and go through the whole thing all over again. All he really had to say was, if one thing was clear to him, it was that Ruth Dickins killed her mother.

White issued a statement that same afternoon. "This case," he firmly declared, "will not be taken up again during my term of office *unless completely new facts are discovered.*" People signed petitions, he added, without thinking. Which was a shame, because "every convict" deserved an opportunity to come before the governor and plead his case. Signed petitions were, in fact, probably the least trustworthy method people employed. In fairness to Mr. Dickins, he had looked into the case, but "there isn't any ground I can find for the governor taking action."

Headline in the Jackson *Clarion-Ledger:* "White's Decision on Clemency for Mrs. Dickins: NO."

Undeterred, even in the face of flat-out rejection, John stayed over an extra night to make a last-ditch appeal. It went nowhere. Three weeks later, he wrote an open letter to "the Citizens of Washington County and the State at Large" in which he strongly condemned not the governor but Doc Witte's statement. Printed in a number of newspapers, it ended, "I know my wife is innocent and when you are right nothing stops you or scares you."

Prison rules limited Ruth to two letters a week, to be sent only to members of her immediate family. In a response to the governor's decision, written on lined, prison-issue paper, she thanked her husband and assured him of her determination to see her confinement out, however long it lasted. White's decision would not, she vowed, alter her, "not in my thinking or my conduct. I know what I know & what I am—Nothing will ever change me regardless of the grind that they put me to. I will stand it & come out of it all a plain human who has learned about people. There is No Need to be bitter—That will only harden us—and make us wrong. I still believe that by doing right, you can win out."

She signed off with "I love you so. Always, Ruth." In a last-minute addition—inmate letters were limited to the front and back of one page—she scribbled across the salutation a reminder, "Get this on to Dell," who was off at school.

For such a straightforwardly blunt woman, Ruth's handwriting is surprisingly whimsical. To pen a capitalized *I,* she starts on the right side of the spine of the letter and whips upward to make an elliptical balloon, then curves down as if in a backward *C* to make a smaller balloon at the bottom. There are many other such balloons, making the tail of the letters *y* and *g,* the entirety of a lowercase *l,* and so on. She capitalizes any word beginning with *N,* even if it occurs in the middle of a sentence. She also likes to use dashes and circles. Looking at one of her pages, the roundedness of her handwriting stands out, those quickly executed loops and balloons.

. . . .

Late that fall, my father delivered the moving company's year-end books to Rob Robertson, the partnership's CPA, in preparation for its requisite annual statement. One morning not long after Robertson finished studying those numbers, he called Billy Keady and asked him to come to his office. It was Sunday, so they'd be alone. Keady rushed right over.

The David L. Fey Storage and Transfer Company, it turned out, was head over heels in debt. As for those upbeat weekly statements, either Daddy or the bookkeeper he'd hired had recorded the firm's total sales, not its gross profits. In addition, while 95 percent of the year's revenues had come from the air base move, what Keady and the other partners didn't know was that the Allied agents who actually owned the vans my father used had not been paid. And neither had the drivers. There were contracts. My father had signed them. Allied Vans was owed some $50,000, a sizable percentage of the profits. In addition to which, local trade creditors' accounts were long overdue.

Meanwhile, the understandably teed-off Judge Keady complained in his memoir, "David's draws of salary and commissions were all shown on the books and indicated that he had enjoyed a highly successful year!"

When Keady informed his partners of "the debacle" they'd been bamboozled into, the three men concluded that my father, "though a good salesman, was devoid of management ability." They considered walking away from the partnership, letting him face the consequences alone. But there were debts they'd be accountable for, including the overdue "sizable monthly building rent." To make matters worse, there was the matter of the government cheese. The highly regarded sprinkler system Daddy installed had inexplicably switched on in the middle of one night. It ran nonstop for hours. The cheese was a total loss. This calamity was not his fault, but still . . .

The partners removed my father from the operations that bore his name. When Keady and the man they hired to take his place traveled to Chicago to negotiate with Allied, they discovered that Daddy had owed a substantial portion of the company's indebtedness *before* they'd organized the limited partnership. In order to get square with Allied, the partners sued the sprinkler company for negligence. Once they won that, they settled with Commodity Credit Corporation over the lost cheese. This took months. Paying off the debt to Allied took longer.

I have no reason to doubt Judge Keady's account of my father's shady approach to friendship and business, and in the end find his remarks to be quite fair. I do, however, question the casualness of his remark about Daddy—and by extension us—having personally enjoyed a quite successful 1953. The Keadys lived a block and a half down Washington Avenue from us. They had to know we'd lost our home. People didn't voluntarily move out of a house they'd just built to relocate into an okay rental they'd more than likely have to vacate within a year.

But judges depend on being right at least a good part of the time. And honestly, a truly expert con man might have known better than to hustle a one-armed man who, as a teenager, played statewide competitive tennis. Duped into suckerhood by my father's flimflam, Keady perhaps felt he'd earned the right to engage in a bit of snark.

Under the new manager's leadership, Keady and the other two investors eventually regained their original investment. Not long afterward, they began receiving dividends. When the new manager offered to buy them out, they were happy to sign over their shares. By then, the Feys were long gone.

. . . .

On December 21, Governor White authorized Ruth's second furlough, to begin December 31. This time around, however, the announcement came and went with little notice. Nobody took umbrage or celebrated. Nobody slammed the governor for yielding to class privilege. Perhaps this was because a lot of people who might be inclined to write in had something else on their minds.

The lawsuit *Brown v. Board of Education of Topeka,* arguing that racial segregation of children in public schools was unconstitutional, had been bundled with similar lawsuits and filed before the U.S. Supreme Court some fourteen months earlier. Word was, the justices might make a ruling before the coming summer. In years past, the South had enjoyed a good many favorable decisions from both the U.S. Supreme Court and the U.S. Congress. But the situation had changed.

Southerners' trepidation had begun to build in September, when Chief Justice Fred Vinson—who seemed likely to vote the segregationists' way—died and President Eisenhower nominated California's governor, Earl Warren, to take his place. Considered "communistic" by many white southerners, Warren posed far more danger than they could bear to think about. Within a month of his confirmation, a white man from Greenwood—the chubby-faced, bow-tied plantation manager Robert "Tut" Patterson—quit his job and started making speeches.

People, he said, should not wait for a decision on *Brown.* They should prepare for battle now. At stake were their God-given and constitutional rights, their vaunted "way of life." The time had come to "stand together forever firm against communism and mongrelization."

In the coming months Patterson added "atheism" and "amalgamation" to his rabble-rousing bundle of buzzwords. He also circulated a phony pamphlet purporting to be written by a Black man who asserted point-blank that what men of his race wanted was not to desegregate the schoolroom but to fulfill the white man's greatest fear by integrating his bedroom.

Most people found Patterson's call to action premature. But talk was building, and white residents of many southern towns, especially those with a majority-Black population—as was the case throughout the Mississippi Delta—began to discuss ways to defy the ruling if it went against them. They gathered over coffee in downtown drugstores and lingered after church services, smoking cigarettes on the lawn, speaking in low tones as the preacher stood in the church door shaking hands. The most popular strategy they discussed was a vague scheme to end the entire public school system and create separate private schools for Black and white students.

Then a member of the state legislature decided to weigh in. In its final 1953 session, the man known as Mr. Delta, Speaker of the Mississippi House Walter Sillers Jr. from Rosedale, introduced a resolution to preemptively create an amendment to the Mississippi Constitution, giving the legislature power to take full control of the state's public school systems, *if and when* a federal ruling defied the state's right to maintain racial segregation in its classrooms.

The resolution created vehement disagreement. Only after four raucous sessions did it finally squeeze through the house in a one-vote victory. The vote in the senate, however, ended in a tie. One vote short of a win, Sillers's resolution died.

Mr. Delta didn't back down. Accustomed to voter agreement with his views, unafraid to reveal his true motives, he contradicted the separate-but-equal argument when he told an interviewer the way to keep the masses satisfied with low wages and the status quo was to keep them uneducated. As for the *Brown* decision, he didn't really care what happened next. Even if Earl Warren and the U.S. Supreme Court ruled against the rightful power of the state to take care of its own damn business, he and his supporters had the numbers and the moral and political justification to do what had to be done.

The Jackson *Clarion-Ledger* made no bones about what Sillers was after: the right of private schools "to deny Negroes entrance to schools attended by whites."

A Rankin County senator blasted the resolution. It was, he said, "conceived in the minds of men of wealth . . . who could afford to send their children to private schools." An unveiled dig at Mr. Delta and every other uppity landowner in that part of the state.

In a *Delta Democrat-Times* editorial called "Good for the Senate," Hodding Carter dismissed the resolution as a fantastical and palpably unconstitutional subterfuge. He praised senators for giving Sillers the "lambasting he got" for attempting the same sort of trickery that resulted in "the South's long failure to make its schools equal" and led directly to the present crisis.

Did I notice any of this? Did my friends? I don't think so. For one thing, change seemed unlikely. For another, we were fifteen going on sixteen and had other things on our minds. If my parents had an opinion, they didn't speak of it. They too were concerned with other matters.

. . . .

Nineteen fifty-three drew to a close. Among his end-of-year reports, Governor White triumphantly announced that Parchman had enjoyed a banner season in cotton production and sales. Having sold some five thousand bales at an average of $34.16 a pound, the penal farm had deposited some $930,000 in the state treasury.

As for the debutante ball, the *Delta Democrat-Times* society editor abandoned restraint and described the 1953 ceremony as "the most beautiful in the history of the organization." The country-club ballroom was festooned with white flowers, gladioli, and smilax. The debutantes wore "frocks of frothy white and carried bouquets of white carnations."

Reminders of whiteness, it seemed, were everywhere.

The Feys waited for whatever came next. The Dickinses prepared for another reunion with Ruth. Many southerners shivered in anticipation of the Supreme Court ruling on *Brown*. Others advised patience. If the decision went against them, they'd handle it. Nothing was going to change.

1954: FURLOUGHS,
DOCTORS, *BROWN*, AND ELVIS

During Ruth's most recent furlough, Governor White received one petition signed by descendants of Idella Thompson and another by a hundred or so Mississippi residents. Both relayed the same message: Ruth had been sufficiently punished, no matter what she'd done.

The governor dutifully answered both but did nothing.

· · · ·

The day after her return to prison, Ruth's doctor, Paul G. Gamble, wrote to Parchman's chief medical officer, Dr. Thomas Robinson, concerning the "irregular and prolonged" menstrual periods Ruth had been experiencing for some years. According to Gamble, the condition had worsened considerably since her imprisonment. Ruth was now forty-five, and Gamble thought she had either fibroids, endometriosis, a uterine polyp, or cancer. His strong recommendation was that she undergo a complete hysterectomy. If Robinson agreed and decided to send Mrs. Dickins to Greenville for the procedure, he would appreciate being notified ahead of time, because he'd be the one to perform it.

And by the way, the Dickins family had assured him, they would foot all bills relating to the surgery and subsequent hospitalization.

Robinson conducted an examination. Seconding Gamble's diagnosis, he proposed to Superintendent Wiggins that because Mrs. Dickins was "apprehensive about having any surgery done except by her family doctor" and was willing and able to assume whatever financial obligation might be incurred, he recommended allowing her to go to Greenville for the procedure. Furthermore, because of her age and the seriousness of her condition, he hoped this could be done right away.

When Governor White received this information, he quickly sent his approval. When a reporter asked why Ruth was leaving prison again, so soon after her furlough, he delicately described the cause as "the most serious operation a woman can have."

The reporter pursued the matter no further. He didn't have to. Back then, having a uterus removed was thought to leave a woman scooped out and sexless. "Not a woman anymore," people whispered.

. . . .

While preparations for Ruth's surgery were in progress, my father's connection to what Judge Keady called his "drayage" business received its public termination when a quarter-page ad in *The Delta Democrat-Times* announced that "GREENVILLE STORAGE AND TRANS-FER CO. (Successor to Fey's Storage and Transfer Co.)" was under new management. Same address, different phone number, same Allied Van Lines logos: the duck, the squirrel, the mama cat.

In essence, we'd lost just about everything. House, business, standing. I think by then Daddy must have gone back to work as a traveling salesman, this time for a company called Brown and Bigelow, a manufacturer of swag, mostly the calendars and datebooks dry cleaners and funeral parlors gave away during the holiday season. My father believed in advertising, but he seriously hated that job. If a salesman didn't fully believe in what he was selling, he had to find a way to pretend. This was one time David Fey couldn't do that. He thought giving away free calendars as a way of increasing business and creating loyalty among customers was a crap idea and crap was what he was selling. When he worked the road as a detail man for drug companies, he was peddling, as much as the product itself, his own expertise. He knew chemistry and anatomy and could talk intelligently about the properties of a drug. Hawking calendars, he was a shill; a two-bit con man people hated to see coming in the door. I never heard him complain about other jobs. But this one, oh yes.

As for me, along with many of my friends, I'd joined Young Life, a nondenominational religious organization out of Colorado describing itself as "created to impress teenagers in high school with the thrill and excitement of Christianity." And, as a side benefit, to combat communism.

We met twice a month in the homes of young believers. Given a particular Bible verse to memorize, we spent the hourlong meeting discussing it, singing upbeat Christian songs, praying, and listening to a talk by our community leader, tall, blond, lively John "Long John" Miller. That winter, "the David Fey home on Main Extended" hit the paper after I volunteered our house for a meeting. And because we were planning a big Greenville-Leland get-together, *The Delta Democrat-Times* sent a cameraman and reporter. The photograph ran the following Sunday, corner of the page, nice and big, thirty or more of us, smiling our heads off.

Over the next two years, some of us would travel to Young Life camp in Colorado for a ten-day summer stay. There, we could enjoy the cool dry air and do some hiking and canoeing while continuing Bible studies. During the final few nights, we gathered at prayer meetings at which we were encouraged to accept Jesus as our Lord and Savior. My girlfriends and I went home filled with conviction. Among the girls' names listed as having attended the camp the summer I went was that of Dorothy Jane Dickins. If I met her—and my friend Sang says I probably did—I didn't make the connection.

Young Life's presence in the Delta came to an abrupt halt when a promotional leaflet featured a photograph of cheerful campers, among whom were two suspiciously dark-skinned boys. The next Sunday, a Greenville preacher, speaking from his pulpit, quoted a letter he'd received, accusing the organization of "communistic" leanings.

Our chapter disbanded. Long John Miller was assigned to a new territory. Our commitment to Christianity grew slack. We hardly noticed.

What remains is the newspaper photo, all of us looking happy, me in the front row, smiling away in the living room of our new and very temporary home.

. . . .

Ruth was hospitalized for more than three weeks. The day before she was scheduled to be discharged, her surgeon wrote to the governor, asking for more time.

Busily drafting "separate but equal" proposals designed to convince Washington that Mississippi's Black children were going to schools physically and educationally on a par with the ones attended by white students, Governor White managed somehow to sign off on an extra thirty days' leave for Ruth, "in order that she might have more opportunity to heal from her recent operation."

Granting prisoners emergency medical leave was not unusual. But if from a distance Ruth's favors seem a bit too easily bestowed, I don't think anyone in the Delta—or in Camp 9—was much surprised, given her age, social standing, skin color, family connections, and—perhaps the clincher—money enough to pay her own way.

Twenty-eight days later, Ruth's doctor was back again with the results of an "intradermal scratch test" for allergies and an accompanying letter explaining that in addition to her "female" ailment Ruth was suffering from an allergic skin condition—a rash—that had spread over her entire body. A direct result, Dr. Gamble felt, of the diet provided by Parchman. Additionally, ever since the surgery, she'd been suffering from a "swimming of the head, a not uncommon response to anesthetics from which she might not recover for two or three months." He was hoping the governor could arrange for yet another extension so that she could receive treatment for both conditions.

The scratch test revealed varying degrees of allergic reactions to an astonishing variety of foods, including bananas, pears, strawberries, tomatoes, eggs, lima beans, and white potatoes as well as yeast, oats, wheat, beef, pork, chicken, and lamb. Gamble omitted any discussion of Ruth's diet prior to her incarceration, which surely included a good many of those basic ingredients. To confirm his diagnosis, he consulted a Jackson dermatologist who agreed with him that the rash was more than likely a nervous condition exacerbated by prison food and the general circumstances of incarceration. In other words, she was allergic to prison?

Disliking the idea of granting her more time while finding it difficult to send her back to prison, White eventually chose what seemed to be the preferable option. He gave her another thirty days at home.

The governor's executive decision put Wiggins in something of a snit. When asked by a reporter when he thought Mrs. Dickins would return to serve out her sentence—because after all hadn't she been convicted of first-degree murder?—Wiggins responded with some petulance. She'd already been given—he couldn't remember, two? three?—extensions of her furlough, and frankly he didn't even know where she was. In many ways, Mrs. Dickins, it seemed, was no longer his prisoner.

Six days before Ruth's return, scheduled for June 7, Dr. Gamble wrote again. While he was certainly aware of and grateful for the governor's leniency, Ruth's dermatitis was still quite bad. He'd spoken again with the dermatologist from Jackson, who agreed that she'd have a difficult time recovering at Parchman. Might she stay at home a little longer?

White's response was brusque: Granting Ruth further leave was impossible. Mrs. Dickins, he said, should return when her time was up.

Given her ten-day furlough in January, the twelve days in February, all of March, April, and May, and six days into June, Ruth ended up enjoying almost four months at home, partially because of health concerns but perhaps more notably because she was wealthy enough to pay for any treatment her personal doctor might deem necessary. In this instance, John Dickins's repeated pleas for fairness seem to have been more than generously granted.

Toward the end of her Leland stay, Ruth was photographed at home by a Jackson reporter, standing before a gold-framed wall mirror, arranging flowers. The shot shows her in profile, emphasizing the swoop of her dark hair over her ear and down to a blunt crop halfway down her neck. Streaks of gray now thread through the blackness, adding definition. She's wearing a boxy suit coat and her hands are busy with the flowers, but her attention is elsewhere. Her eyes have lifted, and she's looking dramatically away from the flowers and the camera, into the distance. Once again, as in other photographs, she looks unwaveringly sad, filled with gloom. But then, her freedom was ending. She was going back.

. . . .

In the years to come, after alcoholism, diabetes, and arthritis had shattered my father's health and mobility, he entered a nursing home. As a special caretaker for him, I hired an orderly to, on a regular basis, bring him to my house for a Sunday afternoon visit.

We'd eat, chat, mess with the dogs, sit outside, and study the clear green river that ran nearby. Pleasant enough. But when his aide got back, Daddy turned dark and sour, and I knew he was regretful, at that point, that he'd come at all, if he had to go back. Nothing worked to cheer him up. The moment was awful.

It occurs to me to wonder if Ruth felt that way when, after so many months at home—long enough to feel she'd restarted her life there—she faced a return to Parchman. Did she feel a similar drop in her spirits as the contrast between home and confinement became a reality and felt like thumbs pressed against her eyes?

. . . .

In early May, Governor White flew with his wife to Washington to attend a White House conference of U.S. governors arranged by President Eisenhower. All forty-eight governors attended. Arriving home afterward, when asked the one question his constituents cared about, he boasted that, concerning desegregation and the *Brown* case, his backbone was a little stiffer than it had been when he left. He didn't think Mississippi would be as bound by *Brown* or any other Supreme Court decision as they'd been led to believe. Washington had no right to dictate policy to the governors of the respective states, and "if we do get an adverse decision, it may be so couched that we can take care of our situation nicely."

Two weeks later, on Monday, May 17, 1954, the Supreme Court handed down its decision. In a unanimous vote, engineered by Chief Justice Earl Warren, the Court ruled for the plaintiff. Segregation—the practice of separating Black and white students by law within a public school system—was declared unconstitutional. Southerners' "separate but equal" argument, which since the 1890s had fueled laws specifically designed to guarantee that white and Black students attended different schools, was iced out of existence. States were ordered to initiate a process of school desegregation. The ruling was called a "sweeping victory for the Negroes."

Within days of the announcement, the Mississippi U.S. congressman John Bell Williams had damned *Brown* on constitutional, educational, and cultural grounds. Calling desegregated schools "sites of anarchy," he dubbed the ruling an event that would forever be known as "Black Monday."

Thomas Pickens Brady (pronounced "Braddy"), a circuit court judge in Mississippi's Fourteenth Judicial District, picked up on the phrase. An effective, if bombastic, speaker, he began making appearances all over the state decrying the *Brown* decision and supporting white supremacy. Black people, he argued, were biologically inferior. They had made no significant contributions to civilization. Integration led to amalgamation. Warren and the other justices were communistic. All Americans had a patriotic duty to resist the desegregation of schools as part of an international conspiracy to destroy the country.

Having been encouraged to publish his remarks, Brady sat down and wrote a ninety-page manifesto he called *Black Monday: Segregation or Amalgamation: America Has Its Choice.* Among other things, it called for the elimination of the NAACP, the abolition of public schools, the popular election of Supreme Court justices, and a nationwide youth educational program on ethnology and communist infiltration.

One of its warnings was especially memorable.

"If trouble is to come," Brady warned, "we can predict how it will start." The instigator he envisioned was a "supercilious, glib" Yankee Black boy who came to the South from his home city for one reason or another and while there made an "obscene remark, or a vile overture or assault upon some white girl." Violence would follow, even killing, for how could it not? Belief in racial equality produced nothing but "riots, raping and revolutions."

. . . .

By mid-June, several other Lelanders had written to the governor to say they'd visited Ruth at home and had been shocked at her skin condition. Her imprisonment, they argued, was aggravating the malady while accomplishing nothing. What good was incarceration doing anybody, whether she killed her mother or not, for her to suffer more? Responding to their pleas once again, the governor asked Wiggins for an update on Ruth's health. In response, the superintendent arranged for the dermatologist who'd examined Ruth previously to pay a visit to Parchman and make a diagnosis.

The doctor was not impressed. Ruth's dermatitis, he reported, was much improved, and furthermore she seemed in altogether good spirits and was quite satisfied with the treatment she'd received at Parchman.

Ruth remained, for now, in Camp 9.

. . . .

After reading Brady's manifesto, Tut Patterson became even more committed to the cause they both espoused. He vowed to spend the rest of his life resisting desegregation, racial mongrelization, and communism. His first move was to go to Indianola and gather together a group of influential citizens, including a banker, a planter, and a lawyer, to discuss strategy. Together, they figured out a plan. The times required a more civilized version of terrorism with the same goal in mind: keeping Black people in their place. No hooded night riders. No burning crosses. They made some rules, named themselves the Citizens' Council, put together a letter-writing campaign and a reading list. They campaigned, crusaded, attracted members and money, first from the Delta and soon afterward from all over the state. "We can't have bloodshed," Brady warned. "If we stoop to that, we lose."

English teachers in Indianola and other towns agreed to conduct contests in which high school students were required to write an essay on the topic "Why School Segregation Is Better for Both Races." The U.S. senator James O. Eastland called for unrepentant resistance to the federal assault on segregation by any means necessary. Byron De La Beckwith, a member of the Sons of the American Revolution, sold *Black Monday* on Greenwood street corners. Massive resistance to federal interference in "our way of life" was called for by white organizers from all over the South.

There were a few dissenting voices. Hodding Carter chided readers who'd been surprised by the ruling on *Brown*. If ever a region asked for such a decision, he wrote, the South did through its "shocking, calculated and cynical disobedience to its own state constitutions which specify that separate school systems must be equal. For seventy-five years, we sent the Negro kids to school in hovels and pig pens, and even now we kid ourselves when we say we are approaching equality."

Governor White went his own way. While Patterson, Brady, and the other loudmouths were out speechifying, he continued working his charm campaign, speaking at Black institutions and conventions, offering a compromise he called "Equalization within Segregation." In July, he invited ninety leaders of the Black community, including some members of NAACP, to Jackson, where he made many hopeful promises, all with the underlying intention of maintaining the enforced separation of the races. When a spokesman for the Black delegation told the governor his people would not support any scheme undermining the Supreme Court's "just and humane decision," he was—as he told reporters—stunned.

With that, he gave up on any notion he'd had of charm as a bargaining chip.

Not long afterward, white Mississippians voted two to one in favor of a constitutional amendment allowing the state to abolish public schools. To limit and control voter registration, they also passed a bill requiring all people wishing to register to first read and understand the state constitution and then offer a reasonable interpretation of a particular passage chosen on the spot by the registrar.

Opposition to *Brown* ran wild-eyed through the South, creating chaos wherever it landed. But in no other section of the country were the leaders of the movement as virulently, defiantly determined as in the Mississippi Delta.

. . . .

The music, nonetheless, and the dancing continued. As if we'd been wound up to do it and couldn't stop or take time to think.

In August, the Fey family took a quick trip to Memphis, maybe two nights in the home of a couple they met when David and I were babies. Their names were Baxter and Scottie, and they had a daughter, Betty, who was a year older than me.

I hadn't seen Betty since we were children. She was sixteen now, and that night, in preparation for a date, she combed her butter-yellow hair in ringlets around her face, put on a tight, fuzzy sweater, and painted her full pouty lips bright red. To my mind, she was a sophisticate, a girl in the uptown know. She looked hard at me and said, "We got you a date." When nobody said I didn't have to go, I got ready.

The boys arrived. We drove to a drive-in food joint, got burgers and drinks, and rode around, checking out places they were interested in, then returned to Betty's house. We parked out front. The radio was on, low, tuned to the local station WHBQ. I was in the back seat sitting as far as I could get from my date, not saying much of anything. The others chatted and laughed. And then, suddenly, Betty shushed us.

Wait, she said. That's him. And she turned up the radio.

Elvis Presley had cut his first single the month before. When the Memphis deejay Dewey Phillips played his recording of "That's All Right, Mama" on his WHBQ radio show the first time, the switchboard lit up like crazy. So he played it again. And again. He followed up with the flip side, "Blue Moon of Kentucky." And then the A side again. In all, Phillips swore he played each of those songs fourteen times that night.

Two weeks later, the skinny boy with the high voice and the suggestive moves opened for the country singer Slim Whitman in the open-air Overton Park Shell, in midtown Memphis. Girls swooned, danced, screamed, went wild. We knew about him in Greenville, but couldn't always get WHBQ on our radios, and so we hadn't actually heard the songs.

A white boy singing Black music changed our little white-girl world. I went back to Greenville bragging to my friends. I'd *heard* him. They had no idea what that was like, to be in Memphis and actually *hear* him.

Girls across the nation soon bought the single. We played the grooves off it.

. . . .

By then we'd been kicked out of 1276 South Main and were living on Fairview Avenue in a much smaller, more run-down house. The neighborhood was respectable, but the house was small and fairly ratty, one of those asbestos-shingled bungalows that cropped up here and there, often the least good house on the block, an obvious rental. The kitchen was tiny. There was no dining room. Everything about the house was slightly shabby. We smushed in together. Mama hung the pictures. Put books on the shelves. Life was definitely going in the wrong direction.

The move, that house, and Elvis are the main things I remember about 1954.

In contrast, the year ended relatively well for the Dickinses. On December 16, perhaps because of the governor's refusal to allow her a fourth leave of absence in the spring, Ruth received notice that her Christmas furlough would begin five days later, on the twenty-first. This meant she'd be home on Christmas Day for the first time since 1948, the year of Idella Thompson's murder.

On Christmas night, Ruth sat down and, taking out a couple of sheets of John's personalized stationery, wrote Governor White a letter. She wasn't sure, she said, that writing to him was appropriate, but she did want to thank him for his trust and for giving her the chance to be with her family on Christmas. She praised his courage and kindness and promised, in return, never to disappoint him. "You are a source of inspiration to so many who are less fortunate than you. Whenever my road gets extra rough or my courage starts to go low-ebb, I think of the way in which you always fight and stand up for what you believe is right."

She piled on the praise.

She and John might well have found reason for hope in the coming year. K. L. "Doc" Witte had died in August. Ruth still had enemies but none as relentless as Doc.

. . . .

The year ended with a somewhat disappointing thud for those who were used to planning their Christmas and New Year's celebrations around attendance at the biggest blowout of the year, the Delta Debutante Club ball. In June, the club's new sponsor, Mrs. Lawrence Paxton, had announced that she and the board of directors had decided that girls ought to be making their debuts a year later than had been the case, once high school graduation was long behind them and they were well into their sophomore year of college.

The girls who, in the summer of 1954, had been invited to make their debuts would slide forward and join the 1955 group. In all likelihood, those girls were not asked to weigh in on this decision.

. . . .

Football crisscrossed with the Supreme Court ruling on *Brown* when the U.S. Naval Academy at Annapolis received an invitation to play in the 1955 Sugar Bowl against the Ole Miss Rebels. The game was a sell-out, the odds were even, and because Maryland hadn't seceded in 1861, a lot of Rebel fans were hot to sink the Midshipmen—who were, after all, enrolled in the U.S. Navy, which was a part of the despised federal government. And wasn't it all of a piece?

The Mid-Winter Sports Association handed out tickets to both colleges for distribution. But when the secretary of the navy received a letter of protest from a member of the NAACP, he turned his ticket over.

There it was, in print:

This ticket is issued for a person of the Caucasian Race and if used by any other is in violation of State Law.

For its entire twenty-year history, the Sugar Bowl had issued tickets with that warning. Assuming it didn't go unnoticed by every fan who'd bought or been given a ticket during that time, we might want to wonder, did anybody think anything about it? Ever?

In response, the navy secretary apprised the MWSA and the press that the navy had distributed its thirteen thousand tickets without regard to racial restrictions and that those tickets "will be so honored regardless of any printing thereon."

When questioned, a Sugar Bowl spokesman said he believed the navy's statement spoke for itself. The following day, the Jackson *Clarion-Ledger* headlined a front-page story, "Segregation Is Out at the Sugar Bowl," while one of its sportswriters called the decision a "blast from the frigid winds of social change," an obvious reference to the *Brown* decision.

The Yankees claimed victory over the Rebels 21–0.

. . . .

A few days later, Johnie Witte—the widow of the late K. L. "Doc" Witte and Idella Thompson's sister—wrote to Governor White "in regard to the recent movement to parole Mrs. Ruth Dickins."

A member of the state parole board, she wrote, had come to Leland recently, specifically to ask if her family would be opposed to Ruth's release. Mrs. Witte replied to the parole board member and then to Governor White in no uncertain terms: her family were "in complete accord with the position of [her] late husband." She was sorry that Mrs.

Dickins was in poor health and hoped that she was receiving proper medical treatment. But the right to sympathy along those lines should not be extended to cover her release and return to society.

Hugh White's response to Johnie Ruth Long Witte was brief. To sidestep the main issue at hand and forestall any suspicion of his complicity in the parole board member's inquiry, he claimed ignorance. He had, he said, no knowledge of the man's visit.

1955: CULMINATIONS

Agitation in the Delta mounted. In March, all hell broke loose, in Greenville in particular, when copies of the new *Look* magazine hit the stands. Within its pages, an article by Hodding Carter called "A Wave of Terror Threatens the South" directly challenged the local Citizens' Council's view of itself as nonviolent and law-abiding. Although things had remained calm so far, Carter wrote, "if today's leaders give way to boredom or anger or despair," the councils could be taken over by hoodlums and thugs and become "instruments of interracial violence," basically, a modern-day Ku Klux Klan.

The backlash was immediate, especially in the Delta. Tut Patterson lambasted Carter's assessment of the organization he'd helped organize while simultaneously assuming that anybody familiar with *The Delta Democrat-Times* already knew of its editor's "intolerance toward the determination of white people to stay white."

The mayor of one Delta town defended the Citizens' Councils as a respectable cross section of "our white male population."

A columnist in the *Jackson Daily News* accused "Clairvoyant Carter" of seeing a Ku Klux Klansman under every Mississippi bed and envisioning an "impending reign of terror." A state of mind, he warned, that would delight both the communists and the "Eastern critics hostile to Southern ways."

Carter refrained from responding but did nothing to prevent *Look* from running a four-inch ad in *The Delta Democrat-Times* touting his article. Illustrated with a stark white burning cross set against a solid black background, the ad posed a hard-sell question: "Will DESEGREGATION bring back the KLAN?" And below that, "Will the lash-wielding, night-riding mobs that once terrorized the South try for a comeback?" Readers who wanted answers should go out immediately and get the exclusive story of how the Citizens' Councils might be used to "threaten the peace of the South," written by Hodding Carter, "noted Southern editor," in its latest issue.

This provoked another spate of bilious comments and even a burning in effigy on the Carter lawn. Threats and nighttime gunshots were followed up by a vote of the Mississippi House of Representatives, which 89–19 charged Carter with lying. The message of his article, the congressmen declared, "drew inferences and conclusions on the flimsiest and most speculative kind of evidence" and was nothing but a "willful lie a nigger-loving editor made about the people of Mississippi."

Carter responded in a sly editorial headlined "Liar by Legislation." Making fine use of his puckish sense of humor, he suggested that now that he'd been resolved a liar by the house of representatives, he felt qualified to serve as a member of that body. As such, therefore, he herewith resolved by a vote of 1–0 that there were eighty-nine liars in the state legislature, beginning with Speaker Walter Sillers and working its way down through the ranks, skipping only the sensible nineteen who voted against the resolution.

"I am hopeful," he concluded, "that this fever, like the Ku Kluxism that rose from the same kind of infection, will run its course before too long a time. Meanwhile those 89 character-mobbers can go to hell collectively or singly and wait there until I back down. They needn't plan on returning."

. . . .

The Mississippi house passed another bill that same week making it unlawful for a member of the "white or Caucasian race" to attend any school attended by a member or members of the "colored or Negro race." Flouting the state law was now punishable by a hefty fine or even a jail term. "This," said the congressman who filed the bill, "segregates us."

Abandoning all pretense of belief in a "separate but equal" school system, one congressman suggested that a white child would be "better off in jail than in a Negro school," a statement that, considering the state of schools built exclusively for Black students, might not have overstretched the truth.

. . . .

Late in April, Governor White made an unannounced trip to Parchman, perhaps to survey the new gas chamber he'd been so high on, which, after several postponements, had recently been the site of its first successful execution. During the visit, White apparently expressed additional interest in Ruth's physical condition. Had it improved? It's not clear what the governor had in mind, but Wiggins must have detected a note of seriousness in his tone, for he wrote to the Parchman medical department right away. He wanted a complete medical checkup of Ruth to be scheduled immediately.

Lacking a prior diagnosis by Ruth's local physician, Dr. Robinson conducted a complete physical workup, including lab tests. His main concern was Ruth's weight. In 1953, during her Christmas furlough, she'd told a reporter she was proud of the thirty pounds she'd lost in prison. She was down, she said then, to a "healthy 120 pounds." Which means that, by her own measure, when she arrived at Parchman in 1950, she weighed close to 150. In 1955, she was down to 105.5, a considerable drop.

Her other vital signs were pretty normal, but the rash was back and there were indications of scratching and swelling. She'd suffered a fall the day before the doctor's visit. It had left her sore and bruised, but an X-ray revealed no fracture or bone pathology. Ruth's only complaint was the sting and itch of the dermatitis. The doctor's final report listed as symptoms the "evidence of weight loss and some emaciation," persistent dermatitis, some inflammation of the lymph nodes, and, because of the fall, contusions and back sprain. He admitted her to the prison hospital and ordered a rigorous diet, along with treatment for the rash, which he still maintained was of allergic origin.

Two weeks later, after his regular Sunday visit, John wrote to Wiggins to thank him for his attentiveness and concern. The diet they'd put Ruth on had greatly helped. Most of the rash had disappeared; in fact, her skin was clearer than it had been in some time, and she'd been relieved of the "constant stinging" and itching, which had "practically worn her out." Though the food regime was rigid, he was certain Ruth would stay on it, determined as she was to get her health back. She'd even gained a little weight. But she was still awfully thin, and her right leg bothered her.

Nonetheless, he was grateful for Wiggins's care and asked him to thank the hospital staff for the fine job they were doing.

Governor White's attention to one inmate's health would have been unusual at any time. By late summer, it was extraordinary. As schools throughout the South were opening for the fall semester, the newly energized Mississippi chapter of the NAACP was threatening to forcibly enroll Black children in all-white schools. Citizens' Council members responded, not always nonviolently. Black men who'd been registering voters for the upcoming fall elections were either fired from their jobs, threatened, or in some cases shot dead on the courthouse lawn. In May, Reverend George W. Lee, a Black preacher, businessman, and NAACP organizer, was killed in a drive-by shooting. In response, the county sheriff called the murder an accident. The metal in Lee's mouth, he said, was not from a bullet but "loose dental fillings." When Black parents showed up to enroll their children in white schools, they were told enrollment had ended and they should return to their regular school and sign up there.

And then, on August 28, a fourteen-year-old boy from Chicago was kidnapped from his uncle's house in the middle of the night and taken by two grown men to a nearby barn, where he was brutally pistol-whipped and murdered, his corpse tied to a cotton gin fan and tossed into the Tallahatchie River. The boy was Black; the men were white. This happened in the Delta, in Leflore County, near Greenwood, where the boy—Emmett Till of course—was visiting relatives. He'd supposedly grabbed the hand of a white woman working in her family's general store, then asked her for a date. Before one of his cousins could pull him outside to safety, Till told the woman goodbye, then—some said— issued a "wolf whistle" at her.

The woman, Carolyn Bryant, closed the store and rushed home to tell her husband what the boy had done. Two days later, Till was dead.

The men who killed Emmett Till showed no remorse. Few local citizens thought they should. By defending the honor of sacred white womanhood, they were fulfilling Tom Brady's *Bloody Monday* prophecy, which declared that if schools were desegregated, racial violence was inevitable. The trouble would begin, he predicted, when "a young Negro from some northern city came down and made some kind of obscene remark" or "vile assault or overture" upon "some white girl."

That would set things off. And after that . . . ? Well, they'd been warned.

. . . .

I keep wondering how long prophecy takes to morph, in the minds of those prone to believe, not just into permission but into something close to a commandment, an obligation to act accordingly, to make certain the prophecy is made manifest. We don't always know how we came to believe a certain thing or what inspired us to carry out a particular action, one we might previously have never dreamed of. Memory has its ways. We think we forget when we don't.

. . . .

By September, Ruth's health had deteriorated again, and according to Dr. Robinson she was in need of an unspecified treatment unavailable at Parchman. Governor White heard about this when a member of the parole board dropped by his office and said he'd heard the news from Hilton Waits, who said Ruth's husband, John, had told him. Knowing of the governor's concerns regarding Mrs. Dickins's health, the parole board member thought he'd want to know. In response, White wrote to Marvin Wiggins to ask if in his judgment Mrs. Dickins should have a "suspension for a while until she can recover from whatever her trouble is."

Some people thought John Dickins's wealth played its part in keeping Ruth's situation alive in the governor's mind, something like a secret payoff deal between the two men, facilitated by Hilton Waits. And while that explanation would be the odds-on favorite among those who believed Ruth should remain in prison, I for one am not convinced. Not because I think John Dickins was too upstanding a citizen ever to have done such a thing—he as much as said he would do whatever it took to get his wife out of prison—but because I figure that John Dickins was smart enough to realize he didn't have to. The tide was slow, but it was moving in his direction.

But time was running out. Hugh White had moved into his final three months in office. On January 17, the current state attorney general, J. P. Coleman, would be sitting in the governor's chair. In a campaign speech, Coleman had made his intentions clear regarding Ruth when he vowed that during his administration she would be released only over his dead body.

If White was going to be the one to let her out, he had to act fast. But he had a problem. Only two years earlier, he had insisted that no pardon or suspension would be forthcoming while he was governor unless new evidence challenging Ruth's conviction had been found. If he was going to pardon her or suspend her sentence indefinitely, he had to find a way to justify a change in his thinking.

Waits was working on that.

. . . .

The day after the governor wrote to Wiggins to ask about Ruth's health, a jury of twelve Tallahatchie County white men deliberated for a little more than an hour before returning a verdict of not guilty for the men who killed Emmett Till. Expecting a much quicker decision, some people thought the length of time they took might well indicate a measure of racial progress. But as one juror explained, it wouldn't have taken that long if they "hadn't stopped to drink pop."

To complicate the situation and give it further nationwide attention, when Till's body was sent home to Chicago for burial, his mother allowed her son's casket to be open so the world could see what southern white men had done to her boy. *Jet* magazine ran a photograph of the boy's mutilated face—unrecognizable not only as who he was but also as a *human*—in its September 15, 1955, issue. An estimated quarter of a million people filed by Till's casket. Other periodicals fell in line and ran the shocking picture in their pages. The world responded. And the rumble of protest began to inch forward into an actual movement.

Governor White issued a brief statement deploring the murder and then returned to other concerns. When Hilton Waits wrote to him in late October to suggest that he think about making a trip to Leland to suss out for himself the town's feelings about Ruth, he was already making plans to go.

. . . .

John and Ruth were longtime customers of the Bank of Leland, which had been founded early in the twentieth century by the two families who'd first hired John to work in their cotton offices. His request to use the bank's Director's Room as a place for the governor to comfortably meet local residents and listen to what they had to say about having Ruth back home again was given quick approval. There were other, more public spaces, but John might have been trying to keep some of the naysayers in the dark by choosing a less obvious spot.

White and his secretary arrived at 11:18 on the morning of November 16. By then, some forty white people had already lined up in the hall outside the Director's Room. Most were middle-aged or older. Once he and the stenographer had set up, he began calling people in, either singly or in groups of two or three.

He'd already heard from a good many of Ruth's supporters, and he was pretty clear on what a lot of Greenville bankers, lawyers, and business-men thought. But petitions were essentially a form of propaganda, and he needed to ask his own questions, come to his own conclusions. Did people in her hometown want her back? As a member of their church and their neighborhood, somebody they might cross paths with every day? What if the jury had it right? Did that mean she had the capacity to commit murder with *malice aforethought* again? Were they afraid that might happen?

The stenographer took notes, identifying each witness by name, re-cording their answers to the governor's questions.

Opinions voiced by the majority group varied somewhat in regard to the question of guilt or innocence, but not in terms of basic support.

She'd served long enough, some said. Too long, according to others.

Her health was suffering. It was a shame—*it was cruel*—to keep a sick woman in prison.

As for the will of the community, the governor should know that many of those who had felt bitter toward her at first had changed their minds and were now in favor of letting her come home. And even if she did kill her mother, some said, the charge should have been manslaughter, not murder. She never *planned* to stab Mrs. Thompson to death. She did it in a "rage of anger," the kind of thing that could happen to anybody.

W. E. Bufkin, the ever-ambivalent school superintendent, still refused to go all out. "I did not approve of her," he said, "and she did not approve of me. But I feel she should be let out."

Some repeated the usual tropes: Ruth was convicted by public opinion and rumors, the newspapers were to blame for the gossip, the five or six people who wanted her to stay locked up were either outsiders or plain "soreheads."

. . . .

The opposition, though many fewer in number, was as resolute as ever, even without Doc Witte. They thought returning Ruth Dickins to Leland would be the worst thing for the community since the murder of Mrs. Thompson. As longtime friends of the Stovall-Thompson family or in some cases blood relatives, they had sympathy for Ruth and especially for her daughters and her fine Christian husband. If she was a "normal person," they wouldn't say a word against her, but everybody knew she wasn't normal and that she and her mother both were high-tempered and difficult. The ladies of Leland, the wives who had previously been Ruth's friends—according to their husbands—would be scared to death if she came home. They'd heard that friends were the ones abnormal people like her attacked. And did the governor know that three people in her family had been murdered: the father who supposedly committed suicide, even though he was shot twice in the back of the head; the husband Ruth's sister killed a long time ago; and now Mrs. Thompson? One person even accused Ruth of killing a rival. Her husband's girlfriend.

But the most potent piece of information communicated to the governor was that Hilton Waits and John Dickins had invited only the citizens they knew to be in Ruth's corner. They were told this was their opportunity to speak up for Ruth and help bring her home. Hilton Waits had eventually called one of the five men who'd been to Jackson to speak against her release but not until that morning, just before White arrived. Others knew nothing about the meeting. And the newspapers didn't cover it. As several people assured the governor, if they'd known in advance, they could have rounded up hundreds of like-minded protesters. But they didn't. The deck, they believed, had obviously been stacked against them.

John, Dell, and Dorothy Jane Dickins testified last. The stenographer did not record their comments.

. . . .

The governor stayed in Leland for about two hours before heading to Parchman. The prison was out of the way, but he made a stopover nonetheless, to have a conversation with Ruth.

White had turned seventy-four in August. Although he came from a family of many children, he had none himself. He was old, fat, and childless, walked with a cane, and would soon be replaced in office. He was also a rich white man with nothing to lose if he made an unpopular decision. It's hard to imagine he didn't have some ingrained feeling for a white woman of forty-nine who had had major surgery, was disturbingly thin, and had been driven near mad with a merciless itch. And there were the daughters, especially the one still at home. She needed her mother.

Aside from certain elements of her personality and her past, Ruth would have been *familiar* to Hugh White.

He didn't stay long at the penitentiary. He'd already made up his mind. Arriving at his office, he wrote a letter to the chairman of the state parole board requesting their recommendation. The next day, November 17, the seventh anniversary of Idella Thompson's murder, he held a press conference.

His announcement was brief: unless he received strong, sensible protests within a reasonable amount of time, he would sign off on an indefinite suspension of Ruth Dickins's sentence. The meeting at the Leland bank had convinced him that the vast majority of Leland citizens wanted her to be given her freedom and to have her back living in their midst. In contrast, the five who showed up to protest it were, he said, "the same ones who have objected all along."

There was also the matter of her conviction. The physical evidence showed "*conclusively,*" he contended, that there had been a fight before Idella Thompson was killed. Furthermore, "*it is known that* Mrs. Thompson had the garden shears in her hands when an argument commenced." And when she struck her daughter with the shears, "*people in Leland think*" Mrs. Dickins wrestled the shears from her mother and struck the fatal blow, not with malice aforethought, but in the heat of passion.

And so the lame-duck Mississippi governor, Hugh White, found it in his heart to slide by his original, sternly worded demand and make use of wobbly speculations voiced by the friends, neighbors, and family of a convicted murderer as a way to justify his actions without acknowledging the discovery of any new evidence at all.

He blasted the jury's charge. "If she was guilty of anything," he declared, "it was manslaughter."

He urged citizens of Mississippi to think of her release therefore as a kind of restoration of justice. For if Ruth had been properly charged and convicted, she'd be up for parole now anyway. So there. As judge and jury, he hoped his constituents would agree with him that that was conclusive proof of Ruth's having served "long enough." He'd held off letting her out thus far, but unless he heard strong protests against it now, he wouldn't do so any longer. He was, however, allowing plenty of time for protests to come in.

Asked if by "plenty of time" he meant, say, about ten days, he said, "Something like that."

Nobody thought it necessary to ask whether the governor agreed with John Dickins's belief in his wife's innocence. He never mentioned innocence. And in fact, by describing the fight between Ruth and Idella and excusing Ruth's actions as having been carried out in the heat of passion, he was essentially accusing her of killing her mother.

Ruth's release wasn't an exoneration or a full pardon. Basically, what seems clear about the governor's thinking is that he just thought Ruth Dickins ought to go home and live her life as wife and mother. After all, there was very little possibility she'd kill anybody else.

And he found a convenient way to do that.

. . . .

Outraged letters of protest began to arrive before he could start packing up his papers. Leroy Allen, his longtime critic from Leland, reminded White that when he and five other men from Leland visited Allen in his office in 1953, the governor had interrupted their declaration to state absolutely that without proof of new evidence he would not pardon Mrs. Dickins at any time during his tenure. They were, Allen wrote, grateful for that statement, "believing then and now that you would fulfill it in every sense."

Allen and the others with him that day were fully aware that the governor had been under constant pressure to release Ruth, especially during recent months when her health became an issue. But as far as he knew, nothing new had developed in her case, no evidence brought forward that might alter the views the governor expressed two years earlier. Furloughs were one thing, but Allen and his friends remained convinced that Ruth's return to Leland as a permanent resident would do much to disrupt the social life of the community and frustrate the ends of justice.

When he received no response from the governor's office, Allen gave a statement to the papers saying he and others who agreed with him had not been notified of the hearing until just before it took place, too late for many who might have wanted to protest to make arrangements to be there.

The matter of the meeting was, Allen argued, "adroitly and secretly handled" by Hilton Waits and others, and if the governor was inclined to think he could leave fair notification of the hearing to the "partisan hands of Mr. Waits," his confidence was greatly misplaced. Allen wasn't completely certain what had been done to secure the overwhelming presence of citizens favoring her release, but even many of the bank officials admitted they had no knowledge of the meeting until the crowd began to assemble. Earlier that fall, there'd been whispers all over town saying the governor was planning to release Ruth before Christmas, but Allen hadn't paid them much attention. Given their previous discussions, he'd been led to believe that, like himself, the governor was convinced of her guilt. In which case, why would he let her out?

Allen also made an obvious reference to the verdict in the Emmett Till trial when he wondered if, now that Mississippi was being denounced all over the world as a "lawless commonwealth," its citizens didn't owe it to themselves to prove that they believed in retributive justice for all?

Eight of Ruth's jurors wired White the day he was in Leland to let him know they knew nothing of the meeting at the bank and objected to parole or pardon for her.

Two people thought the state might as well close up the courts and the jails if governors were going to release murderers like Ruth to kill again.

One woman suggested that, given the national and international publicity of the Emmett Till case, if White now "turned Mrs. Dickins loose on an innocent community," signs would appear all over the country telling people to "bring your victim to Mississippi to murder. Nobody cares."

Doc Witte's widow, Johnie, wrote again to ditto the jurors' complaint. She knew nothing about the public hearing in Leland and wanted to assure the governor that her family had not changed its opinion; they were still in complete accord with her late husband, Dr. K. L. Witte, and would very much oppose Mrs. Dickins's release. A pardon should not be based on a popularity contest. The hearing had once again torn the community apart, as any discussion of this incident always did. If Mrs. Dickins was ill, the families against her release would hope she'd be hospitalized and receive proper treatment at the prison. She didn't have to come home for that.

"Governor," wrote Mrs. W. B. Summer from Jackson, "if you release her you might as well throw open the prison doors and let all criminals out. She killed her mother in cold blood. How many prisoners in Parchman are guilty of a crime so heinous? I do not believe in capital punishment but if anyone deserved the death penalty, she does."

From Memphis: "Ruth Dickins' husband and any others who are active in her behalf should be incarcerated in a lunatic asylum."

From New Albany, regarding the incoming governor: "Mr. J. P. Coleman stated that if you wanted her pardoned you had better do it before the middle of January or she was in for four more years."

There were also letters of support to add to the pile. One from Ruth's brother-in-law Pope McCorkle included a comment she made during a visit he and his wife made to see her. "Pope," she'd said, "you know I have served longer in Parchman than any white woman . . . all others have died, committed suicide or have been pardoned."

McCorkle clearly thought the governor would consider "longer . . . than any white woman" important.

. . . .

The chairman of the parole board replied to White's request for their recommendation within two weeks. The board had interviewed both Dr. Robinson and Ruth and had examined her file, which included a spotless prison record and a statement from Robinson concerning Ruth's poor physical health. Additional material supporting her release were petitions containing a total of 908 signatures, 114 personal letters, and sworn affidavits from three members of her trial jury.

. . . .

Opposing clemency were 33 signed and four unsigned letters of protest—one of them signed by eight of Ruth's trial jurors—and petitions containing 47 signatures.

In conclusion, the parole board chairman wrote, "After a long and careful study and deliberation, taking into consideration the physical condition of this prisoner at this time, the Parole Board feels that the ends of justice will best be served and society will not be jeopardized by recommending to Your Honor an indefinite suspension of sentence" for "Mrs. Ruth Thompson Dickins, MSP No. X-19813, White Female."

By the end of November, Hugh White had exactly the backup support he needed.

. . . .

Friday, December 9, 1955, six and a half years after Ruth was sentenced to spend the rest of her natural life in prison and less than six years after she entered Parchman Farm and donned her up-and-downs, the governor announced the indefinite suspension of her sentence, beginning the moment it was issued. He had not chosen to pardon her, and so she would not be able to reclaim her suffrage rights, but unless she violated the terms of her release—committed another crime, behaved in a wretchedly unseemly manner—she would remain free for the rest of her life.

To defend his decision, Governor White might be said to have skirted the truth. Or perhaps more correctly, to have outright lied. Admittedly, he said, he'd received a "few" letters opposing this decision, but most were "crank protests" from people from out of town who knew little about the case. And he quoted the recommendation of the parole board.

· · · ·

When John Dickins arrived at the penitentiary at eight o'clock the next morning, he found his wife, he said, mopping the floor of her dormitory. All the camps received daily newspapers, and so in all likelihood Ruth knew about the governor's announcement, but until she looked up and saw her husband, or so she said, she'd had no idea she'd be going home so soon. From the women's camp, she and John went to the administration building for processing. When they left at 9:30, John said, "She'll never come back to this place."

A clearly miffed Wiggins warned against entertaining absolutes. "Mrs. Dickins," he said, "could be sent back to prison by any future governor who didn't think she was doing right." When asked about her health, he said it wasn't as bad as the papers said.

Ruth told *The Delta Democrat-Times* she thought she'd done some good for other women in the camp she'd lived in—those whom the Greenville judge Emmett Harty called "the *vilest of womankind*"— talking to them and asking them about their life and problems.

"I'm the best Baptist in the South," she quipped. As for John, he simply said they were hoping to live a normal life now, without publicity.

· · · ·

Dell's engagement to be married to the future congressman Vincent Scoper was announced the next day. In January, she would graduate with special distinction from Mississippi College. The wedding was set for less than a month later, on February 11. First Baptist Church. Leland.

A few days later, Ruth entered King's Daughters Hospital, where she had minor surgery for an undisclosed condition. After three days, she was back in Leland.

The rumors heard by Leroy Allen, it turned out, were true. Ruth was home for Christmas.

Only one newspaper issued anything close to a negative comment about the governor's decision. In his weekly column, Oliver Emmerich, editor of the *McComb Enterprise-Journal,* wondered about other people sentenced to life for murder, people who were "humble, unknown and without influence." Would they receive the same consideration as an influential socialite like Ruth Dickins?

Side by side with newspaper articles about Ruth's release were reports of continued violence against Mississippi Black men. In August, Lamar Smith, a farmer and World War I veteran, was shot dead in broad daylight and at close range on the lawn of the Lincoln County Courthouse while organizing Black voter registration. Three men were arrested. No indictments. Three months later, Gus Courts, an outspoken Black grocer, was shot in front of his store. The police blamed unidentified members of the Black community and did not seriously investigate the shooting.

But on December 4, four days after Rosa Parks was arrested in Montgomery, Alabama, for refusing to give up her bus seat to a white person, a young preacher named Martin Luther King Jr. spoke before several thousand Montgomery citizens at the Holt Baptist Church.

"There comes a time," he told the crowd, "when people get tired of being trampled over by the iron feet of oppression."

Many historians consider this the real beginning of the civil rights movement in this country.

RUTH AT HOME

In one sense, Ruth began a new life, her third. The minute she was released, newspapers no longer referred to her by her given name, as they had when she was a criminal. From that day forward, in the eyes of the press she became, once again, Mrs. John Dickins, socialite, wife, mother.

She could also be as easily said to have picked up where she left off, just as, after a few years away, a seasoned world traveler might decide to come back home. And there she was, the same Ruth as before. As if, with the wave of an outgoing governor's political wand, the past had been erased.

. . . .

On Sunday, February 12, 1956, Dell's quite beautiful wedding portrait, along with a description of the wedding itself, took up fully half of the first page of the *Delta Democrat-Times* society section. Held in the evening, the event was huge. Guests from all over the state. Elaborate flower arrangements, a big reception afterward at the Greenville Country Club. Mildred and Shields Hood were there; Thompsie—now married and the father of three—was a groomsman. Demetra and Wood Thompson drove from Jackson to attend. Demetra hosted the bridesmaids' luncheon that afternoon at her family's home in Hollandale. Ruth wore . . . well, let the society editor describe it: "The bride's mother was attired in a flax Italian silk sheath costume with a yellow-throated orchid." The only missing Thompson sibling was the older brother, Jimmy, who presumably remained at home in the outlying suburbs of Denver.

And incredibly enough, in contrast to the predictions of the protesters who foresaw further violence if Ruth were set free, life did seem to return to something like normal for the Dickins family, just as John had hoped. Ruth was welcomed back into the fold of the Baptist church, first as a substitute Sunday school teacher, then as a regular. She taught adults and for a couple of years took on the Girls' Auxiliary, the Baptist church's special class for teenage girls. She worked in the church library, attended Baptist conventions, chaperoned girls when they took church trips to Memphis.

In Leland, I met a woman who'd been a member of Ruth's GA class. She said she'd never known anyone as kind as Ruth Dickins.

"She was just . . ." She paused, searching for a more descriptive term, then gave up.

"Just," she continued, "*kind.*" After a moment she added, "And she had the lowest voice I'd ever heard in a woman. And the deepest southern accent."

But there was one strange thing about her. She never smiled. Not ever.

So, I wondered, she was kind without smiling?

The woman said she guessed so.

I found that odd, especially for a southern woman, but then, Ruth had always made it her business to challenge conventional—especially regional—expectations.

. . . .

Dell and her husband settled in Louisiana. But Dorothy Jane was still in Leland, a senior in high school, and very much a presence in town. An adventurous girl, in contrast to Dell, she had a predilection for hijinks and edgy fun. When pranksters set a small fire at her school, she told a friend she'd definitely get called in for it. "They blame me," she joked, "for everything."

But in many, if not most, ways her life changed for the better once her mother came home, perhaps partly because as a teenager Ruth had been something of an off-the-charts, fun-loving girl herself, and instinctively knew better than to try to reshape her second daughter in the mold the older sister had set. Dorothy Jane took over the quarters John had had built for the girls' nanny. Presumably because of her artistic skills, when a Who's Who contest was held in her high school, she was voted the senior best known for outstanding "capability."

Like Ruth, after graduating, she went off to a girls' school in Virginia—Sullins, a two-year Methodist college in Bristol. By then, she'd been to Bermuda and after her freshman year at Sullins flew to Hawaii to attend the University of Hawaii's summer session there. Two years later, she spent time in London. She took part in many of her friends' weddings as a bridesmaid, announced her forthcoming wedding in Greenville, even provided names of those who'd be in her wedding party. Then abruptly canceled it.

Ruth went to and gave parties, shared cuttings from her garden with neighbors, helped Dorothy Jane and her cousins with their Latin studies. A joke—actually a stand-alone punch line—that went around town was, *I heard Ruth Dickins showed up at the hardware store to buy a new pair of pruning shears!*

Young people still told scary stories about her, shuddered at the sight of her. One boy swore to a friend that while delivering advertising flyers on Deer Creek Drive, he passed Ruth's house and saw her, outside, on her knees, digging in the flower bed. She waved and called him by name, he waved back, and then a dog from next door appeared, barking and lunging at him. Ruth ran to the sidewalk with a shovel in her hand and smashed the barking dog in the head. Hard enough that he fell down dead. *Dead.*

This was the kind of story that gained traction in some Leland circles and was banned in others. Most seem unlikely to be true.

A man who worked for a television cable company told me he refused to work alone at the Dickins house if Ruth was there. He was serious. He shuddered slightly, remembering.

Another man said that once when, as a teenager, he went to a Greenville restaurant, he looked over and there she was, having dinner. She called him over. "Sit with me," she said. "I don't like to eat alone." Having been reared never to disobey his elders, he picked up his plate and moved to her table.

She asked him about his schoolwork. He answered.

"But," he said, "I was so scared I couldn't eat my French fries."

Small towns love to tell stories about a local boogeyman. In Leland, the boogeyman was, for many years, a woman.

. . . .

The spring of 1956, my last semester at GHS, turned out to be a good one. In October, I became a published writer when an essay I wrote won the Greenville Community Fund essay contest. The subject was "What the Community Fund Means to Greenville," and the contest was open to students from both high schools: all-white Greenville High and all-Black Coleman. A hundred students entered from our school; fifty from Coleman. Two winners were chosen from each, a boy and a girl. All four essays were scheduled to run, one at a time, on the editorial page of *The Delta Democrat-Times*.

Here's my opener: "To you, Reader, the Community Fund may seem to be just another organization that robs your piggy bank blind. But stop a minute and think. Think of a pale thin man lying straight and still on a narrow hospital bed, stricken with that dreaded disease, cancer; a lonesome soldier who longs for his home, his wife and his children, a small child badly in need of a pair of shoes . . . etc. Then, Mr. and Mrs. Reader, consider . . ." It goes on, challenging unseen readers to think beyond their own lives, to dig deep into their pockets and *give*.

I'm not sure I'd have entered that contest without the urgent prodding of an enthusiastic English teacher named Nell Thomas. Mrs. Thomas loved teaching literature, especially books written by Greenville authors. In addition to assigning works from the past, she never quit poking around in the schoolroom bushes to flush out and nurture her town's next great writer. We had a duty, she told us. A legacy to fulfill.

Later that same year, she encouraged me to enter another contest. I won that one as well. A couple of hours after Ruth and John left Parchman for Leland, I arrived at the Hotel Greenville to read my winning Voice of Democracy essay to the junior chamber of commerce. Given the topic "I Speak for America," I employed the same exhortative tone that won me the Community Fund prize. It began, "Communist, Fascist, beware! I speak with a voice that is free."

The Jaycees awarded me a Smith-Corona portable typewriter, which at some point my father took possession of and was still using in 1960 when his latest place of business opened with some fanfare and then quickly closed. And when, a lifetime later, in 1982, my mother began to keep a journal, she often typed her entries on that same little machine. After that, I don't know. It disappeared.

By this time my family and I were living in our next Greenville house—my last—located on a narrow lot some seven or eight blocks due north of the previous ratty one. Again, I don't know why we moved; all I know is, it wasn't by choice. The new house was not as old or as run-down as the one we just moved out of, but it was far smaller and in style totally inappropriate to the neighborhood.

Built of concrete blocks painted white and little more than one room wide, it resembled nothing more than a single-wide trailer placed vertically on a long, narrow lot. The floors were concrete, painted red. The living room and kitchen shared a narrow space, separated only by a breakfast bar. Beyond the kitchen was a bathroom, then David and Eddy's room, hardly bigger than a walk-in closet, and a few steps from there my parents' bedroom. I had the far-back room.

My mother called it "the Florida house."

Life had become touchier than ever by then, any sideways remark capable of setting off a storm.

THE RECKONING

An aerial shot of Idella Thompson's neighborhood, featuring her house and the area around it, between Second Street and Deer Creek Drive, as indicated by the white lettering. The picture was taken by Mrs. J. E. Ahler Jr. and presented to the jury as Defense Exhibit No. 1. It was shot from the rear to show how the man Ruth described might have escaped from the Thompson back porch, across Second Street, toward the cotton compress. It was not included in the trial transcripts but appeared in *Tragedy-of-the-Month* magazine. Although Judge Jordan had banned the taking of photographs inside the courthouse during the trial, the editors of this magazine found clever ways to sidestep that ban and to run pictures of Ruth and John Dickins alongside their lawyers, as well as candid shots of the prosecutors, the judge, the Thompson family, the packed courtroom audience, Doc Witte, Frank Aldridge, and many others. This made *Tragedy-of-the-Month* an immensely valuable visual source.

MASSIVE RESISTANCE

I became involved with Nell Thomas once again when, early on the morning of Monday, February 13, 1956, she called. Instinctively, I wondered if I'd done something wrong. Teachers didn't much call students directly. But no, she wanted me to meet her in front of the high school half an hour or so ahead of my classes. There was something she wanted me to do. And by the way, I should be sure to wear something nice.

. . . .

On the preceding Friday—the day before Dell Dickins's wedding and two weeks after the killers of Emmett Till had nonchalantly acknowledged their guilt to a magazine writer—Senator James O. Eastland, known as the godfather of Mississippi politics and a fierce opponent of racial equality, made a speech at the Alabama Coliseum in Montgomery.

Sponsored by the Citizens' Councils, the rally drew a standing-room-only audience of an estimated eleven to fifteen thousand white people, many of whom had driven there from Georgia and Mississippi. Membership applications to the Citizens' Councils were available for $3.50. Tut Patterson also spoke, but Eastland was incontrovertibly the big gun. The headliner. To champion white supremacy, he ranted, railed, and called for stern resistance to any form of segregation. In response, his audience cheered, gave the rebel yell, and demanded one more rousing round of "Dixie."

The event issued a ringing notice from large numbers of white southerners just how unwilling they were to tolerate racial equality. As such, the meeting was duly noted by the national press, including the

CBS-TV reporter Eric Sevareid, who decided to springboard it into his next Sunday's program by asking citizens of a southern town how *they* felt about desegregation and *Brown*. Greenville was his choice of locales.

Hodding Carter would narrate.

Daddy drove me to school early as Mrs. Thomas had requested. When we got there, we saw a big van, parked not in the street but actually on the wide sidewalk that led to the front doors of the school. A lot of strange men in work clothes, headphones clamped over their ears, were moving in and out of the van, lugging microphones, lights, and thick black electrical cords. Beyond all of this, I spotted Mrs. Thomas, waving wildly. Three other students were with her: my friend Sang and two boys, Eddie and Peter.

Mrs. Thomas hustled us inside and up the stairs to her classroom. We had no idea what was going on or why we were there.

When we got to her classroom, she closed the door and handed each of us a small piece of paper, on which was a handwritten statement in support of the belief that racial integration of our schools was a bad idea, not just for us, but for everybody. Black students included. We sat in one-armed school desks and studied our lines. My assignment was to quote statistics from a study of school integration in Washington, D.C., which proved that the grade point average declined from a desired high before the schools were desegregated to a disappointing low afterward.

We practiced our speeches until we could recite them without looking at our notes, and when we were ready, we went back outside to be interviewed. One by one we stood before the cameras and said what Mrs. Thomas told us to.

The program ran the next Sunday afternoon. I watched with a friend, at her house. I don't think anybody in my family bothered; maybe I didn't even tell them about it. I was just as glad to keep it secret.

The show opened with spot news coverage of the meeting in Montgomery, showing the size of the crowd and featuring clips of the speakers shaking their fists and raising their voices to a wall-rattling high, like Holy Roller preachers.

"These are angry voices," Sevareid told his audience, "but there are others." A picture of Lake Ferguson came on the screen, then downtown

Washington Avenue, and some shots of children on school playgrounds. A nice, quiet town.

After that, spokesmen for racial civility appeared. The banker and Citizens' Council member Conwell Sykes confidently informed the nation that it was inconceivable that integration would take place here and "we are relying on our Negroes" to cooperate. If necessary, the state had laws in place that would circumvent the Supreme Court ruling. Should those laws fail, he and other leaders would shut down the public school system entirely. The state would fund two separate private school systems. He didn't specify the race of the leaders he referred to; he didn't have to.

Two Black men spoke, the businessman Levye Chappel and Dr. H. H. Humes, president of the Negro State Baptist Convention. They both assured the interviewer and the country that local Negroes were not disturbed over integration and, although it was now the law of the land, they believed things should be dealt with calmly and in a timely manner. The planter Leroy Percy said southern people could best solve the problem on their own. Hodding Carter didn't think the rest of the country could possibly know the extent of the long-standing separateness of the races down here, but whatever happened, he was sure the South would not resort to physical violence or civil anarchy in solving its problems.

As for the students, Peter appeared first. The two races, he recited, represented such different cultures he couldn't see how integration in classrooms could exist here. "It just," he said, "wouldn't work right." Sang then pointed out that "Negro" students in Greenville already had a new, modern high school before white students got theirs and she wasn't sure why they'd want to come to ours. After that, the show moved on to its conclusion. Eddie and I ended up on the cutting-room floor.

I was disappointed and relieved in equal measure.

. . . .

Nell Thomas would stay on as a GHS teacher after its student population changed from exclusively white to something like 98 percent Black. She believed in education and the importance of the liberal arts. That *she* was the person who, in 1956, found it necessary to keep our opinions in line with the going racial philosophy of the South is an indication of just how deeply felt the belief went. How general it was, as context, as what we thought held our world together. Except for the color of her skin, she was not otherwise a privileged person. She was, however, living proof that even the good white people were terrified of what change would mean, for them and especially for their children; how utterly *righteous* they felt, speaking not just for themselves but for people of another race. And white kids like Sang and me and the two boys tagged right along and, dumb as fence posts, said what they told us, what we were supposed to say.

A month after the Montgomery meeting, Congressman Howard Smith of Virginia, chairman of the House Rules Committee, introduced what's known as the Southern Manifesto on the floor of the U.S. House of Representatives. Signed by eighty-two representatives and nineteen senators—about one-fifth of the total congressional membership, all from former Confederate states—it attacked *Brown* as an abuse of judicial power and urged southerners to exhaust all lawful means to resist the "chaos and confusion" that would result from school desegregation.

It was, in essence, a call to war. Call it states' righters versus the U.S. government. Call it the white Citizens' Councils versus the NAACP. Truth be told, the battle lines were not that different from the ones drawn ninety-five years earlier when the Confederacy was born and the southern states seceded.

. . . .

On the day after the Sevareid show aired, I was named with five other graduating seniors as a member of the first-ever GHS Hall of Fame, chosen by teachers and the administration for having "distinguished themselves in their high school careers as superior students and class leaders." A large photograph of the six of us was framed and prominently displayed in the school hallway. I was also named best all-around girl and given a $100 award and a medal by *The Delta Democrat-Times* and the Hodding Carter family, who chose me as Most Outstanding Senior of my class. I'd been accepted by Stephens College in Missouri, and my parents assured me I was going there, but somewhere along the way they issued the first hint that the tuition money might not be available after all. I clung to "might not" and got a job as the sole lifeguard at the country-club swimming pool, located about three miles from our house. My hours were nine to noon and two to six, six days a week. David usually drove me to work in the one car we had then, a tiny Crosley. Once I got there, I was stuck until six o'clock. I took my lunch and in my two hours off sat in the women's locker room to eat it, in retrospect a long time to spend sitting on a low wooden bench with nobody to talk to. Maybe I read, I guess I did. As a member of the staff, I'm sure if I'd gone into the kitchen and chatted up the waitresses and cooks, they'd have slipped me maybe a plate of their famous chicken salad or a brownie. But I never tried. You had to be a member, I thought, to expect favors. And so I sat, read, ate. And . . . waited. For . . . ? It all to be over?

In July, everything became clearer when David got in trouble, and to avoid his being sent to the "pea farm"—the state reform school—my parents agreed to enroll him in an Alabama military academy. I registered at Ole Miss, a school famous for football, parties, sororities, fraternities, and driving to the county line to drink beer. I excelled in many ways, none of which appear on that list. Within maybe a month, David had been kicked out of military school for cold-cocking the adjutant general's son. He hitchhiked his way home from Alabama.

During my first semester at Ole Miss, my parents and brothers moved from the Florida house into a bigger, newer one in a recently constructed development off Highway 82 on the way to Leland. The move was a big improvement, but they weren't there long. The sheriff threatened to run them out of the house, I suspect for nonpayment of rent, but in truth I don't know. When my mother told me they were relocating to the Holiday Inn in Greenwood, I didn't ask why. I had a dorm room I was happy to think of as home.

For Christmas that year, Eddy received a collie puppy he named Princeton. The dog also became a Holiday Inn resident.

. . . .

The same magazine article that placed the then inmate Ruth Dickins in secret attendance at her daughter Dell's debut in 1952 also brought her home for Dorothy Jane's entrance into society in December 1957. While the 1952 rumor seems, to my mind, unlikely, the latter one ignores reality altogether. By the time Dorothy Jane would have received an invitation from the Delta Debutante Club—the summer after her freshman year in college—Ruth's sentence had been indefinitely suspended for more than a year and a half. She didn't need a secret furlough to attend. She was at home.

And there is the other bit of news contradicting the story: Dorothy Jane Dickins didn't make her debut. Not in Greenville and not anywhere else. A Stovall cousin told me she had no idea whether Dorothy Jane had been blackballed because of her mother, or if she'd simply decided not to go to the trouble. If perhaps like Ruth getting married in her traveling costume, she had other things to do.

The cousin knew one thing: she and Dorothy Jane were the same age and she'd made *her* debut that year, and *knew* Dorothy Jane didn't participate.

She was right.

. . . .

By this time, now that his daughters were growing up and doing well, John Dickins had become more than slightly dissatisfied with Ruth's status. Her life had leveled out, but it wasn't yet *normal.* He was certainly grateful for Governor White's indefinite suspension, but as things stood, new evidence or a random complaint of criminal behavior could result in her return to the penitentiary. Governor J. P. Coleman had made his position clear regarding clemency; there was no sense asking him for a favor.

Perhaps Ross Barnett, elected in 1959 to take Coleman's place, would see his way clear to accommodate John's wishes.

. . . .

By the summer of 1963, Dorothy Jane had graduated from Mississippi State College for Women with a bachelor's degree in fine arts. She'd also earned another degree at an art school in New Orleans and afterward had landed a job teaching there.

She was, it seemed, on her way.

On August 29, 1963, after consulting with his old friend Hilton

Waits, John sat down with paper and pen. Governor Ross Barnett was—like Hugh White in 1955—nearing the end of his term, the time when governors and presidents were expected to hand out pardons. If John didn't secure Barnett's support before the next governor was inaugurated in January, he'd have to wait another four years.

"Dear Governor," he wrote.

His handwriting is a little scratchy and vertically aligned, as if by ruler, in a uniform slant to the right. He habitually fills his pages with words. They move, leaning, across the page as if in a hurry.

He began by heaping lavish praise on Barnett as a "much more popular, respected and down to earth governor than our state has ever had," despite the trouble "piled on" his administration—presumably a whispered reference to Barnett's rabid encouragement of "massive resistance" to the September 30, 1962, efforts of the Black Mississippian James Meredith to attend the University of Mississippi. Meredith's admission resulted in riots, deaths, and the eventual intervention of the National Guard. It's impossible to know how Dickins truly felt about this infamous spectacle or if he'd supported Barnett—whether he was sincere in his praise of Barnett's "patience, fair-mindedness and admirable decision-making" or simply playing up to the politician to get what he was after. Barnett, who called himself a "vigorous segregationist," was, after all, a Citizens' Councils member and had almost certainly been elected because of that organization's support, despite robust opposition from two former governors. He made his first speech as governor-elect at one of their meetings.

Unmentioned in John's letter is a notable connection between himself and the governor: both graduated from Mississippi College in 1922. John, as we know, served as president of the student body that year. Given the estimate of four hundred enrolled students at that time, it seems unlikely that Ross Barnett didn't recognize John's name.

Whatever his political beliefs, John laid the praise on, thick as cold butter. "As your time comes to a close," he wrote, "people are beginning to realize . . . how you had only the good of Mississippi and our nation at heart in all of your decisions."

This goes on for most of the first page. After which, he gets to the point.

"Some months ago," he reminded the governor, "I was in Jackson and you told me you would attend to our matter as soon as the elections were over." He doesn't spell out the exact meaning of "our matter," presumably feeling no need, but does underline the phrase as if to jog the governor's memory. And then he gets straight to the point.

Ruth wasn't at home that night. Having recently been made assistant church librarian and superintendent of beginners' programs at Leland First Baptist, she had been sent to the Ridgecrest Baptist Assembly in North Carolina to take a course. She also, John told the governor, taught regular Sunday school classes and had recently "carried a bus load" of girls to a convention in Memphis.

"In other words," John summed up, "what I'm saying is that my wife is as she has always been." Not, in other words, a killer, but *Ruth:* wife, mother, dedicated church lady. Respected member of the community.

Fifteen years ago, he went on, he and Ruth had had a "stigma cast on" them. And because people naturally hate to admit when they're wrong, it took time for them to accept their mistake and move on. In the meantime, "all you can do is keep living like you always have." A normal life, in other words.

Why "this thing" happened all those years ago, he'd never know, but in the time since then he never had any reason to doubt Ruth's innocence.

And now he was hoping Barnett would take the final step and grant her a full pardon. And, by the way, if he did see fit to do that, John hoped the governor would refrain from making any mention of her church activities. Ruth, he explained, did not believe in "riding on" her church work.

In closing, he returned to his usual tone of entitlement.

"She has been indicted, convicted, served time, granted a suspension and now we want a pardon . . . I am depending on you to give us that final relief."

Barnett's executive aide answered John's letter the next day with a CC to Hilton Waits. Ruth's case, he assured them both, had been "diaried" for consideration and attention by the governor on September 6, "at which time the necessary will be done."

. . . .

Two weeks after John wrote his letter, Governor Ross Barnett came through with a letter of executive clemency sent to Marvin Wiggins, granting Ruth T. Dickins—convicted of the crime of murder and sentenced to life in the state penitentiary—"A FULL AND COMPLETE PARDON."

In his comments, Barnett explained that during an investigation of her activities since the suspension granted by Hugh White in 1955, he found that the "subject" had lived a "life above reproach" during which she had "demonstrated every attitude toward rehabilitation" by fully assuming her duties "in her home as a citizen" and as a regular attendant in church. Clemency had been recommended by "several hundred officials and prominent citizens" of Washington County. In the "approximate eight years she has been at home, not a single complaint has been filed against subject or against her receiving further executive clemency."

In law, "pardon" is defined as "the use of the executive power of a governor or president to forgive a person charged with or convicted of a crime, thus preventing any prosecution and removing any remaining penalties or punishment."

On September 13, 1963, Ruth's full rights were restored, including suffrage. Her freedom was no longer contingent. She could not be returned to prison based on her original charge or conviction.

A status mighty close to freedom. Not, however, the same as exoneration. Like Hugh White, Barnett did not speak of innocence. And when he applauded her complete rehabilitation, you have to wonder. Rehabilitation from what?

A lawyer I know told me he was in the Washington County Chancery Court one day that same fall when a slight woman in a pale blue dress came in, waving a paper, asking where she could register to vote. He happily passed on the information. When she left the room, witnesses to the scene were shocked he didn't know who she was. Didn't he recognize Ruth Dickins? The woman who killed her mother?

. . . .

Ruth outlived John by nearly twenty years. He died at home in 1977; Ruth, in an assisted-living facility in 1996, forty-eight years after her mother's death and six months shy of her ninetieth birthday. She also outlived everybody in her immediate family: her sister and both brothers, her sister's husband, and her brother Wood's wife.

By the time of her death, she had deeded the house she and John had built to Dorothy Jane, who sold it to an insurance salesman from the Midwest. He lives there to this day. Painted the color of milky mud, 403 North Deer Creek Drive West is now the least-tended-to house on either side of the Drive. Bushes have been clear-cut. An ancient oak tree chopped down. There are no flowers, no palette of color. An abandoned refrigerator lay in the backyard for months. Neighbors and members of the garden club have voluntarily contributed cosmetic improvements. The new, reclusive owner is rarely seen in town and does not readily answer the door.

The original Thompson house, still advertised as an inn, has been for sale for several years. There have been no serious offers. In the absence of family members wishing to move in, the owners, mostly Stovall descendants, are hoping to sell to like-minded purchasers, investors who are eager to maintain its architectural design as well as its life as a bed-and-breakfast. But snagging the perfect candidate to buy the biggest house on that side of the Drive is not an easy thing to pull off, especially in a depressed market like the Mississippi Delta, a part of the country many more people are moving out of than in to.

Idella Thompson's house, halfway between the other two, remains the same. Painted sparkling white, it has recovered its anonymity despite the rapid turnover of its owners.

That side of Deer Creek Drive is now home to a few Black families. Not many.

THE QUESTION OF WHO?

Dorothy Jane Dickins O'Neill has followed in her father's footsteps, insisting ceaselessly on her mother's innocence. I keep trying to find a way to agree with her, to exonerate Ruth myself by coming up with the *real* killer—somebody other than Ruth. After several years of thinking about this and contemplating various possibilities, I have reached a few conclusions, some tentative, some not.

First and most important, Ruth's story, the one she told the investigators lined up at the foot of her bed in chairs provided by her husband on the day of her mother's burial. The story of the "dark-skinned Negro" she discovered hiding in her mother's bathroom. When it comes to this one, I feel no tentativeness.

I agree with the member of the armed posse who saddled up on the night of the murder and rode through Black neighborhoods and, upon his arrival at his Deer Creek Drive home afterward, told his wife, "There's no Negro. It's somebody in the family." And I believe Sheriff Foote knew what he was talking about when he told the press back in December 1948, less than a month after Idella Thompson's murder, that after many interviews and long, careful searches, in the opinion of his investigators, there was "no Negro."

To put it bluntly, he ought to know. For the first crucial days and weeks after the murder, he and his deputies and two chiefs of police, even the private eye among them, searched exclusively for a Black man matching Ruth's description.

He even said so in court. To tell the truth, he said, he was only "looking for a Negro." Because of this, he had personally interviewed a good fifty Black candidates, as had A. E. Crawford. All had verifiable alibis. He and his deputies and cops had combed the crime scene with a fine-tooth comb. And still, they found no trace of a murderous intruder anywhere in Mrs. Thompson's house, in her bathroom, on her porch, or in her yard; none on the wall separating her house from Second Street; none within or under the floor of the cotton compress. Nobody saw a man running wild through the neighborhood in the middle of the afternoon, covered in blood. And while, admittedly, there wasn't a lot of evidence to be found, there was some. Buttons, fingernails, hair, the handkerchief, the washed pruning shears. Anything not derived from Mrs. Thompson came from Ruth.

If not as irrefutable as today's scientifically supported forensic methods, there was also the soundness of local knowledge concerning racial realities in the Delta. Nobody, Black or white, thought a Black man would freely and without invitation enter a white person's house in the middle of the afternoon and stick around long enough to slash into the body of a tiny woman more than a hundred times. Case in point: the arrest of the Black man Arthur Jones in Clarksdale for "malicious trespassing" simply for knocking at a white person's back door and asking for a handout. And as Ruth's jury foreman told a reporter, nobody Black or white believed a Black man would walk around with a lacy linen handkerchief in his pocket like the blood-soaked one found in Idella Thompson's bathtub. Even the state supreme court emphasized these regional assumptions in its denial of Ruth's appeal.

If no homicide investigation can be called perfect and most can be said to have been "botched" to some degree, the search for Idella Thompson's killer can surely find its place high on the list of candidates for those more thoroughly bungled. But the crucial, early mistakes and the tunnel vision traveled in one direction only: the unblinking trust in the word of the only person available to tell or create the story of what happened as well as the assumption that, first off, only a man would commit such a crime and, also, surely that man would be of the race known to commit—*genetically disposed* to commit, some would say—that kind of crime.

. . . .

Second. If there was no Black man, why did Ruth say there was? Why else would she, other than to divert suspicion from . . . well, from whom? Herself? Or somebody else? She didn't say she *thought* she saw a Black man. Hers wasn't a far-off viewing of a person she'd seen on the run, through a screen door or window, but a man she stood face-to-face with, with whom she energetically tussled in a nine-by-eleven bathroom that within that small space held a bathtub and toilet, a sink, a heater, a small closet, and, on the floor near her feet, the body of her mother.

If he *was* there, she not only *saw* him; she felt his skin, the painful pressure of his hand around her forearm, the clutch of his fingers around the handles of the shears.

. . . .

Third. If I accept my first contention—that Ruth's "Negro" was a fabrication—and still want to join the Dickins family in her exoneration, I can come up with no explanation other than that she was protecting if not herself, then someone else. But who?

There's only Jimmy. The brother who depended on Ruth to take care of him, to be responsible for collecting an overdue rent check made out to him and then driving him to Greenville to—in order—deposit that check, make out another, withdraw some cash, mail the second check to his creditors, hand him the cash for his own use. The brother who testified in court, in her behalf, that she had been taking care of him ever since his father died some nine years earlier. The fragile older brother. The one who, in the Easter finery photograph taken when the four Thompson siblings were children, is looking with suspicion—or perhaps fear—at something or someone to his left.

Who, according to both himself and his sister, went to Greenville on the day of Idella's murder but did not return to Leland with his sister but stayed over allegedly to get a haircut and, by the way, never said *how* or *with whom* he managed to get home from Greenville later that afternoon, after he heard about his mother's death. And so one of the speculative questions to mull might be, what if he *didn't* stay over in Greenville to get a haircut? Hector Townsend, the barber who testified about the sighting of Ruth and Jimmy in the café, never said anything about Jimmy coming back to the shop later to get his hair cut, and neither did Jimmy, although, to be fair, we have to remember that because during the trial nobody *asked* him or Hector about a haircut, there was no call for either of them to point that out. Nobody asked, nobody said.

So. Say the haircut and the staying over in Greenville were lies. Say Jimmy rode back to Leland with Ruth and stayed with Idella when Ruth drove her car the two houses down Deer Creek Drive to get the box of shavings given to her by Louise Azlin of Azlin Drugs to use as a bed for her mother's kittens. And say that when Ruth returned to Idella's house, parked her car in back instead of out front as she usually did, and entered the house through the porch door, she saw her brother Jimmy whaling away on their mother with the pruning shears she had left on the radiator some one hour or so earlier.

Horrified—she was after all the caretaker daughter, the smartest member of the family, the sibling who managed and protected her mother, her brothers, and her sister—she threw herself between victim and slayer, thus managing to become injured as well as covered head to toe in blood from both herself and her mother. Suppose then, once they realized Idella was beyond help, brother and sister managed to lay their mother half on and half off the bathroom rug and pull her into the bathroom, where her body would be hidden from view.

Jimmy was of substantial heft but not exactly a big man. His draft card has him at five nine and 170 pounds. It might have taken him a number of blows to successfully kill Idella, but the coroner's estimate of 150 and "too many to count" seems excessive, even for a smallish man. But to continue.

Fourth. Say we have this right and Jimmy was the offspring who fell into a deep hot rage at his mother on November 17, 1948—more than likely because of a tiff of some kind about money because what else was there?—and was discovered by his sister in the act of killing her. What comes next?

When I imagine Ruth—she was a quick thinker, her mind facile enough to switch directions on a dime—telling her brother to run, run, she would take care of things for him as she always did ... I then think:

To where exactly would Jimmy run? He *lived* in his mother's house, just down the hall from where she—the woman who deemed him her favorite and the only one of her children who wasn't mean to her (whether in jest or not), the woman he drove to Colorado every summer and spent weeks alone with there in the cool mountain air, away from the torpid heat and the polio scare, until his sister arrived—lay butchered and dead. Frank Aldridge said when he got there, only minutes after Doc Witte called, the house was "neat as a pin," everything in its place. No mention of disorder anywhere in the house, no trace of bloody clothes *other than* the ones Ruth was wearing. Which were *covered in blood*, one cop said. *Soaked*, said another. The gray suit jacket and skirt, the soft silk blouse with the buttons missing, the outfit she took off at home, quickly put to soak in a tub of water by Beatrice Smith. All of it. The blood was on her clothes and body and, until the sheriff agreed to have it mopped, standing in a lake on the bathroom floor.

But to continue the hypothetical trail of possibilities:

Say Ruth quickly comes to the realization that if she tells the truth, Jimmy will go to Whitfield and more than likely die there, but if she creates another reality—the "dark-skinned Negro"—she can protect him. She can describe the Black man vaguely so as not to incriminate any of their devoted employees and simply plead uncertainty if or when they produce a suspect. That might be her first plan.

But *what if* the unthinkable happens and her friend Hughey and the other cops including her friend Mr. Frank Aldridge eventually begin to suspect her? What then? Surely, the place white women hold in the minds of white men would protect her. No southern man would be able to *imagine* that—would, in the words of Emmett Harty, "find it hard to conceive that"—she, a woman of some local prominence, a mother and Sunday school teacher, could have done anything so heinous, so far beyond the scope of *unthinkable as to become even unimaginable?* And even if she was arrested, what grand jury would indict her? What jury of her peers—all male, a plus for her side—would find her guilty, much less send her away to prison?

The Jimmy scenario has holes. Deep ones. Not least among which concerns Ruth's family. Could she persuade the others to join in the conspiracy and let her—*help* her—take the hit for her brother? Would John agree to the risk that she might, against all odds, be indicted, convicted, and sent away, leaving two young motherless daughters behind?

Could they all pull it off? Ruth, I have no doubt about, but all of them? Even Mildred? Jimmy?

Belief doesn't come easy.

On the other hand.

Ruth liked being in charge. She was good at telling the others what to do. I get the feeling her intelligence sometimes ran too fast for her to keep up with. Maybe she simply got carried away with the lie and the certainty of her privileged status, and took the others with her.

And there's the question of why in the world Wood and Demetra took off with Jimmy *one day* before the state asked the grand jury panelists to indict Ruth for the murder of her mother, which by then had become a fait accompli in the minds of the citizens of Leland and Greenville? Leaving behind jobs, work, homes, land, and, for Demetra, her very active participation in the local Junior League? And stay away through Ruth's indictment until they were subpoenaed to appear in her trial six months later, having spent time in Memphis, Mexico, and far west McAllen, Texas? Was it possibly because of the need to hustle Jimmy away from trouble? Not that he'd do anything to hurt Ruth, but that conversely he might up and confess to his own guilt and send himself off to the insane asylum?

And why, once the trial is over and Ruth is sent to Parchman, does Jimmy disappear, not just from Leland, but from further participation in Thompson family life? To live, die, and be buried alone in Denver?

It's all deeply, deeply odd.

The craziness (what we now call the dysfunction) of my family was always if not instantly obvious, then shimmeringly close at hand. We were unattached and on our own, dispensable and simply *out there*. But then, we had little choice, given our desires. The Thompsons/Dickinses, on the other hand, maintained their place in Delta society, even after at least two and maybe three violent and mysteriously committed deaths within the space of, if we include the rumored shooting of the other husband sitting in his living room during the 1927 flood, twenty-one years.

In the end, I am, personally, unable to create a credible story of the murder of Idella Thompson that includes a guilty verdict for two members of the Thompson family: murder for the brother, accessory to murder for his sister.

And so I come to this:

If Ruth didn't kill her mother and there was no Black intruder, who else is there? A question I throw out to the universe. So far, no answer has appeared. And I keep coming back to two nagging, underlying questions.

One concerns Doc Witte. Unquestionably, his testimony—his staunch certainty about what happened on November 17, 1948—was the key to the prosecution's case and Ruth's conviction. He was a member of her family, and yet he never let up. When John Dickins began to collect signatures asking for his wife's release from prison, it was Doc who led the resistance to it. Why? For one thing, he was a man who didn't think his word ought ever to be challenged, and as he straight-out said, he knew who the killer was the minute he walked in Idella Thompson's bedroom and saw Idella cut to pieces on the bathroom floor and Ruth looking the way she did, her pruning shears and shoes washed and all. To support his position and the eyewitness testimony he knew he'd be asked to give, he test-drove his route from the clinic to the Deer Creek Drive house and looked up questions about rigor mortis.

Maybe personal resentments paved the way: the fact, for instance, that Ruth didn't choose him as her personal physician. One Lelander with a low opinion of Doc thinks he acted out of pure meanness.

But give him this: he was there first. He saw what he saw. His wife was the victim's baby sister. And maybe John Dickins's declaration—when you know you're right, nothing scares you—applies equally to the motivations of Dr. K. L. "Doc" Witte.

. . . .

The other question lurking in the cracks of this story is, beyond actual guilt or innocence, why Ruth's jury convicted her of first-degree murder. Governor White had it right when he suggested manslaughter as the proper charge. But even then, odds stonewalled against the chance of her conviction.

When asked if there was a turning point in their decision, jury foreman Wilson Webb said they went through the evidence three times and he thought the turning point was Ruth's own statement to the police. In addition, he said, the cleaning of the pruning shears and the bloody handkerchief in the bathtub also "carried a lot of weight." My friend, longtime Leland lawyer Josh Bogen, was not surprised by the foreman's statement. He considers John Dickins's insistence on not hiring a lawyer until Ruth's arrest the biggest mistake the family made. Hubris—and perhaps the advice of Billy Wynn—tripped him up. Convinced that no one would dare dispute his or his good wife's word, he ushered investigators straight into her bedroom. Even had chairs lined up and ready for them.

As for the motive the state came up with? Those loans Ruth kept secret from John? So what?

The only answer I can come up with is, those twelve men didn't like her. When I described Ruth's courtroom appearance to a prosecutor I know, including clothes, hairstyle, and shoes, he agreed with me. It was, he said, the shoes. The clunky shoes.

We laughed. But I didn't think he was kidding. Not completely.

. . . .

Chroniclers of real-life events aren't supposed to become enamored of their subjects, but I can't help admiring Ruth Dickins for her willingness to play out her oddballness as far as she could take it. She was, indeed, a rare bird, a species of which, to my mind, we have far too few. I'd like to have known her.

On the other, other hand, admiration aside, I can come up with no plausible story line that doesn't pinpoint her as the murderer of her mother.

EPILOGUE

In 1977, the U.S. Commission on Civil Rights, established in 1957, issued a Mississippi Advisory Committee staff report titled *School Desegregation in Greenville, Mississippi*. As background, the report describes Greenville as, in many ways, "an atypical Southern city" that—because of its locale and function as a river port to and from which people have traveled freely for commerce and pleasure for generations—has become a "proud and friendly community of openness to new ideas and cultures." Although very much a part of the rural Mississippi Delta farmland—not known as a particularly progressive region of the state, politically or socially—Greenville was notable for its absence from the roster of communities promoting "flareups of organized racial violence" during the civil rights turbulence of the 1960s. The town had begun to liberalize racial access to its public facilities some fifteen years before the school desegregation order had been issued and by 1964 had initiated its own plan for majority-to-minority crossover of students on a freedom-of-choice basis, infuriating Governor Paul Johnson, who—a member of the Citizens' Council himself—wanted all school districts in the state to join together in what was known as massive resistance. A coded expression that can be translated as "whatever it takes."

By the early 1970s, the Civil Rights Commission report states, "Desegregation of the Greenville, Mississippi schools is very nearly total." The town was "a model of voluntary school desegregation."

A brief moment of change. Lost and gone by the time the report was officially presented to the nation. When meetings were held to organize the first private, or "segregation" or "Christian," academy in Greenville in 1969, a solid community of white people displayed its abject rejection of the new ideas touted by the government pamphlet. If they couldn't shut down the state public school system as a way of keeping white schools white, they could at least form their own private institutions.

There were those who tried to make the new system work.

When his father died, Hodding Carter III stepped in as editor of *The Delta Democrat-Times*. He, Billy Percy, and my English teacher Nell Thomas were among the white people who met with Black administrators, teachers, and community leaders to establish a setup that might work. Together, they created new attendance rules: first and second grades in this school, third grade in that one. Black children side by side with white. If an option was offered, students were given "freedom of choice" to pick the school that suited them and their parents best.

Billy Percy and Hodding Carter III kept their children in the public system. Hodding's daughter graduated from Greenville High. Billy's four children stayed throughout elementary and middle school and left only when they reached the tenth grade, when they enrolled in traditional prep and boarding schools outside Mississippi, as he had done himself.

"It wasn't easy to pull off," Billy told me, referring to the attempt to follow the government mandates. "We all struggled, Black people and white. But it was working. There were times when my daughter told us she wanted to bring a friend home. We didn't know he was Black until he walked in the door." She was, he expects, about fourteen at that time.

Hodding has often recalled the day he heard about the organization working to establish the segregation—called "seg"—academies. He sent a reporter to the community center to check out what was happening over there. When the reporter asked why, Hodding said, "Just go."

The reporter stayed long enough to figure out what was up before being kicked out of the meeting.

. . . .

The privately supported seg academies, many of which named themselves "Christian" instead of "white," opened wherever organizers could find the space, often in church basements. They found teachers, bought books, made contracts with the parents, whose bank accounts were docked monthly to pay for salaries and supplies. People who couldn't afford to pay found a way to come up with the money one way or the other. They voted down bond issues calling for a tax increase. As a result, potholed streets were left unrepaired, the roof of the public library continued to leak, city services declined. It's hard to know whether the members of the Citizens' Council ever realized that by subordinating every other concern of state government—roads, education, the health and well-being of its citizens—in defense of what they called their way of life, what they accomplished was the beginning of the end of it. This was especially the case in the Mississippi Delta, where the white resistance to change had been organized and remained strongest.

"White leadership did what it always does," Hodding said when asked about the failure of desegregation in his town. "It ran like hell. Nothing peculiar to Greenville. What was peculiar was that we tried."

In yet another blow to the town's pride of place, in 2011, after forty-six years in business, Hugh and Mary Dayle McCormick, owners of the McCormick Book Inn, closed up the store and moved out of the Delta altogether. The town had changed, sales had plummeted, neighbors and even churches were making purchases on the internet; an armed robbery of the store seemed one vexation too many. They now live in what Mary Dayle calls "the la-la-land of the Atlanta suburbs." Describing herself as a disappointed idealist, Mary Dayle remains gloomy about the future of the region they left behind.

"After our generation is gone," she predicts, "I doubt anyone will remember much about the Delta we knew except for the ugly, hateful stuff."

The wrecked and ravaged town I see when I visit Greenville now is, I believe, a direct result of the events—the "ugly, hateful stuff"—of this time. Not because of the *Brown* decision, but because of the response to it: both the failure of the general white imagination to envision a world even slightly different from the one it knew and the organized rise to power of the Citizens' Councils. This may not be the only factor, but it's a big one.

. . . .

Greenville's private academy, Washington School, opened in the spring of 1969. In 2016, one of the first of more than three hundred students enrolled there remembered the experience. "My parents told me I would be going to Washington School and that was all there was to it," she told a reporter. "The party line was that we would get a better education . . . I hated every day of that school." Once she graduated, she left for college and never went back.

When Hodding Carter III left Greenville to work in the Jimmy Carter administration as assistant secretary of state for public affairs, his brother Philip took over editorship of *The Delta Democrat-Times.* He didn't stay long. And in 1980, their mother, Betty, sold the paper to an ultraconservative chain called Freedom Newspapers, reportedly for somewhere between $14 and $16 million. The sale provided yet another challenge to Greenville's belief in itself as better than other parts of the state.

· · · ·

I don't hear farmers calling themselves planters these days, although they may hold on to the habit and pleasure of it when in their own confabbing groups. "Plantation" as a descriptive term is on its way out. "Place" is its substitute. I lately heard somebody refer to "the Dickins place over there." When I asked if the family still owned the Thompson land, the local farmer said, "Well, it's still called that."

· · · ·

That I do go back from time to time—not only to participate in Delta Hot Tamale Festivals, conduct interviews, and search through files and records but just to go, to see people and carry on with them—has been, for me, a revelation. Whoever would have guessed how much at home I'd feel there? Certainly not me. But there it is and maybe it's normal. Maybe we all, or most of us, long to go back to the place we thought we'd live "for ever," despite lingering memories of loss and disappointments. The language is just so familiar, its rhythms and wit, and so is the need for music and excellent meals, the very tone of a greeting one new friend called out when he saw me and said, "Welcome HOME, girl!"—these things are familiar enough, comforting enough, to draw me back.

To live? Sang asks.

Oh, well, no. Not to live.

As for the Dickinses, the Lelanders among the family have all left—not just their hometown, but, the last I heard, the Delta itself.

Keeping the faith, shushing the memory of November 17, 1948, has been left up to Stovall relatives, many of whom remain. The "brother did it and Ruth covered up the truth with a lie" theory still crops up among them—and among Thompson descendants—and is sometimes curiously offered as the reason for the shushing. When a Greenville theater group chose Ruth's grave as the locale of one of the local dramas they regularly acted out, somebody from Leland strong-armed them into abandoning the idea. I recently met a distant member of the Stovall cousinhood who was visiting the Delta. She assured me that a Leland friend of hers, one of Idella's relatives, would absolutely talk to me. This person, she said, was more "evolved" than other people in town. And she showed me a photo of the woman, in her mid-seventies, sitting on a cemetery stone in a soft colorful dress. She was smiling away, her hair was cut stylishly short, she sat up nicely erect, all of which gave her the look of a much younger woman.

My new friend asked if I'd like her to ask the woman to talk to me.

I said sure, go ahead.

Within minutes I received a text. The woman said she would not talk about that. Not to anybody. Not even to absolve her relative from blame.

So it goes in the town of Leland.

ACKNOWLEDGMENTS

Although in trying to gather details of this story, I ran into many roadblocks and evasions of the "we don't talk about that" variety, especially but not exclusively in Leland, many people were not only willing to talk to me about the murder of Idella Thompson and the subsequent arrest, trial, and conviction of her daughter, but were also puzzled, many of them, that—as one native Lelander put it—so many people thought 1948 was yesterday.

Among the Mississippi Delta residents who provided help, encouragement, housing, meals, memories, and conversation are:

Josh Bogen, who grew up in Greenville and has practiced law in Leland for more than fifty years. Josh came up with a copy of the Dorothy Turk book *Leland, Mississippi: From Hellhole to Beauty Spot;* a rare copy of the tabloid *Tragedy-of-the-Month;* and one of *Whatever Happened to Main Street?*, a book about the decline of downtown Greenville. He did this on his own, without my asking. He was also ready with answers to questions about Mississippi law, Greenville lawyers, the Delta Debutante Club, and many other topics of local and enduring interest.

Humphreys McGee and members of his family. Unlike other notable "top-tier" Leland families, the McGees were willing to spend time with me and answer any questions I came up with. Also a lawyer, Humphreys provided information about Parchman and Mississippi law.

Anne Martin Vetrano. Bill Vetrano. For connections, books, information, housing, and down-home hospitality, and love, extended not just to me but also to my enchanting canine companion, Walter.

Frank Abdo for valuable stories as well as information about Leland history and general architectural, astrological, and decorative trends. Also, friendship.

My brother David and my friend from third grade through now Sang Roberson, for memories of those years and facts I never knew or had forgotten.

Hank Burdine, Delta raconteur and scribe, for quick answers to offbeat questions as well as meals, welcome, and levee board history.

ACKNOWLEDGMENTS

Gayden Metcalf, indispensably informative and helpful in many directions.

Brucie McKamy Mintz, for significant Leland family information, leading to conversations with Dudley and Peggy Baker Cannada. Also generosity, housing, entertainment, and openhearted hospitality.

Lynn Taylor Baker, who grew up on Deer Creek Drive and was willing to talk about it. Holmes Adams for stories and experiences.

Jimmy Robertson, for memories, connections, and general assistance, both legal and personal; Linda Thompson Robertson, for research, especially the discovery of that important death certificate. Stephanie Patton for Thompson House and *Leland Progress* information, as well as friendship and introductions. Nellie Taylor for chancery court research. Lisa and Cedric Bush for stories and information about Black Lelanders in the aftermath of the murder; also Matthew Johnson, husband of Lisa's secretary, Diana, for information and open discussions.

From the Stovall cousinhood: Mary Stovall Boteler, who—despite general warnings from all over—invited me into her home to speak about Leland history and horticulture as well as remembrances of her friendship with and kinship to Ruth Dickins's family. Also her daughter, Jody Huddleston, who pulled back the rug in the library of the Thompson House B and B to show me the large, wine-dark stain she and others believe to be blood from a family death by gunshot. Dick Harbison, a member of the Stovall cousinhood who attended every day of Ruth Dickins's trial. And was willing to talk about it.

Also from Leland: Gaila Oliver, who provided real estate information and a rare copy of *Leland of Old*, a reproduction of the 1904 trade edition of the *Leland Enterprise*, which her mother, Nancy Tate, brought to fruition. Historian and teacher Daryl Lewis. Rich Schroeder, current owner of the John and Ruth Dickins home. Morgan Gulledge, for Leland stories and connections to friends he thought could provide special inside information; not his fault they declined. Rocky Landi, for meals, friendship, long conversations, and quick texts in answer to burning questions especially regarding the families he tagged "top-tier."

From Greenville: Billy Percy, Lisa Percy, Camille Collins, Claire Lake, Mayor Erick Simmons, Benjy Nelken, Mary Sferruzza, Paul Watson, Donna Shirey, Randall Lauderdale. Valerie and Kurt Rankin. Betty Lynn Cameron. Gaines Dyer. Hodding Carter III. Washington County circuit clerk Barbara Esters-Parker. Peyton Prospere. Mary Dayle McCormick.

For Parchman help: Leonard Vincent. Marilyn Corbin. Christy Gutierriez.

For general encouragement: Gary Fisketjon, Bryan Burrough, Ann Patchett, Virginia Carmichael. Over-the-moon thanks to Nancy Faye Smith, friend and enthusiastic, patient reader of several early, much longer, versions of this book.

I am also forever indebted to Katie Blount, director of the Mississippi Department of Archives and History, for unstinting research guidance as well as housing, meals, and great book discussions with her and her excellent husband, David Blount. David Pilcher and the entire reference staff at MDAH also provided tireless assistance.

Thanks as well to Erin Mazzei, digitization expert at the Texas State University's Alkek library, for making a seventy-two-year-old tabloid magazine accessible and safely preserved. Also to the Wittliff Collection's Katie Salzmann for the introduction and assistance.

Endless thanks to my editor, Carole Baron, and her (and my) right-hand man, Rob Shapiro and the incredible staff at Knopf, including publisher Reagan Arthur, production editor Maria Massey, and Jenny Carrow, who came up with the brilliant jacket cover. I feel lucky every day knowing that the Knopf family has my back. My agent, Anne-Lise Spitzer of the Spitzer agency, served as an integral part of my publication team. It was she who came up with the title, which seemed to have been waiting for somebody to wake up and realize it was the one we'd been searching for.

And as always, Colin and Andrea, my support system.

Finally, I deeply regret that some of the people who provided various forms of crucial assistance no longer walk among us and will not be around to read this book. Journalist and Greenville first lady Julia Reed facilitated my return to my hometown by inviting me to participate in the Hot Tamale Festival's Culinary-Literary Mash-up. She also provided encouragement and handy research tips. The magnificent Lelia Wynn emceed and oversaw that literary festival I went to in 1982. She and I enjoyed long and illuminating conversations about Greenville in the 1950s and her thoughts on the Delta Debutante Club. Rabbit Jenkins introduced me to the Highland Club brunches, where I met people in the know, some of whom agreed to talk to me. He also gave me rides to and from the Belmont Plantation and Lake Washington, saving me from getting lost on my own. Retired judge from Indianola, Charlotte Buchanan, the original innkeeper of The Thompson House, came up with sassy Leland information I otherwise might never have figured out. Knopf publisher Sonny Mehta? Without his support, *Deer Creek Drive* might still be waiting for somebody to say yes to its publication. And, from Austin, my dear friend Claudette Lowe, who said time and again, "I can't *wait* to read that book!"

I didn't write this book *for* these folks but I certainly had them in mind as potential, eventual readers of it.

After the verdict: Ruth on her way to county jail, her sentence of life in prison for all of her natural-born life having already begun. Sheriff Hugh Foote is leading the way, in his hand the court order given to him by Judge Jordan to give to the jailer. John, on her right and Ben Wilkes, on her left, seem to be pretty much holding a very frail, desolate Ruth upright. Behind her, one step up and on her left, is her nephew, Thompsie Hood. Beside him, a man who may be his father, Shields Hood. And at the top of the stairs, defense attorney B. B. Wilkes, who will soon take over Ruth's case. Not even the sheriff looks happy here, even though—because the case was his—he, along with the prosecutors, could claim victory. The guilty verdict, after all, was what he was after. This photo seems to me to illustrate just how difficult the crime and the trial were for people to wrap their minds around. Even one of the prosecutors, when asked for a comment, said that nobody was smiling about the outcome. The photograph appeared in *Tragedy-of-the-Month*.

NOTES

ABBREVIATIONS

DDT: *Delta Democrat-Times,* Greenville.

GC: *Greenwood Commonwealth*

HA: *Hattiesburg American*

JCL: *Jackson Clarion-Ledger*

MCA: *Memphis Commercial Appeal*

MDAH: Mississippi Department of Archives and History

MEJ: *McComb Enterprise-Journal*

I. THE CRIME

"Looking Back" merges memory with interviews and my own general ruminations regarding time, place, and the inevitable drift this way and that of cultural trends and attitudes.

The information in "November 17, 1948" is derived, for the most part, from testimonies in *The State of Mississippi v. Ruth Thompson Dickins,* the transcript of which is housed in the digital files of the MDAH in Jackson. Much of the Leland historical material found in this chapter and throughout the book comes from Dorothy Turk's book, *Leland, Mississippi: From Hellhole to Beauty Spot,* and Nancy Tate's reproduction of a 1904 collection of *Leland Enterprise* photos and notes, called *Leland of Old.* Descriptions of individuals mentioned were made from photographs found in various newspapers and the tabloid magazine *Tragedy-of-the-Month.* I have had no personal experience with the racially motivated practice of locking the back door while leaving the front door open but have heard of it from many Delta friends. The practice was also mentioned by the anthropologist Hortense Powdermaker in her book *After Freedom: A Cultural Study in the Deep South.* Many Greenville-Leland details— Mink's Dine and Dance, Lillo's Supper Club—are from personal experience.

NOTES

Some material throughout the book comes from interviews with local residents who prefer to remain anonymous.

"Whiteness and the Mississippi Delta." The physical Delta has been described many times in books, stories, oral histories, speeches, and movies. Those of us who lived there heard and watched them all, even the ones shot through with mistakes. I remember reading Lewis "Buddy" Nordan's very funny novel *Music of the Swamp,* and when I came to a passage in which a storm flooded the basement of a house built in the Delta, I laughed out loud. A basement? In the Delta? Buddy wrote that little inside joke for *us.* The historical information comes from a number of printed sources, including the memoirs of Henry Tillinghast Ireys, the history of the Mississippi Levee Board, and innumerable memoirs and histories written by local residents as well as scholars and writers. They include, among the many I consulted, David Cohn, James C. Cobb, Rupert Vance, Helen Dick Davis, Hodding Carter Jr., John Barry, and of course William Alexander Percy. Cobb's book *The Most Southern Place on Earth: The Mississippi Delta and the Roots of Regional Identity* was particularly helpful throughout the writing of this book, from start to finish, and could be mentioned in many citations recorded here. I found the New Orleans photographs of the honeymooning Idella and Wood Thompson on the internet; the portrait of the Thompson children in a scrapbook available to guests of the Thompson House bed-and-breakfast. Information about J. W. Thompson's life and ancestry—as well as quotations from interviews with him—is from government documents, U.S. census data, Leland and Greenville newspapers, and ancestry.com, as well as the Turk book and the Tate reproduction.

Most of "Ruth's Turn" can be found in Ruth Dickins's statement to the investigators as well as in various testimonies by the attending lawmen, included in transcripts of the trial. My observations, however, can be traced, as always, to my own, perhaps idiosyncratic, reading of her long, rambling statement. The Hollins yearbook photos of Ruth are included in the online digital archives of *The Spinster,* as is John Dickins's photo in the Mississippi College yearbook, *L'Allegro.* Notice of the Dickinses' real estate purchase was found in 1935 Washington County Chancery Court files and mentioned in the local newspaper; description of their home is from personal visits; the description of Ruth's exuberant flower garden is from a photo provided by Frank Abdo. Specific newspaper sources are often included in the text itself to establish contextual as well as factual information. As for Ruth's statement, I have tried to plumb it for its specific rhythms and tonal quality as well as its aura of speed and intimacy, without constantly relying on a Q-and-A approach. What is known about the death of J. W. Thompson comes from the official death certificate as well as newspaper obituaries and my own experience at the Thompson house. Yellow fever epidemic and historical details of Tallahatchie County are from various histories as well as the indispensable *Mississippi Encyclopedia* (mississippiencyclopedia.org), issued by the MDAH.

"The Run-Up" is an attempt to zoom through time instead of dwelling overlong on specific occurrences, in that way to get a sense of what happened in the lives of the two families the book focuses on, the Feys and the Dickinses, along with concurrent information about their home turf, the Mississippi Delta, up to the point when the events previously described took place. Believing that nothing happens out of nothing, I wanted to provide an idea of how, in my view, things got to where they did, going year by year, from the mid-1930s, through the war years, right up to the night before Idella Thompson was murdered in November 1948. Information is from various sources, including memory, family journals and albums, deeds filed in the Washington County Chancery Court, and newspaper articles, mostly from the *DDT*, found online at newspapers.com, as well as military and census records located on ancestry.com. Mississippi history is from entries in the online *Mississippi Encyclopedia* and various books cited there.

"Grand Jury." Information about the makeup of the jury and the hearing itself is from various newspapers including the *DDT, MEJ, GC*, and *JCL*. Lizzie Borden clothing description from internet sources and Cara Robertson's book, *The Trial of Lizzie Borden*. Descriptions of Ruth's trial attire, both here and in future chapters, are from the newspapers listed above, among others, and from newspaper and magazine photographs. The flight of Wood, Demetra, and Jimmy Thompson from trial transcript.

"The Importance of Beatrice Smith." Information is from the motion for continuance brought by Ben Wilkes, during which he questioned Smith's personal physician. Found in the official trial transcript.

"Waiting." Memory fuels the girlhood passage. Details about the house plans my mother studied are from the *Better Homes & Gardens* clipping, found in a box of various articles, invitations, and letters she managed to hold on to. Deed to the 830 South Washington lot as well as records of the sale of 313 Deer

Creek Drive are in the Washington County Chancery Court records room. Bob Marks's last-minute *MCA* interview of Ruth with accompanying photograph found in an MDAH subject file.

II. TRIAL

"The Jury." Day-by-day coverage of the trial found in all newspapers listed above, among others. Physical details found in this entire section, including the courtroom, the lawyers, the judge, the audience members, the concessionaire selling hot dogs, and Ruth and her family at the defense table and on her way with John out of the courthouse, derive from newspapers, including the *MCA* and the *JCL,* and the tabloid periodical *Tragedy-of-the-Month.* Because the voir dire was not included in the trial transcripts, I depended chiefly on the extensive coverage run by the *DDT,* with backup and details found in other Mississippi newspapers. Information about Brown's Pastry Shop is from interviews with Greenville residents who remember either the shop or stories about it. For some reason, I never went there.

"Opening: Stanny," "Day Three," "Saturday Morning," and "The Catalyst" depend primarily on the trial transcript for basic information and witness testimony, with added details from newspaper coverage. Description of the clump of hair found in Idella Thompson's fist comes from personal experience at the MDAH, where the one surviving box of trial evidence—small brown evidence envelopes containing buttons, fingernails, hair—is stored. The envelopes are approximately 2" x 4", many of them still sealed shut with old-fashioned cellotape. In its banner-headlined story, "PROSECUTION RESTS CASE," the *DDT* ran extensive, directly quoted passages from the prosecutor and the witnesses called by the state to provide a motive for the murder of Idella Thompson. This story took up a big section of page 1 and almost all of the following page.

"Weekend." The quite detailed story of the transformation of the courtroom into a church ran in the *JCL* and the *GC* but not the *DDT.* My assumption that therefore the jurors had been sequestered is based on rationale—there being no other reason for the switch to have taken place—and a later *JCL* article citing the jury's nighttime schedule of returning to the courthouse with Ruth's fate in their hands after eating supper. Tidbit news about Dell and Dorothy Jane Dickins's camp attendance from *DDT.*

"From the Defense" and "Defense Rests." The ovation for Stanny Sanders was noted in the *HA* and the *DDT.* Bern Keating information from various internet sources, interviews, and the memories I retain of him and especially his wife, Franke. The photograph mentioned was on display at the McCormick Book Inn. Details of "the Rule" from Josh Bogen and internet websites explaining legal terms. Questioning, testimony, and decisions by the judge are all from trial transcripts.

"Closings." I have long been puzzled by people's willingness to accept a jury's decision as proven fact. This seems especially true in the case of family members seeking "closure." Musings about this are all mine. Story of the Sweet Potato Slayer is from the *DDT.* Alex Clark's locally famous pro bono attorney was Howard Dyer Jr. The existence of a Parchman Farm "Long Chain Man" (also known as Long-Chain Charlie) is recorded in various books about the penitentiary, as is the use of the lash to discipline and control inmates. Details of closing arguments are from the trial transcripts. The story of the trapped pigeon is from a detailed front-page story in *The Shreveport Times. JCL* photos of the jury and the courtroom on the final day of the trial provided visual details.

"Verdict." Information comes from every newspaper listed in these notes, and others. I consulted whatever I could come up with, in order to grasp a sense of what the trial of Ruth Dickins was like, not from a modern perspective, but as it happened.

"Appeal." News of Wilkes's death from his obituary, which ran in a number of places. The state supreme court's lengthy and very forthright opinion regarding Buck Conn's appeal, known as *Dickins v. State,* can be found at leagle.com and other legal websites.

"Late 1949, Early 1950." Stories about my family during this period are as I remember them, as well as from photographs, letters, and my mother's journal. The Leland Christmas tree story ran in the *DDT.* The New York *Daily News* story is in a subject file at the MDAH. Ruth's departure from Washington County Jail is from the *DDT* and other newspapers.

III. PRISON

"1950: A New Life." Indianola history is from the *Mississippi Encyclopedia* as well as Mississippi history books. Parchman details, including its history, come from David Oshinsky's book *Worse Than Slavery* and William Banks Taylor's *Down on Parchman Farm,* as well as newspaper stories, the *Mississippi Encyclopedia* and the MDAH's digital files, plus personal interviews with former employees. Other than her inmate number, however, all of Ruth's Parchman entrance records have been either lost or removed from the MDAH digital files. When a former Parchman employee told me that she removed some of her father's inmate files from the system, I came to terms with that possibility, generally. "Temperament of a rattlesnake" description of Marvin Wiggins is the historian Dennis Mitchell's. Details of Irene Locke Hughes's murder of her husband found in the *MEJ;* Brister information, *JCL;* Countryman in *DDT;* information about Dickins's daughter and John, also Hilton Waits, from *DDT.* Fey material is as I remember it and from articles, ads, and photos in the *DDT* and family albums.

"Suspects, Escapes, Captures, and Ruth." Charlie Ferguson escapes, crimes, captures, and presence in Whitfield lineup from the *DDT, GC,* and *JCL,* as are A. E. Crawford's and Buck Conn's participation, descriptions of Ferguson, testimony of his family, and Ruth's identification procedure. Escape of Parchman inmates Countryman, Locke, and Blackwell from those same newspapers and the *Blytheville Courier News.*

"Letters from Leland." All letters and petitions sent both to and from Governors Fielding Wright, Hugh White, and Ross Barnett, among which are those from John Dickins, Dell Dickins, Ruth Dickins, Hilton Waits, Marvin Higgins, and a great many local citizens from Leland and Greenville, are located in the Mississippi governors' files at the MDAH. The Dickinses' 1951 Christmas decorations from the *DDT.*

"A New Year." Junior Cotillion information and other news about Dell Dickins from the *DDT* society pages. History of debutante and cotillion tradition from Kristen Richardson's book, *The Season,* and columns written by the sharply observant eyewitness reporter Sara Criss Evans, Leflore County bureau chief for the *MCA* for thirty years. Her column can be found at daughterofthedelta.com. Details of the parole board meeting and response as well as John's statements to the press are from the *DDT.*

"A New Governor, Another Suspect." Hugh White information from the *Mississippi Encyclopedia* and various books mentioned here. Parchman photo files from MDAH, *A New History of Mississippi* by Dennis Mitchell, and various newspaper articles. Arthur Jones material from *JCL* and *DDT.* Parchman interviews with Ruth and Janie Brister, *DDT, JCL.* Regional Council of Negro Leadership and NAACP details from Mitchell, Cobb, and newspaper sources.

"1952: Year's End." Fey and airbase information and moving and storage company information are from the *DDT* and personal memories and photos. Keady record of my father's scam, from his book *All Rise: Memoirs of a Mississippi Federal Judge.* Fey ads and photos, Dell Dickins photo, and other Greenville and Leland information from this chapter are from the *DDT.* Parchman news about female inmates, *JCL.*

"Furlough." Marvin Wiggins's letter to Hugh White regarding a request for Ruth Dickins's furlough, which had been approved by the sergeant assigned to her living quarters, is from the governors' files, as are letters from Lelanders reporting on White's response.

"Mr. Marvin, Ruth, and the Press." Stories about the Sonny McGraw arrest, murder charge, and confession along with citizen responses, Tom Karsell articles, and Hodding Carter editorials appear in various newspapers around the state including the *MEJ* and the *JCL,* and are lengthily cited in Karsell's and Carter's work published in the *DDT.*

IV. CHANGES

"The Feys, the Dickinses, the South." Record of 830 South Washington foreclosure and deed transfer from Washington County records. Letters to and from Hugh White are in MDAH governors' files and Ruth's prison letter to her family. David Fey removal from moving company partnership included in Keady's book. First reactions to *Brown v. Board of Education,* from various sources including citations mentioned above.

"1954: Furloughs, Doctors, *Brown,* and Elvis." Doctors' letters to Wiggins and the governor located in governors' files, MDAH. Young Life information and photo, *DDT. Brown* decision, Patterson and Brady response, Citizens' Councils details from every Mississippi newspaper cited as well as all Mississippi histories, the *Mississippi Encyclopedia,* and various magazine articles. Letter from Ruth to Hugh White and one from her aunt Johnie Long Witte from the governors' files. Sugar Bowl ticket information, from *JCL.*

"1955: Culminations." Hodding Carter's responses to segregationists' activities and threats in response to *Brown* and his *Look* magazine article can be found online. Ann Waldron's book *Hodding Carter: The Reconstruction of a Racist* provides excellent coverage of the terrorist threats and actions visited upon the

Carter family. Emmett Till murder and subsequent trial and acquittal of his killers are from many sources, including, especially, Timothy Tyson's book *The Blood of Emmett Till*. Reports of Hugh White's visit to Leland are from various newspapers, including the *DDT*. Letters in response both for and against clemency for Ruth are in the governors' file. His announcement of an indefinite suspension also variously reported in all newspapers cited above.

"Ruth at Home." Dickins family information from newspaper society sections and ancestry.com passport collections, personal interviews.

V. THE RECKONING

"Massive Resistance." Eric Sevareid show details from personal interviews and memory, also a *DDT* front-page story covering the newscast. News of the Citizens' Council rally in Montgomery reported in many newspapers and books. John Dickins to Ross Barnett and his executive aide's reply in governors' file. News of John Dickins's death, Ruth Dickins's death from obituaries. Record of the sale of their home from chancery court deed. Description of it, from personal visit.

"The Question of WHO?" "I take full responsibility for speculations and the unraveling of possibilities regarding the murder of Idella Stovall Long Thompson contained in this chapter. In an effort to determine who else might have killed Mrs. Thompson if Ruth didn't, I have, once again, reviewed her bedridden statement to the police as well as investigation reports from the police and testimonies of various witnesses in the trial in order to come to a final conclusion. Mistakes and misconceived notions are all mine.

"Epilogue." Information on Greenville's response to *Brown* and the organization and foundation of Greenville Christian Academy and other so-called seg academies derives from the 1977 pamphlet issued by the U.S. Commission on Civil Rights and a long substantive article by LynNell Hancock, published by the Hechinger Report in 2006, reprinted in the October 4, 2016, issue of *The Nation*. Other information about the town's shocking decline can be found in *What Ever Happened to Main Street?*, written by students of the writer Curtis Wilkie and produced by the Meek School of Journalism and New Media at the University of Mississippi. Other information comes from personal interviews. Opinions are mine.

A NOTE ABOUT THE AUTHOR

Beverly Lowry was born in Memphis and grew up in Greenville, Mississippi. She is the author of six novels and four previous works of nonfiction, and her writing has appeared in *The New Yorker*, *The New York Times*, *The Boston Globe*, *Vanity Fair*, *Rolling Stone*, *Mississippi Review*, *Granta*, and many other publications. She has received awards from the National Endowment for the Arts, the Guggenheim Foundation, the Texas Institute of Letters, and the Mississippi Institute of Arts and Letters. She lives in Austin, Texas.

A NOTE ON THE TYPE

This book was set in a modern adaptation of a type designed by the first William Caslon (1692–1766). The Caslon face, an artistic, easily read type, has enjoyed more than two centuries of popularity in the English-speaking world. This version, with its even balance and honest letterforms, was designed by Carol Twombly for the Adobe Corporation and released in 1990.

Composed by North Market Street Graphics,
Lancaster, Pennsylvania

Printed and bound by Berryville Graphics,
Berryville, Virginia

Designed by Betty Lew